CHINESE MENU

For my own "happy family": my husband, Alex, who learned
to cook Happy Family from The Complete Chinese Takeout Cookbook
(by Kwoklyn Wan), and my daughter, Hazel, who happily eats it

About This Book

The cover, section, and food spot illustrations for this book were done in Turner Design gouache on hot press Saunders Waterford watercolor paper. The story illustrations were drawn in pencil on tracing paper and then scanned, retouched, and colored in Adobe Photoshop. This book was edited by Alvina Ling and designed by Jessica Dacher, with art direction by Saho Fujii. The production was supervised by Lillian Sun, and the production editor was Annie McDonnell. The text was set in Calluna and Houschka Rounded, and the display type is Aristelle Sans.

Copyright © 2023 by Grace Lin • Case gold foil texture image © janniwet/Shutterstock.com • Cover illustration copyright © 2023 by Grace Lin. Cover design by Jessica Dacher • Cover copyright © 2023 by Hachette Book Group, Inc. • Hachette Book Group supports the right to free expression and the value of copyright. The purpose of copyright is to encourage writers and artists to produce the creative works that enrich our culture. • The scanning, uploading, and distribution of this book without permission is a theft of the author's intellectual property. If you would like permission to use material from the book (other than for review purposes), please contact permissions@hbgusa.com. Thank you for your support of the author's rights. • Little, Brown and Company • Hachette Book Group • 1290 Avenue of the Americas, New York, NY 10104 • Visit us at LBYR.com • First Edition: September 2023 • Little, Brown and Company is a division of Hachette Book Group, Inc. • The Little, Brown name and logo are trademarks of Hachette Book Group, Inc. • The publisher is not responsible for websites (or their content) that are not owned by the publisher. • Little, Brown and Company books may be purchased in bulk for business, educational, or promotional use. For information, please contact your local bookseller or the Hachette Book Group Special Markets Department at special.markets@hbgusa.com. • Library of Congress Cataloging-in-Publication Data • Names: Lin, Grace, author. • Title: Chinese menu : the history, myths, and legends behind your favorite foods / Grace Lin. • Description: New York : Little, Brown and Company, 2023. | Includes bibliographical references. | Audience: Ages 8–12 | Summary: "The origin stories of each Chinese dish told using the framework of Chinese cuisine—oftentimes based in folklore, both ancient and contemporary."—Provided by publisher. • Identifiers: LCCN 2022039636 | ISBN 9780316486002 (hardcover) | ISBN 9780316486392 (ebook) • Subjects: LCSH: Cooking, Chinese—History—Juvenile literature. • Classification: LCC TX360.C6 L56 2023 | DDC 641.5951—dc23/eng/20220922 • LC record available at https://lccn.loc.gov/2022039636 • ISBNs: 978-0-316-48600-2 (hardcover), 978-0-316-48639-2 (ebook) • Printed in Vietnam • APS • 10 9 8 7 6 5 4 3 2

CHINESE MENU

The History, Myths, and Legends
Behind Your Favorite Foods

GRACE LIN

L **B**
Little, Brown and Company
New York   Boston

TABLE OF CONTENTS

WELCOME!

Have you ever eaten at a Chinese restaurant? Yes, I know, the food was so good! Yum! I get hungry just thinking about it.

But have you ever been curious about the names of the dishes you ordered there? For example, General Tso's Chicken—have you wondered who General Tso was? Or Buddha Jumps Over the Wall—why would Buddha do something like that?

Well, I can tell you! Because those names are all clues to the tales behind the food. Almost all dishes on a Chinese menu have a story behind them. In a way, the menu at your Chinese restaurant is the table of contents for a feast of stories.

And this book is that feast.

Because this book is going to tell you the stories that make up your favorite Chinese dishes. From fried dumplings to fortune cookies, here are the tales behind your most ordered foods.

Now, I know you want to ask, "Are these stories real?"

Yes. These stories are real. They are real legends, real myths, and real histories. I did not make any of them up from my own imagination. They have all been researched (you can check the bibliography!) and there are a few stories that are not only real folklore but factually true, too!

That said, even though I did not fabricate any of these stories, I did, however, embellish some of them. Many of these stories are my own adapted retellings, combining various versions of legends together with imagined details and dialogue. But even when I did so, I tried hard to stay true to the spirit of the original tales and keep as many details as possible. For example, important female characters in the legends were sometimes nameless, so I gave these women names, with ones that would be appropriate for that time and place. But when the stories did name characters, I kept true to the tale—if the characters had no last name in the legend (such as Kun in the chopstick story), I left them with a single name. And, speaking of names, in Chinese tradition, the last name is said first and written before the given name. So, General Ding Baozhen—a real historical person— has the last name of Ding. The general's first name is Baozhen. You can read Baozhen's story while learning about Kung Pao Chicken!

And while you read these stories, I hope you also begin to see that this book is actually not about Chinese food. Just like hot dogs were invented in Germany (hot dogs are also called frankfurters because they came from Frankfurt, Germany) and apple pie has Dutch origins (there are Dutch apple pie recipes dating as far back as 1514); egg rolls, Sweet and Sour Pork, and General Tso's Chicken are just as American.

In fact, what we in America consider Chinese food is really just a small sliver of Chinese cuisine. China is a huge country with more than one billion people. And every area has its own specialty—from the dim sum and seafood of coastal Guangdong to the lamb and dairy dishes of the grassland tribes of Inner Mongolia. There's a wide, wide range of Chinese food and we've only gotten a tiny taste.

We are also less familiar with its stories. So, pull up a chair, have a seat, and get ready to eat! I hope you're hungry, because here comes your story feast! While the tales you are about to read might be magical, funny, exciting, or a bit unusual, I know I can say with relish that they are all delightfully satisfying.

Happy reading...and eating!

CHINA

Xinjiang

Heilongjiang

Jilin

Inner Mongolia

Ningxia

Liaoning

Beijing

Gansu

Hebei

Tianjin

Qinghai

Shanxi

Shandong

Shaanxi

Henan

Jiangsu

Shanghai

Tibet

Sichuan

Hubei

Anhui

Zhejiang

Chongqing

Hunan

Jiangxi

Guizhou

Fujian

Yunnan

Guangxi

Guangdong

TAIWAN

Guangzhou

Hainan

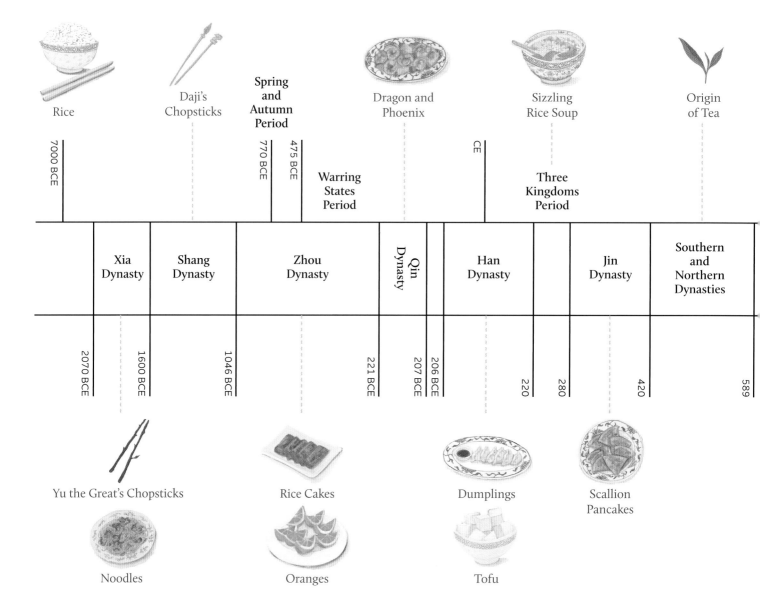

Rice

Daji's Chopsticks

Spring and Autumn Period

Dragon and Phoenix

Sizzling Rice Soup

Origin of Tea

7000 BCE

770 BCE

475 BCE

Warring States Period

CE

Three Kingdoms Period

| Xia Dynasty | Shang Dynasty | Zhou Dynasty | Qin Dynasty | Han Dynasty | Jin Dynasty | Southern and Northern Dynasties |

2070 BCE

1600 BCE

1046 BCE

221 BCE

207 BCE

206 BCE

220

280

420

589

Yu the Great's Chopsticks

Rice Cakes

Dumplings

Scallion Pancakes

Noodles

Oranges

Tofu

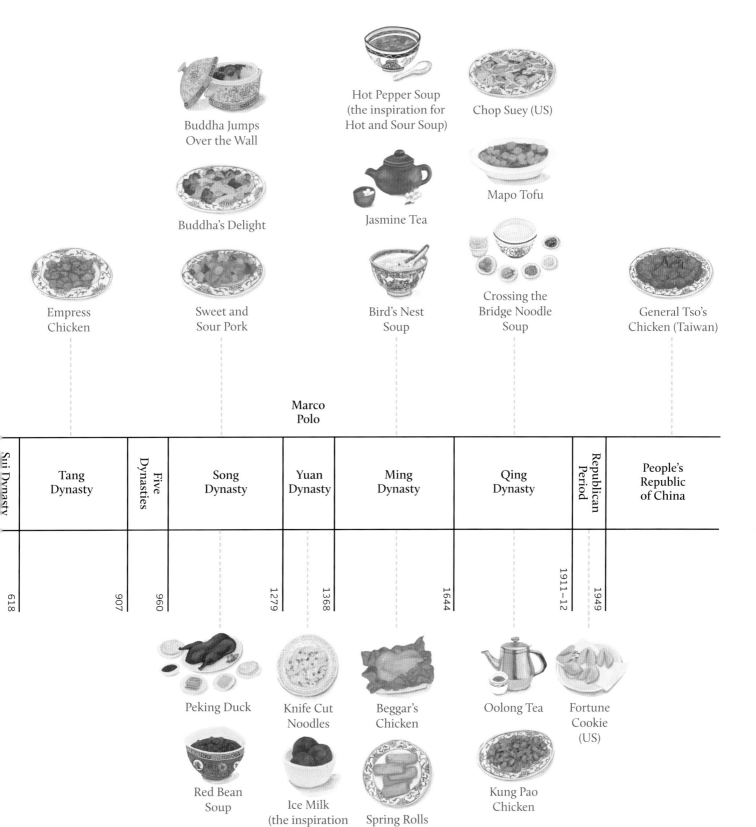

Buddha Jumps Over the Wall

Hot Pepper Soup (the inspiration for Hot and Sour Soup)

Chop Suey (US)

Buddha's Delight

Jasmine Tea

Mapo Tofu

Empress Chicken

Sweet and Sour Pork

Bird's Nest Soup

Crossing the Bridge Noodle Soup

General Tso's Chicken (Taiwan)

Marco Polo

Sui Dynasty	Tang Dynasty	Five Dynasties	Song Dynasty	Yuan Dynasty	Ming Dynasty	Qing Dynasty	Republican Period	People's Republic of China
618	907	960	1279	1368	1644		1911–12	1949

Peking Duck

Knife Cut Noodles

Beggar's Chicken

Oolong Tea

Fortune Cookie (US)

Red Bean Soup

Ice Milk (the inspiration for ice cream)

Spring Rolls

Kung Pao Chicken

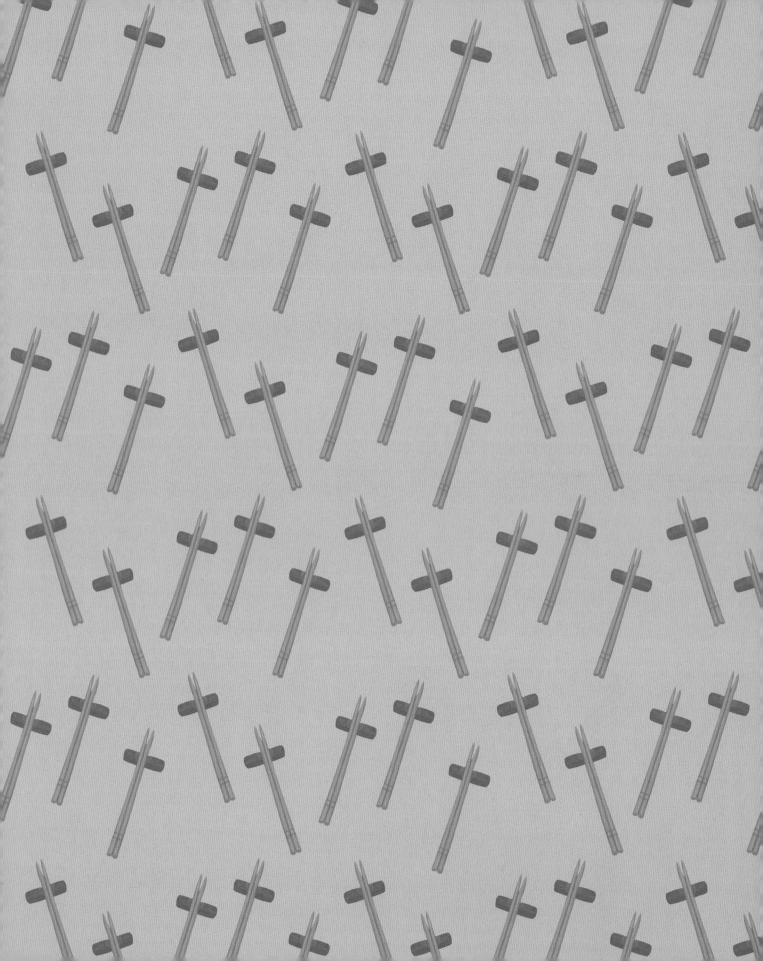

INTRODUCTION
緒論

Confession time! I don't use chopsticks correctly. My parents, immigrants from Taiwan, served Chinese food for almost every meal and we would dutifully set the table with chopsticks.

However, my parents never actually taught me how to use them. Maybe they thought that the skill would simply be passed down in our genes. And perhaps it was and it just skipped me, for both my sisters—older and younger—seem to have mastered using chopsticks correctly.

Yet I have not. Don't get me wrong, I can eat with chopsticks. When I was a child, I grabbed those chopsticks at every meal and figured out, in my own way, how to get the food to my mouth. Still, I hold my chopsticks "wrong" (as my older sister likes to tell me) and, even now, my skills are fairly limited.

Which is why I sympathize with the uncoordinated eaters who find chopsticks the bane of their Chinese dining experience. While a waiter or waitress can probably locate a fork, you usually have to ask for it. Which, of course, causes many to ask—why didn't they have forks in China?

Well, they did. In fact, the fork may have even been invented in China. Archaeologists have found three-pronged forks carved from animal bones in Shang dynasty tombs around 1200 BCE.

And it was also about this time that chopsticks were probably invented, too—archaeologists have found chopsticks in those same tombs. During the Shang dynasty (1600 BCE to 1100 BCE) or Western Zhou dynasty (1100 BCE to 771 BCE), chopsticks were most likely used as cooking tools—they were long and made of bronze in order to reach into deep pots and hot oil.

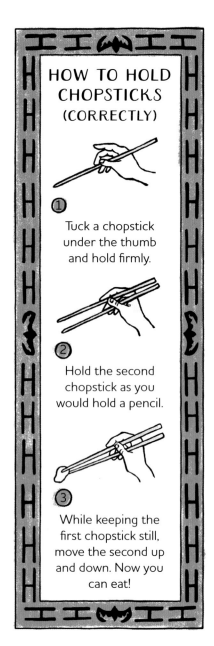

HOW TO HOLD CHOPSTICKS (CORRECTLY)

① Tuck a chopstick under the thumb and hold firmly.

② Hold the second chopstick as you would hold a pencil.

③ While keeping the first chopstick still, move the second up and down. Now you can eat!

As chopsticks evolved from bronze to bone to wood, the everyday use of chopsticks was also encouraged in society. Confucius, a great Chinese philosopher, had begun to advise people to use chopsticks at meals. He believed the sharp knife and fork reminded one of weapons—symbols of destruction and brutality. Dining, however, was a noble custom that could and should promote harmony and order. Replacing the metal fork and knife with refined, polished chopsticks could help people develop benevolent, cultured thoughts. Influenced by his teachings, people began to perceive knives on a dining table as uncivilized.

But everything really changed around 400 CE. At that time, there was a growth in population—such an increase that cooks needed to figure out how to save cooking oil. One way was to cut all the meat and vegetables into small pieces; chopsticks were perfect for maneuvering these small pieces into one's mouth.

And with that, the practice of eating with chopsticks became commonplace. Probably due to Confucius's influence, chopsticks were given a rounded, blunt end. They were shortened for convenience and ease—though they are longer than the Japanese chopsticks, as Chinese food tended to be shared, so longer chopsticks were more useful. Chopsticks even became an art of their own—some were intricately carved and decorated and made of ivory, jade, silver, or gold. Of course, the ones found in restaurants now are usually machine-made of plastic or disposable wood. Today's chopsticks are much less expensive!

Originally, the Chinese called chopsticks zhu. But as time went on and the usage spread, many who lived on the coast resisted using the word. *Zhu* sounded exactly like another word that meant "stop," which to the superstitious boat people implied that the ships would be unable to sail. So chopsticks were renamed kuaizi with *kuai* sounding like the word *fast*—suggesting that now ships would move quickly!

That is not the only superstition associated with chopsticks—there are quite a few! For example, when you set the table with chopsticks, make sure they are placed together near the cups—never with the cup in between—to prevent a quick (*kuai*) separation. In addition, make sure they are placed flush together. An uneven or unbalanced pairing invites bad luck. And speaking of bad luck, never place your chopsticks upright in your food. At tombs and temples, incense sticks are placed straight up and are burned as offerings. Placing the chopsticks in the same position of incense sticks among the living is like calling for death!

Other chopsticks taboos include: knocking an empty dish or glass with your chopsticks (it makes you look like a beggar), holding your chopsticks over the communal plates while you decide what you want (it's seen as plain rude: you should decide what you want before reaching for the food), and stirring or searching for a specific food on a communal plate (also rude and called colloquially as "grave digging"). Lastly, try not to drop your chopsticks on the floor—it disturbs buried ancestors!

But even with all these rules, using chopsticks is a delightful way to eat Chinese food. Many people think food tastes better with chopsticks—and they are right! Because once you get the hang of it, you'll find using chopsticks helps you eat more precisely, with smaller mouthfuls so that you consume your meal slower. This allows you to truly taste the flavors of your food and savor every bite. Even if you hold your chopsticks "wrong"!

There are also many stories about chopsticks to savor as well. Here are some of them.

⎯⎯ Yu the Great Invents Chopsticks ⎯⎯
大禹創造筷子

There are a few different stories about how chopsticks were invented but this is the one that is most commonly known—the one that relatives or Asian elders would tell me when I asked. But it's probably not true, for the use of chopsticks was not widespread until long after this story could have occurred. Also, while chopsticks are an important and vital part of Chinese culture and cuisine, their invention is mentioned in this story as a mere side note. But maybe that is not surprising, as Yu the Great is a well-revered figure in Chinese mythology, and people like to give him credit for lots of things. There are many stories about him, and this is only one of them.

In very, very ancient China (think prehistoric times), the Yellow River continually flooded, causing havoc and destruction. The floods were so devastating that Emperor Yao tasked a man who was known only as Gun to find a way to control the river. Gun was a good choice for the job, for he was said to be part god and a descendant of Huangdi—the Yellow Emperor and the originator of all Han Chinese culture (Han Chinese is the ethnic group native to China and represents about 90 percent of the population).

Gun decided that in order to stop the flooding, he must build dams and dikes around the Yellow River. But no matter how high he built the dams, it continued to flood. In desperation, Gun went to the Heavens and stole some "renewing earth"—a magical soil that could continuously grow and expand. By using this earth in the dams, the walls were able to grow as the water rose, and the flooding stopped.

But only temporarily. Because after nine years, the walls extended so high they collapsed—causing even greater ruin than before. And unfortunately, by now the heavenly gods realized that Gun had stolen from them and had him killed as punishment.

However, a strange thing happened to Gun's body after he was killed. It did not decompose or decay. Instead, it lay untouched and unchanged—as if waiting. During this time, Emperor Shun came to power, and the people still suffered greatly from floods.

After three years, Emperor Shun came across Gun's body and sliced it with his sword. As he cut Gun's stomach, a young man popped out. He was Gun's son, Yu.

"You must finish the job your father could not," Emperor Shun commanded. "You must stop the floods."

Yu nodded. "I will control the river," he vowed.

But Yu decided to approach the floods differently than his father. As he surveyed the river and the land and spoke to numerous tribes, he saw that controlling the water was like ruling the people. While he could force his will upon it, that would only work for a short while. Eventually, the water—like people—would rise to a point where it could not be restricted. The best rulers, Yu realized, were those who guided their people—and he would have to do the same with the water.

So Yu decided to build an elaborate irrigation system for the river, digging enormous ditches to redirect the water. He would lead the water to where he wished it to go.

This, however, was a project of such an ambitious scale and scope that it seemed preposterous. But Yu was undeterred. Even though he was married and had a son, he declared he would not return to them until he had stopped the floods. "The river has caused thousands of people to be without a home," he said. "I cannot rest in my own home until my task is finished."

Unfortunately, that task took thirteen years.

It was a hard, difficult, and ceaseless thirteen years of work. Not only did Yu direct the work, but he dredged and shoveled along with the workers—ate and slept with them, too. But because the work was so endless, Yu even resented the time he spent doing that. So he slept as little as possible and ate as quickly as possible.

One day, after beginning work before dawn, Yu worked so intensely that he did not stop to eat until late afternoon. Of course, by then he was ravenous. Yet, just as Yu's food had finished cooking and was being dished into a bowl, a minor emergency occurred upstream and the workers called for him. Yu quickly grabbed his bowl and tried to eat it as he raced to the problem. However, the hot food burned his fingers. So he grabbed two twin sticks from a nearby branch. They were thin and small enough to hold easily but strong enough to pick up the food from the bowl. Using the two sticks, Yu ate his food as he ran.

He quickly realized afterward that eating with two sticks was not only convenient but practical. With the sticks, he neither burned his fingers nor needed to wait for his food to cool. Immediately, Yu began to eat all his meals this way and introduced this method to all the workers. They, too, saw the advantages of eating with sticks and began to use them as well, which made the work go (slightly) faster.

Yu's irrigation project was successful. Once it was completed, the Yellow River no longer flooded. This made Yu extremely popular—so popular that Emperor Shun decided to name Yu as the next emperor instead of his own son. And even after Yu became emperor, he continued to eat with two sticks, which caused everyone—from nobles to commoners—to do the same. Emperor Yu, remembering the lessons he learned from controlling the river, ruled so wisely and well that Yu the Great is still honored to this day. And perhaps, just perhaps, part of his greatness was due to his invention of and devotion to eating with chopsticks.

Daji Invents Chopsticks
妲己創造筷子

Here is another story that tells the origins of chopsticks. This one is not as well-known, but it is interesting, especially because of how it contrasts with the story of Yu the Great. This story features the infamous character Daji, who has just as many stories told about her as does Yu. But unlike Yu, all the stories of Daji tell of how awful she was! So while Yu invented chopsticks as part of a heroic, selfless act, here they are created as a result of laziness and extravagance.

These two stories about chopsticks make a compelling pair! Which one do you believe?

There are many famous emperors in Chinese history. Unfortunately, a few of those emperors are famous because of how absolutely horrible they were. Emperor Zhou, the last ruler of the Shang dynasty, was one of these: He was a vicious and brutal tyrant who cared only for his own pleasure and indulgence.

Emperor Zhou had a famous companion named Daji—a woman of incomparable beauty. Unluckily, her immeasurable beauty was coupled with her immeasurable selfishness, which is perhaps why she and Emperor Zhou were so well matched. Daji was so heartless to others that people could not believe she was actually human. Rumors (that still live on to this day) began that she was really a fox spirit—an evil, supernatural being who took the form of a woman.

Emperor Zhou and Daji were very devoted to each other, while everyone else feared and hated them. Truly, the only person who felt affection for Emperor Zhou was Daji and the only one who cared for Daji was Emperor Zhou. They were quite a pair.

Now, Emperor Zhou was very picky about his food. Not only did he have ministers or advisors tortured and killed if they dared to criticize him, he also had chefs executed if he didn't like the food they had prepared. But Daji, who enjoyed her food, grew annoyed that her favorite dishes were not available because the cooks were killed.

So to try to keep some of her favored servants alive, Daji began to taste all of Emperor Zhou's food before he ate it. However, this grew time-consuming and boring to her and one day, out of laziness, she did not try his food ahead of time.

But when a plate of steaming food was set before the emperor, she knew he would rage at its temperature.

With an alluring smile, she pulled two jade hairpins from her hair.

"Let me feed you, my darling," she said. And with a quick, graceful motion, she plucked the food from his plate. She gently blew on it and then offered it to Emperor Zhou. Her hair flowed over her shoulders, and her coquettish gaze gave her the power to use her beauty to its fullest effect.

Emperor Zhou was naturally captivated and allowed her to place the food in his mouth. The food, now at the right temperature, was greatly enjoyed.

"From now on," Emperor Zhou demanded, "you must always feed me this way."

Daji was happy to do so, but disliked putting her beautiful jade hairpins in food, potentially ruining them. So she ordered jade workers to create special elaborate jade sticks just for food. These were, at least according to this story, the first chopsticks.

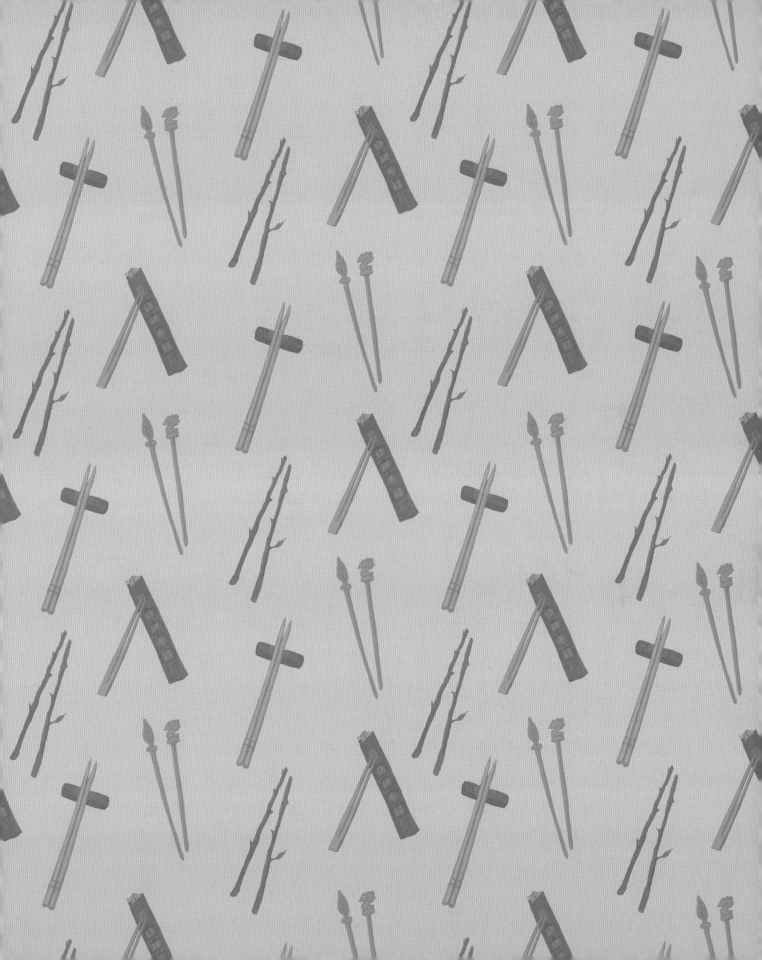

— How Chopsticks Prevent Poisoning —
筷子防止中毒

When I was a child, my father would often act out this joke:

"The emperor always used chopsticks," he'd say, "to make sure his food wasn't poisoned. Chopsticks will smoke if they touch poison." Then, making a grand gesture, he would gingerly place his chopsticks into his rice.

Nothing would happen.

"Good!" he would then declare. "I'm safe!"

Now, this joke was probably born out of the belief that ancient Chinese emperors used silver chopsticks to detect poison in their food. The idea was that the silver would react to poison and turn black if exposed. We know now that silver doesn't have any reaction to poison, but where did this idea of chopsticks being able to detect poison come from?

Most likely, it came from a story that has roots in actual history featuring a real person. Jiang Ziya was an important advisor to King Wen of the state of Zhou and later to his son, King Wu of Zhou, who eventually overthrew the Shang dynasty emperor, King Zhou, and established the next dynasty. (I know it's a little confusing—the emperor that ruled all of China during the Shang dynasty was named Emperor Zhou, while King Wen and his son King Wu ruled the state of Zhou during the same period.) In this story, Emperor Zhou is the same emperor who played a role in the story of Daji inventing chopsticks.

However, even though there really was a Jiang Ziya, this legend is just like the belief that silver detects poison—not true!

Jiang Ziya was a wise and honorable minister who faithfully served the rulers of the Shang dynasty—except for the last. That last Shang emperor—Emperor Zhou—was so depraved and corrupt that the appalled Ziya knew he could never help him. However, Emperor Zhou was extremely vicious (any minister that tried to advise him against his vulgar desires was immediately tortured and killed), so Ziya had to be very cunning in order to leave with his life. Using his elderly age to his advantage, Ziya pretended to be hapless and senile. His ruse worked perfectly, for Emperor Zhou was disgusted by Ziya's feebleness and had him exiled with nothing to Lake Pan in the vassal state Xiqi.

Now far from the court, Ziya and his wife lived in poverty. This did not bother Ziya, who believed he would eventually be called upon to aid a new dynasty to power. He spent his days fishing, patiently biding his time.

Ziya's wife, Shen, however, was quite bothered. She felt betrayed by Ziya, for not only had Ziya's ploy of being demented caused them to lose all rank and respect, her life was now one of drudgery and hardship. As she struggled and labored through the days, a bitter resentment began to grow inside her. Soon, every time Shen saw her husband she was filled with a furious anger.

One day, while Ziya was out fishing, old acquaintances from the court happened to be passing by. Shen burned with embarrassment as her old friends could not hide their pity and disgust at Shen's dingy clothes and shabby home. As they left, they gave Shen the leftovers from one of their meals of braised pork.

Shen prepared the pork for dinner, which would be a rare treat. But as she heated the food, Shen could not help remembering the expressions of shock and repulsion on the faces of her friends. Shen looked out the window and saw Ziya peacefully ambling home with his fishing rod over his shoulder and whistling a pleasant tune. An irrational rage swept over her. How dare he be so content! So happy, so pleased, when they were living in such misery!

"That stupid, lying, old fool! He thinks he will be called upon to help a new dynasty!" she spat. "I'd be better off without him!"

And with that, Shen seized some poison and sprinkled it onto his food.

Unsuspecting, Ziya came into the house.

"What smells so good?" he said, sitting down at the table. "I'm hungry!"

Shen said nothing but placed the poisoned meat before him.

As Ziya reached for the meat, a bird flew into the house! It swooped right over the food and pecked Ziya's hand.

"Ow!" Ziya cried out, waving his arm. "Go away! Go away!"

But the bird would not leave. Whenever Ziya tried to eat, the bird swooped again and pecked his hand.

"You don't want me to eat this, do you?" Ziya said to the bird. It twittered at him as if trying to say something and then fluttered out of the house. Ziya followed.

Outside, the bird waited for Ziya on a branch. As soon as it saw him, it began to sing:

> Jiang Ziya, Jiang Ziya!
> You must not use your hands to eat that meat!
> Here, here,
> Use what is under my feet!

And then the bird flew away. Ziya took the two bamboo sticks that the bird's feet had been resting on and looked at them curiously. "Use these to eat the meat?" Ziya mumbled to himself as he went back inside, his wife watching intently.

So, using the two sticks, Ziya picked up the meat in his bowl. To his surprise, as soon as the sticks touched his food, the tips turned an ugly, foul color.

"What did my food do to these sticks?" Ziya held the meat out to Shen, a gray smoke wisping from the darkened ends of the sticks. He looked at her guilty face and suddenly understood. "Is the meat poisoned?"

Shen turned white with shame. She now saw that Jiang Ziya was right, that he would be called upon to help begin a new dynasty and that the gods were protecting him. Shen confessed and begged pardon, promising to support him faithfully from there on.

Ziya—who soon after was found by King Wen of Zhou and did become an important advisor to start a new dynasty—was ever compassionate and understanding and forgave his wife, but never ate without chopsticks again.

TEA

茶的故事

INTRODUCTION

緒論

The first thing you will be served at a Chinese restaurant, even before you order, is tea. I know some parents don't let kids drink tea because of the caffeine in it, but my parents never had any such reservations. I learned to appreciate the drink pretty early on—and enjoyed it!

So, when the white teapot and a stack of teacups was waiting for us at our table, I was always eager to pour it. And even though my family and I never followed the proper tea-serving etiquette (usually, the host serves from oldest to youngest and themselves last), everyone accepted and enjoyed a cup—usually many cups.

That is because tea is an important part of Chinese culture. In ancient times, when the water quality was not always reliable, people depended on tea (the boiled water in tea made it safer to drink) and wine as beverages. Tea was actually first used as a medicine, but people enjoyed it so much that it soon became a daily drink!

China was the first civilization to cultivate tea—they began the whole system of growing tea leaves and processing them so that the flavor and fragrance would not be lost. Drinking tea became an element of the Chinese identity as well as cuisine. Teahouses became meaningful meeting places where people would come and discuss ideas.

During the Tang dynasty (618–907), a scholar named Lu Yu wrote the famous *Classic of Tea* treatise, writing with great detail about the methods of growing and preparing tea, the varieties of teapots and instruments, and even water qualities! People loved it. Yu's book became so famous and well read that he became known as the God of Tea. Tea shops often display porcelain statues of him—even now. However, whenever business is bad, store owners pour hot water over the statue!

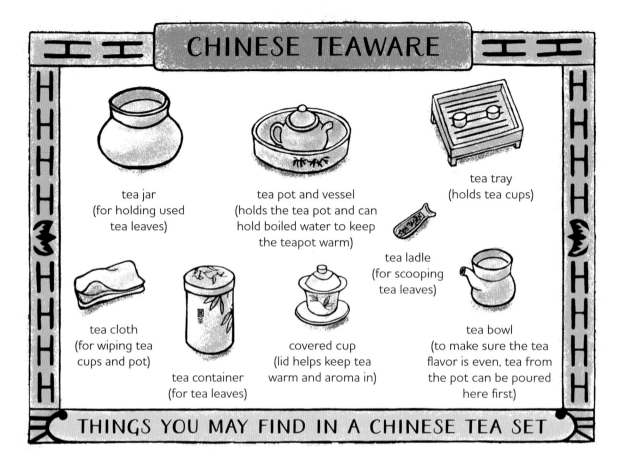

CHINESE TEAWARE

tea jar
(for holding used
tea leaves)

tea pot and vessel
(holds the tea pot and can
hold boiled water to keep
the teapot warm)

tea tray
(holds tea cups)

tea ladle
(for scooping
tea leaves)

tea cloth
(for wiping tea
cups and pot)

tea container
(for tea leaves)

covered cup
(lid helps keep tea
warm and aroma in)

tea bowl
(to make sure the tea
flavor is even, tea from
the pot can be poured
here first)

THINGS YOU MAY FIND IN A CHINESE TEA SET

But tea and tea drinking were and still are taken very seriously. It is often considered an art form. The tea ceremony is a ritual of contemplation and respect. Today, serving tea remains a custom to honor elders.

Tea can also be very valuable. In the past, tea was especially prized. People used to say, "Not for all the tea in China!" when they wanted to declare that they would not change their minds for anything. To refuse "all the tea in China" meant no treasure in the world could move you!

The tea served at a typical Chinese restaurant is probably not the expensive sort. But it should still be very pleasant and aromatic. You might also notice that your teacup has no handle; feeling the warmth of the tea through the cup is part of Chinese tradition. If the cup is too hot to hold, then your tea is too hot to drink!

It also might be difficult to tell exactly what kind of tea you are drinking. There are many kinds of tea—so many that the varieties are broken up into categories such as: green, black, white, oolong, yellow, dark, and scented. Each tea has its own special qualities and comes from a different region of China. And each one has its own story, too.

So, sit down and have a cup of tea (I'll serve you before I pour a cup for myself!) while I tell you some of them.

TEA ETIQUETTE

Serve tea by pouring the tea into cups in order. The cups should be ⅔ full.

Tea should always be served to the eldest guest first.

Do not gulp your tea. Sip it slowly and savor the flavor!

HOW TO SERVE AND DRINK TEA POLITELY

DRAGON WELL TEA
龍井茶

A dragon well is something that pops up fairly frequently in old Chinese myths, much like fairy rings in European tales. So whenever a dragon well is mentioned in a story, I always prepare myself to be enchanted. In Chinese culture, dragons are associated with water—be it rain, a lake, the ocean, or a well! So sometimes—or at least in some legends—a dragon will be a guardian of a special well, often living in it. Those wells are the dragon wells and must always be treated with respect.

Now, Dragon Well is also the name of one of China's most famous green teas. Dragon Well Tea, or longjing cha, is heralded for a flavor that is smooth and delicate and never bitter.

This popular tea is from a village in Hangzhou in Zhejiang Province. This village is actually named Dragon Well Village. And yes, this village has a well. Now, does that well have a dragon? Did the dragon make the tea? Listen, and I will tell you....

Once, a long time ago, there was a village that lay huddled in the mountains. It was a poor village, and it was only made poorer when a drought occurred. The ground turned dusty. The plants withered. The ponds became puddles of hardened mud, and villagers' empty buckets clanged like death bells as their wells dried up. The people searched everywhere for water as the sun blazed down on them through the clear sky.

Finally, they found an old well. It was no wonder they had not seen it earlier, for it was not in the village, but in its far outskirts, and was almost hidden by jutting rocks. And the well was not merely old, but ancient. One could tell by its worn, carved stone covered in jade-colored moss—the only green the villagers had seen in months.

"How can this well still have water?" one of the villagers asked as he stared into a deep hole, the black water reflecting sparkles of sun.

"Who cares?" another answered, tying a rope to a bucket. "It's water! Let's get it!" The other villagers agreed and all readied to gather water from the well. But an old woman, who had been silently studying the carved stones, stepped in front of the well.

"Stop!" she shouted. "Stop! A dragon lives in this well!"

The villagers looked at her in silence. "Why else would this well have water?" The old woman cried out, "Look at the green moss! Look at those carvings! Are those not honored marks for a dragon?"

"She's right," a village elder agreed. "I remember my grandparents telling me of a dragon who lived in a well near here. This must be that well. We dare not disturb his home."

"But we need water!" the other villagers protested. "What should we do?"

"Let us ask this dragon for help instead," the village elder said.

So they gathered around the well and bowed and prayed, asking the dragon for help. They surrounded his home with incense sticks and lit them as offerings. As the incense sticks burned, the wisps of smoke seemed to twist together, creating a thick, silvery cloud. The villagers squinted. Was it in the shape of a dragon? It was hard to tell with the glare of the sun. But they could tell that the cloud was growing larger and larger. As it grew, it floated higher and higher into the sky. Only when it had risen above them and blotted out the sun did it stop.

And that is when the villagers began to hear a low rumble. Was it...? Yes! It was!

"Rain!" The villagers whooped and shouted, raising their arms to feel the cool, wet drops cascade upon them. Many began to dance with joy; others just stood with their mouths open.

But the old woman did neither. Instead, she threw herself before the well in a humble kowtow. "Oh, thank you, honored dragon," she said again and again. When the villagers saw her, they quickly joined in. Soon, all were bowing with gratitude.

"Yes," the village elder said. "We thank this great dragon for his kindness. From here on, we shall now call our village Dragon Well, in honor and appreciation of this dragon in his well."

And so the village of Dragon Well survived the drought. However, it was still a poor village and recovery was difficult. It was particularly hard for the old woman. She lived in the poorest part of the village and was a widow without any children or family. The most she had was a tea bush in front of her house, but the leaves had been bitter in the best of times. Now, after the drought, the bush was scraggly and almost bare.

One evening, soon after the rains had come, the old woman heard a knock at her door. A strange man stood at her doorway asking for shelter for the night. The man was strange in more than one way: Not only was he unknown to her but his clothes were old-fashioned, and his thick, shaggy eyebrows were so long and wild that they almost seemed like two horns jutting out from his large, angular forehead. However, his smile was kind, and his request was respectful and polite, so the old woman ushered him in without hesitation.

"I'm sorry I have only this bitter tea to offer," the old woman said as she poured him tea made from the leaves of her bush. "I'm afraid I'm a poor woman and this is all I have."

"Poor woman?" the man said, as if in surprise. "How can you be poor when you have such a treasure?"

"Treasure? What treasure?" the woman replied, with even more surprise. "Do not make jests at me."

"It's no jest," the man insisted. "The treasure is right outside in front of your door."

The woman opened her door only to see the old millstone mortar that her husband had abandoned there before his death. In the many years since then, the old woman had discarded various bits of rubbish and waste into it, and it was thickly caked with grime.

"Do you mean that?" she asked, pointing at the millstone.

"Of course," the strange man said, nodding.

"If that is the treasure," the old woman said, "you may take it."

"That wouldn't be fair," the man said. "But I'll buy it from you. I'm telling you, it's a treasure."

As the sun began to rise and the man was still asleep, the old woman looked again at the mortar. The morning light did not make it look any better—it was still terribly dirty and filled with a blackish muck. She would be glad to have it taken away. *But if he is going to buy it*, the old woman thought, *I should clean it for him.*

She quickly dug out the filth, throwing the sludge under the tea bush. Then she rinsed it, also dumping the muddy water onto her bush. When she was finished, the mortar was cleaner than it had ever been, with every crack and crevice showing on the gray stone. *He'll be pleased*, the old woman thought.

But when the stranger woke and saw the mortar, a look of dismay came over his face.

"What happened to the treasure?" the man gasped.

"It's right here," the woman said, pointing at the stone mortar.

"Oh, that was not the treasure," the man said, shaking his head. However, when he looked at the old woman, his eyes were twinkling. He smiled. "Make sure you share," he said.

The woman frowned in confusion as she looked again at the mortar. But when she turned to speak to the strange man again, he was gone.

The old woman remained confused until a few days later she found her tea bush lush with new green leaves, the same jade-green color as the moss on the dragon's well. What was even more surprising was that these tea leaves were not bitter—oh no, far from it! These new leaves were soft and tender and made a tea so fragrant that the entire village could smell its scent in the air. Soon, all came to the old woman's house to try this new, enticing tea. And the old woman, mindful of the stranger's last words to her, was generous. Not only did she serve endless cups of tea, she gave the villagers cuttings from her bush so that they could grow their own.

Before long, the old woman's tea plant was growing everywhere in the village. It became famous. People from faraway towns and cities heard about the wonderful new tea, and soon everyone, even the emperor himself, came all the way to the now prosperous village of Dragon Well to have their own cup of Dragon Well Tea.

JASMINE TEA
茉莉花茶

Every once in a while, the teapot at a Chinese restaurant will be holding Jasmine Tea. When this happens, I always feel happy. Because not only is Jasmine Tea one of my favorites, I get to feel smart that I can tell what kind of tea it is without having to see a label.

Though that is not really an impressive thing to brag about, because it's pretty easy to identify Jasmine Tea. The flowery aroma gives it away. However, even though it has a flowery smell, the flavor of the tea is rich and not at all cloying—which is why I like it.

But while the tea is distinctive, I was surprised to learn that there isn't really one kind of Jasmine Tea. Green, black, or white tea is infused with jasmine blossoms, giving the tea its fragrance. Jasmine Tea is one of the most popular scented teas in China.

This story tells of how Jasmine Tea came to be. If this tale is really true (which I, romantically, like to think that it is), it probably occurred in the late Ming dynasty (1368–1644).

Chen Guqiu was a tea merchant from the capital city of Beijing. Though he was a kind man, he was much more captivated by tea than he was with people and often traveled widely to find and trade fine and precious teas. Once, as he was traveling south, he stopped at an inn. Even though his thoughts were full of tea, he could not help but notice a sobbing girl also at the inn.

"What's wrong with her?" Guqiu asked the innkeeper.

"Her father just died and she has no money to bury him. She also has no money to go home." The innkeeper sighed and shook her head. "I don't want to cast her out, but I may be forced to soon."

"Poor girl," Guqiu said. He reached into his purse and took out some bars of silver. "Give this to her. It should be enough to pay for the funeral and get her home."

Then Guqiu packed up his belongings, dreaming of the rare tea he might find on his journey. As he readied to leave, the girl rushed to him.

"Thank you, thank you, kind sir!" she said to him, her face alight with gratitude. "The innkeeper gave me your money and..."

"Oh, it's nothing, nothing," Guqiu said and, slightly embarrassed, tried to wave her away.

"If there is anything I can do for you...," the girl continued eagerly. "Please, oh please! I do so want to repay you! What is it that you wish for?"

"Ah, I only wish to find a new tea for my trade," Guqiu said, "and you cannot help me there."

"Oh." The girl looked down in disappointment. Guqiu climbed upon his horse.

"Do not worry," Guqiu said to the girl. "Bury your father and return home. Good luck to you."

And with that, Guqiu left. He did not look back at the girl, who stood watching until he disappeared from sight. Within a few minutes, he had forgotten all about her—thinking only of the new tea he hoped to discover.

A few years later, Guqiu stopped at the same inn. The innkeeper was excited to see him again.

"You!" she said. "I have something for you. That girl you helped, do you remember? She came back and left this for you."

She handed Guqiu a carefully folded packet. "So sad about that girl," the innkeeper said, shaking her head. "I heard she died soon after she gave this to me."

Guqiu tucked the packet inside his sleeve, his face clouding over the somber news. But, as usual, his thoughts quickly returned to his tea. He had collected various lovely teas on his travels, but none was the special, unique tea he had hoped for. He knew he would be meeting with a tea master when he arrived home and had hoped to offer something impressive. *I will have nothing extraordinary to share with him*, Guqiu thought gloomily.

So Guqiu returned home downhearted. To his dismay, the tea master was eager to see him and came to visit almost immediately.

"I cannot wait to try the incredible teas you have brought back from your journey," the tea master said. "How many treasures did you bring back this time?"

"Oh," Guqiu said, slightly flustered. "Not many."

"Nonsense! You are too modest," the tea master laughed, grasping Guqiu's arm with goodwill. "You always have something that amazes me!"

"Perhaps not this...," Guqiu began, but the tea master's good-natured shake had dislodged the packet in Guqiu's sleeve. Like the petal of a dying flower, it fluttered to the ground.

"And what is that?" the tea master asked, his eyes sparkling in anticipation. Guqiu only shrugged as he picked up the packet and carefully opened it.

Immediately, an enchanting fragrance filled the air, and both Guqiu and the tea master saw that the packet was filled with an unusual tea.

With great haste, Guqiu heated water and prepared the tea sets. As he poured the water over the tea leaves, a figure appeared in the steam. It was the girl! She smiled and held out the jasmine flowers in her cupped hands. Then she disappeared.

The tea master gasped.

"This must be Returning Kindness Tea!" he whispered. "I have heard of this tea—it is of such wonder that a tea fairy appears in the steam! My friend, I thought this tea was only a story! How did you acquire it?"

Guqiu recounted the story of the girl as they sipped the delicate, exquisite tea—stopping often to delight at the enchanting drink.

"The girl must have used all her life energy to create this tea," the master said when hearing of her death. He stopped to savor a sip. "It is unlikely that we will ever taste a tea like this again."

"Perhaps...," Guqiu said slowly, "but did you notice that she carried jasmine flowers? She held them out to me. I think she was trying to tell me something."

The tea master sniffed the remaining tea leaves. "It does smell of jasmine blossoms," he agreed. "Do you think she was telling us to add jasmine flowers to our tea?"

After that, Chen Guqiu began to add jasmine blossoms to his tea—creating the beloved, sweet-smelling Jasmine Tea.

OOLONG TEA
烏龍茶

The complimentary tea that is most often served at a Chinese restaurant is usually Oolong Tea, a very popular and traditional Chinese brew.

Oolong literally translates to "black dragon," so I often imagined that the tea was a gift from a legendary black dragon or maybe—in the typical Chinese fashion that adores stories with sad endings—it was some tragic story of a dragon who died and from his black ashes grew the tea. It seemed to me that a tea with such a mythical name should also have an epic, legendary story. Or at least have a magical dragon in it! But it does not.

During the Qing dynasty (1644-1911), in the village of Nanyan in Xiping Town, Anxi County, Fujian Province, there lived the Long family. They were tea farmers and had a son with dark skin. As the boy grew older and spent more time outdoors, his skin became darker and darker until it was as black as an iron cooking pan. Because of this, he was nicknamed Oolong—or Black Dragon.

Now, Oolong worked on the family farm diligently—as was expected. But he much preferred hunting to picking tea leaves. So, when working in the fields, he would often bring his spear with him just in case he saw something he could hunt for dinner!

One day, he did see something. As he was returning home after a full day of picking leaves, a beautiful deer jumped in front of Oolong. With his basket of leaves still on his back, Oolong gave chase. The leaves bounced and shook inside his basket, but Oolong did not stop—instead following the deer deeper and deeper into the forest. Finally, the deer grew tired and Oolong was able to slay it.

Exuberant, Oolong flung down his tea basket to examine his kill. As he heaved the deer carcass over his shoulder, he forgot all about his basket and returned home. His family butchered the deer and enjoyed a dinner with fresh venison meat.

It was only the next day that Oolong remembered his tea basket. He retraced his steps and found his basket in the forest, exactly where he had left it. Only when he looked to examine the tea, the leaves were now withered with dried edges. Still, not wishing to waste a whole day's work, Oolong decided to prepare the leaves for tea anyway.

Oolong began to roast the tea, and a unique and pleasant aroma wafted from the leaves. This caught the attention of the rest of his family, who came to investigate the delicious scent. The tea was quickly brewed, and all enjoyed cups of this new rich-smelling tea, with a fruity and flowery taste.

"Where did you find this new tea?" his family asked. "We must grow it on our farm!"

"It's not a new tea," Oolong insisted. "It's our tea! It's the same tea we already grow!"

After many experiments, the family was finally able to determine what had happened. The leaves, well-shaken on Oolong's back when he was running and then left outside when he had forgotten about them, had fermented before he roasted them—making the tea unusually fragrant and flavorful. They added these steps to their tea-making process and a new favorite tea was born. Interestingly, the dark leaves, after being oxidized and twisted, seemed to take the shape of an unfurling dragon.

"Ha!" The family looked at the tea, then at Oolong, then laughed. "The leaves look like a black dragon—just like our own Black Dragon!"

So, from then on it was called Oolong Tea.

White Hair Silver Needle Tea
白毫銀針

The first time I had white tea was when I was a child in Taiwan. I remember my mother carefully passing me the small, delicate cup of tea and all the adults around me slowly sipping it as if the tea were some sort of magical elixir. I'm sorry to say I have no recollection of the flavor of the tea, but the hushed reverence of my family drinking it definitely left an impression.

That is because white tea is considered to be the most delicate of all teas. The tea plant is picked while its buds are still covered with fine white hairs—which is why it is called white tea. In the past, this tea was difficult to transport without spoiling, so one rarely enjoyed it outside of Asia.

Now, however, you can probably find white tea available in a fine Chinese restaurant, or you can order it from a specialty store. If you see white tea on the menu, look for White Hair Silver Needle Tea (Baihao yinzhen 白毫銀針), and give it a try. You won't be disappointed—it is the most famous white tea in China. It has a sweet and delicate flavor that is unlike any other tea.

It also has this wonderful story. Perhaps you can share this tale while you pass a small, delicate cup of white tea to a friend, and maybe it will be a magical elixir for you, too.

Long ago, in a small village in the Fujian Province, a terrible, deadly illness began to spread. As people started dying, the villagers remembered the long-told stories whispered by their elders. There was a plant, the elders had said, that must have grown from seeds that had accidentally fallen from the heavens, for it—when made into a tea—could cure any disease or illness. It grew at the top of their highest mountain where a sea of clouds hid all from view. Unfortunately, there was a curse upon that peak—for no one who scaled up it ever came down.

However, as more and more villagers began to die from the disease, people began to search for the plant. Many left, promising to bring back the cure for the village, but none returned.

In this village lived the Zhi family of three siblings: Zhi Gang, the eldest brother; the second brother, Zhi Cheng; and the youngest sister, Zhi Yu. As more and more neighbors fell ill and died, the three came to a decision.

"We cannot just watch our friends die," Gang declared.

"And wait for our own deaths," Cheng added.

"Then, brothers," Yu said, "we must go search for that magic plant."

The others nodded in agreement, and Gang drew out his sword and placed it on the table.

"As the eldest, I will go first," Gang said. "If this sword begins to rust, it means I have failed and one of you must then make the attempt."

So, Gang left his younger brother and sister to find the plant. When he arrived at the foot of the mountain, he met an old man whose white beard seemed to sparkle like silver needles in the light. The old man looked at him sadly.

"Are you here to get the plant at the top of the mountain?" the old man asked.

"Yes," Gang said eagerly. "If it truly exists, I will get it."

The old man sighed. "Yes, the plant does exist and can cure the disease that plagues your village," he said. "But the plant is growing next to a dragon well—a well that is a dragon's home. Unfortunately, the dragon that lives there has become corrupt and wicked. He will stop you, using trickery and magic, just as he has done to the many others who have come before you."

"I still must try," Gang said.

"All right," the old man said. "Then remember this—when you climb the mountain, do not look back until you have the plant in your hand. No matter what you hear—do not turn around for any reason until you have the plant."

Gang began to climb the mountain. The path was very steep and rocky, without any plants or animals around. There was not even a twittering of birds. Gang climbed for hours, hearing only his own heavy footsteps and the wind. When he was halfway up, he encountered a strange rock garden.

Large stones, all as big as he, stood before him—like a forest of giant, grotesque tombstones. Some were weathered and worn, others jagged and pointed. And all had a strange nightmarish quality to them. The entire area filled Gang with dread, and he decided to leave. He had only just begun to step away when he heard a shout.

"Don't go!" a loud, commanding voice echoed. "You cannot go!"

Surprised, Gang looked to see who was calling. As Gang looked back, he was turned to stone.

The mountain had gained another rock.

Back in the village, Cheng and Yu waited for Gang to return. One evening, just as the sun was swallowed by the horizon, a beam of light cascaded through the window upon Gang's sword and the blade immediately covered with rust. Cheng and Yu gazed at each other sadly, but with resolve.

"Gang has failed," Cheng said to Yu. "It is my turn to try to find the plant. I will leave in the morning."

The next morning at dawn, Cheng said goodbye to his younger sister. Before he left, he handed her one of his arrows with a steel tip.

"If the point of this arrow rusts," Cheng said, "it means I have failed, and you must make the attempt."

So, Cheng left his sister to find the plant. Like his brother, he went to the foot of the mountain and met the silvery-white-haired man who issued him the same warning. Cheng nodded soberly, determined not to meet the same fate as his brother.

But the path up the mountain was just as difficult and steep for Cheng as it was for Gang. He, too, reached the midpoint of the mountain and met the eerie, looming forest of stones. The bleak rocks seemed to be warning him, and one rock in particular gave him an odd sense of familiarity. As he gazed upon it, he shuddered as if an icicle had been placed upon his heart. Cheng quickly moved past it, but just as it was behind him, he heard someone call out.

"Brother! Brother! Come back and save me!"

It was Gang's voice! Without stopping to think, Cheng turned. As Cheng looked back, he was turned to stone.

And there was another rock for the mountain.

At home, Cheng's silver arrow tip turned brown. When Yu saw the rusted point, her eyes closed with grief. But when they reopened, they were filled with determination. Yu packed a basket with some pounded rice cakes (niangao 年糕) and drink. Then, after tying Cheng's rusted arrow and Gang's rusted sword onto her back, Yu left for the mountain.

And just like her brothers, Yu met the silver-haired man. When he heard that she, too, was attempting to get the plant, he looked so sorrowful that she offered him one of her rice cakes.

"My friends are dying in the village," Yu told the old man as he ate the rice cake, "and my brothers have probably died as well. So I have nothing to lose, and I am not afraid. I must try to find the plant."

The old man said nothing until he finished eating. He had eaten the entire rice cake except for two small pieces. These, he put in each of her hands.

"There is a better use for these than to fill my stomach," he said to her. The hair of his beard glistened like needles of frost, and his eyes pierced into hers. Then he pulled his ears. "Remember, the wicked dragon will try to trick you. No matter what you hear, you must not turn around for any reason until you have the plant in your hands."

Yu looked at the small, ordinary pieces of rice cake the old man had pressed into her hands. When she looked up to question him, the old man was gone. There were not even footprints on the ground to show he had been there.

Yu bit her lip. The old man had been trying to tell her something, she was sure. But what? She stared at the pieces of sticky rice cake in her hands, thinking about what he had said and how he had pulled his ears. Then she smiled.

Taking the cake pieces the old man had left her, she stuffed one piece into one of her ears and the other piece into her other ear. Immediately, she could hear nothing. With her world now silent, Yu began to climb the mountain.

Just as it had been for her brothers, the path up the mountain was difficult. But when halfway up the mountain, Yu came across the ghoulish collection of rocks, she only shivered and hurried onward. She did not hear the commands of a ruler, the questions of her neighbor, the wails of a baby, or even the begging of her brothers. The rice cakes in her ears blocked all sound, and she continued up the mountain.

Finally, Yu made it to the top of the mountain. It was so high that the clouds rolled like ocean waves, and sprinkling mist coated everything with silver. But Yu did not see any of that. She looked only for the plant. And finally she saw it.

It was growing next to a well, just as the old man had said. Its green leaves dripped with dew, and as Yu plucked the plant, she noticed the fine, white-and-silver pointed hairs covering the closed blossoms. They reminded her of…

But just then, a violent wind threw her to the ground. She could feel the air and the earth tremble, and as she looked up, a monstrous beast emerged from the swelling clouds—its eyes glaring malice and malevolence. The wicked dragon!

Yu had packed the rice cake so tightly in her ears that she did not hear the dragon's thundering roars or angry bellows, but she could hear her own screams as the dragon's spiked claws lashed at her. He only barely missed—his knife-sharp talon slashing the skirt of her dress—and Yu, clutching the plant, squeezed herself between two rocks to hide.

Yu knew that her hiding place would not last long. And she was right. For in an instant, the boulder concealing her was smashed into pieces and the wicked dragon flew before her with a look of satisfied viciousness, set to strike Yu a fatal blow.

However, Yu was ready. Swiftly, Yu pulled Cheng's rusted metal arrow from her back and, with all her might, flung it like a spear at the dragon. The arrow flew fast and true and lodged itself in the dragon's eye. The wicked dragon, in shock and agony, fell to the ground. Yu, without hesitation, then grabbed Gang's sword and plunged it into the dragon's other eye.

The dragon was now unable to see and writhed in pain and outrage. Breathless and panting, Yu snatched the precious plant she had dropped and prepared to run. But as she grabbed the plant, one of its damp leaves flew from her hand and landed on the injured dragon. The dew from the leaf seemed to grow and spread, washing over the dragon and, within moments, the dragon had turned to stone.

Yu could only watch with her eyes and mouth open in awe. When the dragon stopped moving, she knew she could safely leave. With the plant in her hand, Yu turned and made her way down the mountain.

When Yu was halfway down, she hesitated at the strange forest of rocks. For the rocks had changed. No longer jagged or deformed, Yu now saw that the rocks were actually shaped like people. And two of them...Yu gasped. Was it Gang and Cheng? Were these two rocks her brothers?

A drop of water from the plant ran down Yu's clenched hand. She looked at the plant, wet with silvery dew, and then at the rocks before her. Her eyes widened. Dew from the plant had made the dragon turn to stone. Would it turn a stone back into a person?

Slowly, Yu shook the plant over the rock-shapes of Gang and Cheng. As the droplets fell upon the stone, the wetness spread. The rocks seemed to soften and color until finally, the real Gang and Cheng stood before her, warm-blooded and smiling. The siblings hugged in joy and happiness.

Quickly, the brothers and sister sprinkled dew from the plant onto the rest of the stones—

returning all the villagers back to their human form. With great rejoicing, they climbed down the mountain and returned to their village.

The plant, after Yu carefully harvested its seeds, was made into a tea. It was then quickly served to the sick villagers—who all drank it and recovered. Yu planted the seeds and tended to them so conscientiously that they flourished. As the plant thrived, Yu generously shared the leaves and seeds with all the villagers. Soon the plant grew everywhere in the village, and the tea made from its leaves was treasured by all.

And what was the plant called? Yu named the tea plant White Hair Silver Needle, in honor of the old man who had helped her at the foot of the mountain. She was convinced that he was a spirit of the plant or an immortal tea fairy, for the delicate, white, pointed hairs on the plant's buds were much like the hair of his beard. And who knows? Perhaps she was right.

THE ORIGIN OF TEA
茶的起源

This is just one of the many legends of the origins of the tea plant. Like almost all the stories in this book, there are multiple myths—full of imagined fancies that historical evidence points to as unlikely to be true. This one is no different, for the tea plant was most likely around years before the time of the main character Da Mo (roughly the fifth century). But the story is certainly memorable.

If you are squeamish, you might want to skip over this one, as it is a little gory. Which is rather surprising because this story is about a Buddhist, and Buddhism is a religion that generally opposes violence. However, tea drinking and Buddhism are often intertwined—so this story shows that even with its possibly violent origins, tea has grown into a substance for peace.

Hundreds and hundreds of years ago, there was once a devout Buddhist monk named Da Mo. He was especially devoted to the Buddhist discipline of meditation—the practice of calming one's thoughts and focusing on achieving enlightenment. Da Mo would sit for hours and days, training his mind to be calm and clear. He believed that if he practiced enough, he could be free of all the earthly sufferings that surrounded him and that his spirit could achieve perfection.

So, Da Mo practiced meditation a lot. He was so serious about practicing meditation that he traveled to Henan Province and found a remote cave on Wuru Peak. There, inside the cave, he sat down and stared at the rock wall to meditate.

He sat there meditating for *nine years.*

And as the years passed, his spirit became more and more pure. However, during his seventh year of staring at the wall, he accidentally fell asleep. When he woke up, Da Mo was so angry at himself that he vowed he would never fall asleep again. And to make sure, he took a knife and sliced off his eyelids!

However, Da Mo's spirit had become so pure during those first seven years of meditating that when his sliced eyelids fluttered to the ground of the cave, they sprouted. From those sprouts, a plant formed—a plant whose swaying leaves were the same shape as Da Mo's eyelids.

Inspired, Da Mo plucked some leaves from the plant and boiled them in water. As he sipped this newly created beverage, he found that it was delicious and it refreshed him. He no longer felt tired.

With this drink, Da Mo was able to meditate without stopping for two more years and was finally able to completely perfect his spirit. He then founded his own temple, spreading what would be known as Zen Buddhism throughout China. And at his temple, to help their meditation practices, his followers always sipped heated water brewed with the leaves of this plant—the drink that we now know as tea.

APPETIZERS

開胃菜的故事

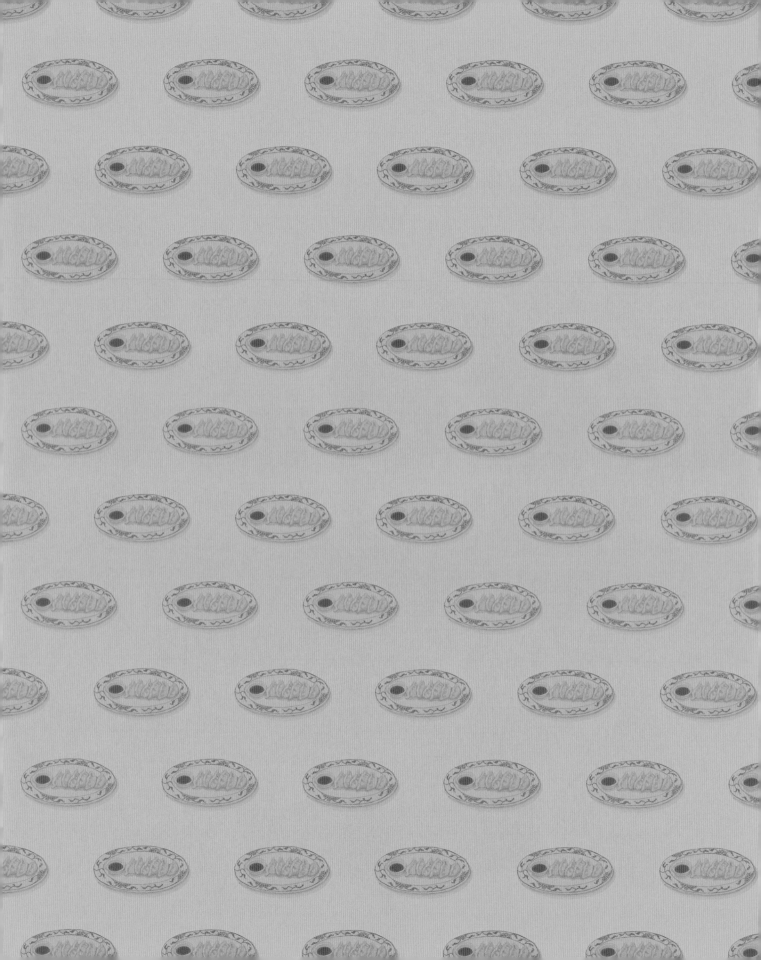

INTRODUCTION
緒論

The dinners my mother cooked at home usually consisted of soup, rice, and three or four hot dishes all served at once. I didn't know this at the time, but this is pretty traditional for an ordinary Chinese meal eaten at home. It's how many Chinese people eat even to this day.

However, Westerners are used to restaurants having categories of appetizers, side dishes, and dessert, so the Chinese immigrants who first established restaurants here in the United States hurriedly tried to fill those categories with what seemed most appropriate from their cuisine.

The idea of an appetizer—a smaller-portioned dish served before the main meal—was slightly challenging to Chinese cooks. At Chinese banquets, they did serve an appetizer of sorts—a first course of cold food that might include slices of tofu, jellyfish, and seaweed. But Chinese chefs were very mindful of American tastes and quickly determined that such foods would probably not be well received.

So, restaurateurs looked through their rich repertoire to see what might work instead. They brought out their snack and street foods, like scallion pancakes and roasted meats on skewers. Yes, all those meat-on-a-stick appetizers can likely trace their roots to old peddlers on the city streets of China, who were, perhaps, selling the very first fast food!

The chefs also presented their festival food, like dumplings and spring rolls. In China, these were usually only eaten during holidays, but in America they quickly became foods to eat every day!

For other appetizers, they "borrowed" from American menus—such as Crab Rangoon, which is a completely American invention! Victor Jules Bergeron (also known as Trader Vic) created it for his tiki bar and restaurant chain (called Trader Vic's after his own nickname) and gave it a false, "exotic" Asian background (sometimes claiming it was Burmese) to help sell it to patrons. But Chinese restaurateurs quickly saw how popular it was and decided to embrace its made-up Asian history to sell to their own customers.

POPULAR STREET FOODS

fried dough sticks
(youtiao)

steamed pork bun
(bao zi)

stinky tofu
(ghou tofu)

tea egg
(cha ye dan)

Chinese hamburger
(rov jia mao)

Chinese meat
kebab (chuan'r)

What might surprise you is that Crab Rangoon—a mixture of crab, cream cheese, and seasonings fried inside a wonton wrapper—has no roots in Chinese cuisine. That is because there isn't much of a history of cheese culture for Han Chinese. The amount of land available for grazing animals was quite limited, so the Chinese did not keep many animals, especially large ones like cows. Across the northern steppes, with its vast grasslands, dairy was consumed by the Mongols and other populations from that area. But, in general, most of the Chinese looked at their cattle as beasts of burden— they were there to plow fields, not to supply milk.

So, that is why the scallion pancake needed Italian Marco Polo to turn it into pizza (really just a myth, but a fun one), and spring rolls are eaten every season, not just spring! And why not? Anything that whets your appetite, be it a street or festival food, is still a great appetizer, right? Anyway, I hope these stories whet your appetite for more!

DUMPLINGS
餃子

There is a common Chinese saying that goes:

Nothing is more delicious than dumplings; no position is more comfortable to sleep than lying down.

好吃不如餃子, 舒服不如倒著

Haochi buru jiaozi, shufu buru daozhe

Personally, I have to agree with both of those statements! For not only do I like sleeping lying down, Chinese dumplings might be my favorite food ever. I can eat them anytime, night or day, sitting up or lying down! And I love all the different types of Chinese dumplings—including wonton with its delicate skin (mentioned in the soup section), the round, squat pork-and-shrimp siu mai found at dim sum, and the famous xiao long bao soup dumplings bursting with steaming liquid as you eat them. It's impossible to count how many kinds of Chinese dumplings there are! And each kind is not only filled with meat and vegetables but also with legends, traditions, and cultural significance.

Usually, when someone says Chinese dumpling here in the United States, we almost always picture jiaozi (餃子)—the crescent-shaped, meat-filled dumplings that are steamed or fried.

And while we now see those dumplings on the menu every day, jiaozi was traditionally considered a festival food. They were shaped like gold ingots—the gold currency of ancient

China—so eating them at Lunar New Year promised a prosperous year. Sometimes families would even hide a coin inside one of the dumplings to bring extra luck to the eater. No cheating, though! Breaking a dumpling before eating it—even by accident—is considered bad luck.

Heaping dumplings in a jumbled pile on the serving plate is also considered bad luck. The boat-shaped dumplings should be served in an orderly line to symbolize moving smoothly through life. In fact, the word jiaozi sounds much like a Chinese expression that means "moving from old to new," which is why dumplings are essential for celebrating the new year.

Yet, the expression does not have anything to do with why these dumplings are called jiaozi. Some think the name comes from the horn shape of the dumpling because the pronunciation of the Chinese word for horn is also jiao (though the written word, or the character, is different). But most believe the name is from the word jiao er, which means "tender ears." Weird, right? What do ears have to do with dumplings? Well, eat some jiaozi and you can hear the story with your own tender ears.

During the Eastern Han Dynasty (25–220), more than 1800 years ago, there was a doctor named Zhang Zhongjing. Now, Zhongjing was an extraordinary person for his time. Terrible illness was widespread and many uneducated people were regularly swindled by doctors who had little knowledge or care. Zhongjing, who had trained and studied medicine from a young age, railed against such doctors and did his best to truly help anyone—rich or poor—who was in need. He studied, experimented, and created medicines, and most important, he recorded it all. As this was a time where medical knowledge was rarely shared or explained and often forgotten, Zhongjing purposely made his findings available for others and tried to make them as easy to remember as possible, all to be helpful.

One winter, after a long time away, Zhongjing went to visit his family's home for the Lunar New Year. The cold, icy wind was like a whipping rod, and he hurried as quickly as he could. But when Zhongjing heard a man scream from inside a home, he stopped.

"What is wrong?" Zhongjing yelled, much alarmed.

A man burst out of the house, quickly followed by a woman. The man was covering one of his ears with his hands and wailing like a child.

"My ear!!" the man sobbed. "It hurts!"

"You are being ridiculous!" she snapped.

"Your husband seems to be in a great deal of pain," Zhongjing said. "What happened?"

"Nothing happened! This rice bucket," the woman scoffed, nodding toward the moaning man, "decided again to go play games with his buddies instead of chopping us some firewood like he was supposed to. All I did was pinch his ear and now he is bawling like a baby!"

"Let me see," Zhongjing said as he leaned over the man. As the man uncovered his ear, Zhongjing saw that it was as gray as smoke and hard like crusted snow.

"No wonder it hurts!" Zhongjing exclaimed. "Your ears are frostbitten!"

"What's that?" the man blubbered.

"Your ears are starting to freeze," Zhongjing explained, "because they are too cold."

"It's not just my ears, sir," the man said. "It's all of me. I'm too cold in my arms, my shoulders, my chest—I'm too cold everywhere. It's winter! Everyone is too cold!"

"Hmm, yes," Zhongjing said, stroking his beard. "But right now, you must go inside where it is warmer. And you"—Zhongjing looked at the wife—"don't pinch his ears again."

The couple went back inside, and Zhongjing continued on his way home. But now he frowned as he noticed the many sickly villagers shivering with cold, all of them with ears as pale as tofu. "They *all* have frostbitten ears!" he said to himself. "They are too cold! I must help them."

When Zhongjing arrived home, he immediately began to research and think up a remedy. "They need to be warmed from the inside as well as out," he decided. "Therefore, I must make something that will promote blood flow. That means I must make something nourishing, with hearty meat and warming herbs, and if I could make it in such a way that will remind people that this will help their ears…"

With those thoughts, Zhongjing minced lamb meat and mixed it with warming medicinal herbs, like black pepper and ginger. He then wrapped the mixture in a small dough skin and made it into the shape of an ear. After he had made a good many, he boiled the ear-shaped, pocket-wrapped food in a broth. This, he ladled into a bowl and brought to the man with the frostbitten ears.

"Try this," Zhongjing said to him.

"What is it?" the man asked. "Those things look like ears."

"Yes," Zhongjing said. "That is because it is Qu Han Jiao Er Tang—Dispelling Cold from the Tender Ears Soup! Your ears hurt because you are too cold. Eating this will warm your body and your ears and make you feel better."

The man sniffed and smiled. Then he took a bite of one of the "ears" and grinned. He said no more until the bowl was empty.

"How do you feel?" Zhongjing asked.

"Wonderful!" the man exclaimed. "That was good! Can I have some more?"

"You should eat this until the Spring Festival," Zhongjing said. "It will prevent more frostbite and keep you healthy."

"Sounds good to me!" the man said, his grin even larger.

"Please tell everyone in the village who suffers from frostbitten ears to do the same," Zhongjing said. "I will give anyone who needs it the jiao er, these tender ears."

"I sure will!" the man said with relish.

Soon, people from the village lined up for Zhongjing's jiao er soup—perhaps more for its satisfying taste than for its frostbite protection. Because after Zhang Zhongjing left, people copied his recipe and continued to eat the jiao er—the tender ears that were China's first dumplings.

Egg Rolls and Spring Rolls
蛋卷和春卷

For me, Chinese takeout is just not complete without an order of egg rolls or spring rolls. Those crispy, golden deep-fried cylinders filled with savory goodness are the perfect way to start a meal, as well as a satisfying snack for later! While they have both long been classic offerings at Chinese restaurants, the egg roll and the spring roll are slightly different.

Egg rolls are enclosed in a thicker and crispier wrapper than a spring roll and are dipped in egg before frying—hence the egg in the name. And they are always fried. A spring roll, on the other hand, can be ordered fresh—served cold, with an almost translucent white wrapper—or can be baked or fried until golden and crispy. Spring rolls also have a rice-flour wrapper that is thinner than that of an egg roll. So you can see they are not quite the same thing. In fact, they might not even be the same thing to those in different parts of the United States, as friends of mine from the West Coast claim that their spring rolls are always served fresh, never fried. And those same friends also say they have never had a batter-fried egg roll, either!

But there is plenty of history to show that fried rolls have been around for a while in the United States. Though there is a bit of debate on who invented the egg roll. According to Chop Suey: A Cultural History of Chinese Food in the United States by Andrew Coe, a chef named Henry Low is said to have invented the egg roll for his Cook at Home in Chinese cookbook published in 1938. But a chef named Lum Fong opened a Chinese restaurant in 1925, and various newspaper articles around the same time reference the "egg rolls" one could get in his restaurants, which places Lum Fong before Henry Low. However, in The Chinese Cookbook by Shiu Wong Chan, there is also a recipe for Egg Roll, and that book was published in 1917!

While no one is quite sure who invented the egg roll, almost everyone agrees that the egg roll is an evolution of the spring roll, which has deep roots in Chinese cuisine. The spring roll is most often eaten during the early spring—which is why it was called the spring roll—when people are busy preparing offerings for the Qingming Festival, when one honors one's ancestors and partakes in cold food. However, spring rolls can be eaten at any time for they have always been a food of convenience. And it is this convenience that caused the spring roll to be invented.

During the latter part of the Ming dynasty, in the late 1500s, there was a high-ranking minister named Cai Fuyi. He was industrious, diligent, and dedicated. Unfortunately, he suffered from a number of ailments that gave him a limp and a hunched back, and one of his eyes did not work properly. Still, none of this affected his work, and he was quite brilliant at his job. In fact, he was always able to do his work twice as quickly as anyone else.

But his appearance did give an excuse for his jealous colleagues to bully him. Some of the other ministers, small-minded and petty, were eager to gain importance by getting rid of the competition, and Fuyi's appearance seemed an easy way to do so.

"Fuyi is too ugly to be an imperial minister," one said. "I'm sure the emperor cringes when he sees him."

"Yes," another said peevishly. "Fuyi's appearance is an embarrassment to the whole palace."

"Yes!" another declared. "He should be ashamed and not show himself here."

However, the complaints about Fuyi were quickly dismissed by the emperor.

"What you think of his appearance is your opinion," the emperor said. "And not only do I not agree, I do not care. The only thing I *do* care about is his work. That is very pleasing to me."

And then the emperor called Fuyi to the throne room.

"The report you wrote on the Guangzhou area was well done and very promptly delivered," praised the emperor, in front of all the other ministers. "In fact, I expected it much later and was surprised to see it waiting for me so soon. Fuyi, you are an exemplary official."

Of course, this only made the other ministers even more jealous.

"He always finishes all his work before us," they said to each other with much resentment, "And as long as he does that, the emperor will favor him."

"Unless," said one of the more spiteful ministers, "we make the emperor think Fuyi is dishonest...."

Soon, the malicious ministers hatched a plan and began spreading a string of lies.

"Fuyi is a fraud," one of the ministers whispered to members of the court. "No one person could write that report that quickly. He must be cheating somehow...."

"Yes, Fuyi is deceiving the emperor," another murmured. "Someone or something else is doing Fuyi's work...."

Of course, it was only a matter of time before these rumors reached the ears of the emperor. He frowned. The emperor did not care about his minister's appearance, but he did care very much about his character. A dishonest minister had no place in his court. He called Fuyi in for an audience.

"Cai Fuyi," the emperor said, "are you completely responsible for the reports you have provided me?"

"Of course, Your Majesty," Fuyi said, a little startled. "I have written them all myself with my own hands."

"Liar!" one of the ministers hissed. "That was an extensive report on the Guangzhou district, and you finished it in one week. It should have taken two weeks to write, maybe three! How could you have completed it so fast?"

"That is a good question," the emperor said. "Fuyi, how are you able to accomplish your work so swiftly?"

"Well, Your Majesty," Fuyi said, bowing low, "I admit I do have an unusual advantage. I am able to write with both hands at the same time."

"Impossible!" another minister cried out. "No one can do that!"

"I can," Fuyi replied calmly. "My right hand can write one sentence while my left hand can write a different one. In that way, I am able to do my work in half the time it would require someone who only writes with one hand."

"Absurd! You think we are fools?" The ministers jeered at Fuyi.

"I can," Fuyi insisted. "I will do it for you right now, if you wish."

"Well, anyone can write with two hands for a few moments," one of the ministers sputtered. "But to write a whole report? To do all of your work with two hands? Preposterous!"

The emperor raised his hand for silence.

"Very well," the emperor said. "I will let you prove your ability." He turned to the guards. "Bring me the Yellow Registry Archives."

The Yellow Registry Archives were population surveys of the entire empire. The records filled nine boxes, each large and weighty and requiring two men to bring in each box. As they were arranged, the boxes seemed to close around Fuyi.

"I will give you forty-nine days to hand-copy the Yellow Registry," the emperor said. "If you can truly write with both hands, it should be an easy feat for you to do alone. If you are unable to, we will know you have been dishonest, and you will be dismissed from my service."

Fuyi nodded but gulped as he stared at the wall of records. He knew that even using both his hands, he would have to work nonstop to finish in time. He quickly hurried home, the nine boxes of records accompanying him.

Now, Fuyi had a wife—Li. She was kind, clever, and, best of all, wise enough to see past Fuyi's physical afflictions and appreciate his kind and true nature. As he entered their home, he quickly told her of the challenge that lay before him and immediately got to work.

Li did everything she could so that nothing would distract him. But when he refused to eat, she became concerned.

"I cannot stop to eat," Fuyi professed. "I am afraid if either of my hands pauses, I will not finish in time."

"Then I will feed you," Li declared.

However, this was not a simple matter. Spoonfuls of soup and bowls of rice were not only very awkward to be fed while writing, but they could also possibly spill onto his precious work. Fuyi often waved her away with a shake of his head. But as the days continued and Fuyi began to grow weak, Li knew he needed nourishment.

I must make something that will be easy to eat neatly as well as be satisfying, Li thought. So, she went to the kitchen and pondered deeply.

Soon, Li lifted her head and went to work. Mixing flour with water, Li made a thin dough skin. She sliced fresh vegetables and wrapped the vegetables tightly with the dough skin so that it made a cylinder shape—one that could be easily held. Then she heated some oil and fried it golden.

Li brought this to Fuyi, who could easily bite off a chunk from the roll as she held it. Not a crumb fell to the table.

"Delicious!" Fuyi said, and began to write with renewed energy. "Can I have some more?"

Li was very pleased and continued to make the rolled food for Fuyi until he finished copying the nine boxes of records. He completed it just in time.

On the forty-ninth day, he presented the copied records to the emperor. The other ministers inspected the papers, attempting to find errors or trickery. But they could not find any. The registry had been copied in its entirety.

"How can we be sure he wrote everything himself?" one of the ministers challenged.

The emperor waved. A guard came to attention.

"Report," the emperor ordered.

"Your Majesty, I guarded the home of Cai Fuyi for the last forty-nine days. No one except for his wife entered and exited the house," the guard said. "As you ordered, I observed from the window numerous times. At all times, Minister Cai was sitting at his table writing with both hands. On occasion, his wife would feed him a roll-shaped food."

The emperor nodded and looked at the other ministers. They looked at one another in defeat, and all bowed begrudgingly to Fuyi, conceding that he had copied all the documents himself, and his talent of writing with both hands was, in fact, true.

Soon, all was in the past. Fuyi remained a minister of high regard. The others were forced to give up trying to get rid of him and had to begrudgingly accept him. Perhaps the spring roll, too, would have been forgotten had Fuyi not continued to ask Li for the rolled food he had enjoyed so much while he had been copying the records. And even though he now fed himself, he still found it very convenient. As did so many others centuries later, for we still eat the wrapped, round spring roll—delighting in its delicious, satisfying ease.

Scallion Pancakes
蔥油餅

We did not make scallion pancakes often at my house, but when we did, it was great fun—at least for the kids. I have vivid memories of playing with the dough like it was clay. I would sprinkle green onions onto a flat rectangle of dough and then roll that rectangle into a long, lumpy snake. After that, the snake would be coiled into a tight circle that was supposed to be rolled flat with a rolling pin. My sisters and I would eat those scallion pancakes as soon as my mother flipped them out of the frying pan, even if the rest of the dinner wasn't ready yet.

So, I can understand why so many Chinese restaurants list scallion pancakes as a choice for an appetizer. The flaky, chewy-crispy layers of the scallion pancake are the perfect pairing for any meal. Called congyoubing (蔥油餅) in Chinese (literally translated as "scallion oil pancake"), the scallion pancake is a savory pancake with green onions—but instead of using a batter, it uses a rolled and flattened dough (like I described above) that is pan-fried. The scallion pancake is commonly sold as a tasty and toothsome street food in Taiwan and China as well as in Chinese restaurants all over the world.

But where did the scallion pancake come from? Some say it was invented in Shanghai, as there was a large Indian population there and scallion pancakes are similar to the paratha, an Indian flatbread. However, the scallion pancake is also connected to Buddhist monk Zhi Dun, who lived during the Jin dynasty (265–420). Many say he invented the scallion pancake—at least a primitive version of one—called Zhi Gong Cakes (Zhi Gong Bing 支公餅, literally "Master Zhi's Cake"). He was said to be so fond of these cakes that he carried green onions with him whenever

However, the most enduring legend of the scallion pancake is not about its own origin but how it inspired an even more famous favorite food—the pizza! While historians broadly agree that this tale is likely a fable, I remember being told this story as fact, as a child, and feeling rather proud. I believed it! So, even though the term pizza was recorded in Italy well before Marco Polo returned from China in 1295, and many point out that the first printed version of this tale is actually a parody story from a Chinese newspaper (!), I still think it is a super-fun myth to share with you. And it also shows the connections we can make with foods from all cultures.

Marco Polo was born to a family of Venetian merchants in 1254. When he was around seventeen years old, he accompanied his father and uncle on a journey to Asia that lasted twenty-four years! Upon his return, Marco fought for Venice in a war against Genoa over control of the Mediterranean Sea and became a prisoner for about a year. There, inspired by his romance-writer cellmate, Rustichello da Pisa (the first Italian to write about the King Arthur legend), Marco began to compile the stories of his travels. This was to become his famous, influential book *The Travels of Marco Polo* (cowritten with Rustichello da Pisa), which sparked interest in China.

But before he became entangled in Italy's wars and wrote his book, Marco Polo was just happy to be back home in Italy. However, he did miss many of the things he had gotten used to in China.

One thing Marco Polo yearned for was the food!

In particular, Marco Polo craved the scallion pancakes. How he had loved them! He longed to taste them again. They could not be hard to make, could they?

Alas, Marco Polo was a poor cook and his attempts were unsuccessful. In frustration, he complained to his friends.

"There is a very skilled chef in Naples," one of his friends told him. "He is supposed to be very smart and can understand flavors and ingredients like no other. He has created dishes never tasted before. Why don't you go to him and tell him what you want? I am sure he could make it for you."

So, Marco Polo went in search of the expert chef. When Marco finally found him and explained his problem, the chef was intrigued.

"Describe this dish to me,'" the chef urged. "Any detail will help."

"It is crisp but chewy," Marco Polo said, "thin and savory. It's rather round but you cut it into triangular pieces and then it can be easily eaten by hand. Oh, and there are sliced green onions inside."

The line between the chef's brows deepened, but he raised his chin. "Well," he said, "let us try to make this scallion pancake."

So, the chef, with Marco Polo at his side, made his attempts. But their labors were unsuccessful. While they were better than Marco's solo efforts, their cakes were nothing like the scallion pancakes of China. They were too crispy, or they were not chewy or flaky enough, and never the right flavor! Marco Polo grimaced as he swallowed each one.

"Perhaps it is the way the onions are being cooked," the chef said, pursing his lips. "I am not sure how they are able to be inside the dough while cooking and also have the dough be crisp and chewy."

"Maybe," Marco Polo said, "they put the onions on top before they place it in the oven?"

"Yes, perhaps the onions sink in when cooking," the chef mused. "Let's try!"

Unfortunately, this did not work, but it was the closest to Marco Polo's memory of the scallion pancake of any of their other tries. Still, Marco was crushed.

"It's impossible!" Marco said, throwing his hands up in the air. "We shall never make scallion pancakes!"

And with that, Marco Polo abandoned the venture and left Naples.

But the chef was not as easily discouraged. Long after Marco left, he continued to experiment. Even if he could not make the scallion pancake of China, he felt he could make something just as appetizing. Instead of only using onions, he began adding some local ingredients such as tomatoes and cheese on top before he baked the dough.

When he sampled his result, the chef beamed with delight—as did everyone else who tasted it then—and now! For, ecco! Even though the chef did not make scallion pancakes, he had created the beloved and everlasting pizza!

Fried Shrimp
炒蝦仁

An appetizer I often see on a Chinese menu is fried shrimp. Now, I like fried shrimp, but I'm always hesitant to order it. Because when you order fried shrimp, you can't be exactly sure which fried shrimp recipe will be used. The shrimp might be battered and deep-fried similar to American fried chicken or Japanese tempura. Or it could be prepared in a Cantonese style with bread crumbs, ginger, onions, and peppers from a recipe that originated in typhoon shelters off Hong Kong in the mid-1900s. Or it could be salt-and-pepper fried shrimp, a completely different but also Cantonese recipe. Or, at higher-end restaurants, the shrimp could be stir-fried with green tea—which was invented when the Qing dynasty's Emperor Qianlong (1711–1799) asked for fried shrimp with green tea (meaning a dish of fried shrimp with a pot of green tea), and the chef, scared to displease the emperor, took him literally and put green tea in with the shrimp as he fried it. Don't worry, it worked out well, as the dish became a favorite of the emperor and is a recipe that continues to this day.

So as you can see, when you order fried shrimp, it can be a bit of a surprise when you get your dish. Good thing they are almost always delicious no matter how they are prepared, and you are unlikely to be disappointed (at my local Chinese restaurant, they have a particularly tasty shrimp appetizer sauteed in a spicy, red sauce—which I am told is just the cook's invention!).

But regardless of which fried shrimp dish you are served, shrimp has had a long and important place in Chinese cuisine. In Erya, the oldest existing Chinese dictionary (dated from the third century BCE), shrimp is mentioned. And in the Qimin Yashu, an ancient text dating from the Northern Wei dynasty (500) there is a shrimp paste recipe. Records from the Tang dynasty remark, "Southerners buy shrimp more often than vegetables...." as part of another recipe. And Marco Polo wrote about how he saw so much shrimp in the marketplaces when he was in China all the way back in 1280 in The Travels of Marco Polo.

Anyway, while I am not quite able to serve you a story about your specific fried shrimp appetizer—mainly because I don't know which fried shrimp dish you are eating—I can offer you a Chinese story that involves shrimp themselves. Even though not exactly related to food, this is a myth that has probably been shared since the Ming dynasty. That said, for all its age, it's a story that is more slapstick than serious—portraying Chinese dragon kings more like squabbling children than regal rulers! I really enjoyed it and hope you do, too!

A long time ago, when the mythical Dragon Kings ruled the Four Seas, the Black Dragon King of the North Sea found a beautiful jewel. This jewel was so exquisite that everyone in each of the Four Seas burbled about it and, before long the murmurs reached the ears of the Green Dragon King of the East Sea.

"So, Black Dragon has a new jewel, hmm?" Green Dragon brooded. There was always a bit of jealousy among the four Dragon Kings, and they often competed with one another over trivial matters. "Tell me," Green Dragon asked his Gold Croaker General. "What does this jewel look like?"

"There's been no specific description, Your Majesty," the brilliant yellow fish replied, "just that it is of surpassing beauty."

"Well...it would be nice to see it. Perhaps someone could go and get it for me, so I could take a look?" Green Dragon then added archly, "Maybe without Black Dragon knowing about it?"

Silver Eel General spoke up. "Smooth-Shelled Crab is smart and strong, Your Majesty," he said. "I think you should send him."

Gold Croaker made a protesting noise. He secretly worried that if Crab was successful, Crab would be promoted and given a greater rank than himself. It was not only the Dragon Kings who were jealous of others!

"This is a search mission," Gold Croaker argued. "Smooth-Shelled Crab is all muscle and power. He's a fighter, not an investigator. This needs someone more skillful. I'll go."

Green Dragon agreed, and Gold Croaker set off to search for (and steal) Black Dragon's new jewel.

It must be some sort of jade or crystal, Croaker thought. And off he went.

He searched and searched. He searched all four seas, looking for the glint of a crystal or the polished shine of a piece of jade. But he found nothing and saw nothing. Only after he searched for an entire year did he return to Green Dragon, defeated.

"Your Majesty," Silver Eel said, "perhaps we should send Smooth-Shelled Crab now?"

Green Dragon nodded and immediately Smooth-Shelled Crab was sent out.

Smooth-Shelled Crab methodically and slowly made his way to the North Sea. On the way, he thought deeply. *If Croaker was unable to find the jewel after a year, it must be hidden in something... like a pearl in an oyster shell....Perhaps it even is a pearl....*

So, Smooth-Shelled Crab spent the next few months observing Black Dragon's kingdom and palace. As time passed, he noticed something interesting about the Royal Garden. It was beautiful and well cared for, as fitting of the Dragon King's home. But there was one section that was not growing the usual colorful corals and graceful swaying seaweed found in the rest of the garden. Instead, there was one bed growing moonflowers—large, white, and radiant. And, even more interesting, Smooth-Shelled Crab noticed that these moonflowers seemed to be perpetually blooming—never closing at any time of day or night. This was quite unusual for moonflowers, which were known to open only at night.

"The gem must be hidden in there!" Smooth-Shelled Crab deduced.

And that night, when none were around, Smooth-Shelled Crab crawled to the bed of moonflowers and began to dig. With his strong, massive claws, he was able to dredge and excavate the bed in minutes. And after those few minutes, he pulled out just what he suspected—a brilliant, glowing pearl. Black Dragon's gem!

The pearl was beautiful but heavy and awkward for Smooth-Shelled Crab to carry. He struggled for many hours tying it to his back and only succeeded right before daybreak. Just in time! He was able to make his escape from Black Dragon's kingdom to the East Sea.

When Smooth-Shelled Crab arrived home and presented the pearl, he found he was smooth-shelled no longer! The pearl, with its weight and constant shifting, had created dents all over his back.

But no matter! Green Dragon was delighted to have the jewel. All gasped and admired it, and already Green Dragon considered the dazzling pearl his own. He was just about to reward and promote Crab when jealous Gold Croaker stepped in.

"I saw nothing of that gem for a whole year, but Crab found it in only three months," Gold Croaker proclaimed. "That can only mean that Crab is allied with Black Dragon! Crab is a traitor!"

Green Dragon frowned, but unfortunately for Crab, he found Gold Croaker's words believable.

"Take Crab to prison!" Green Dragon ordered.

But just as Crab was being locked away, Black Dragon of the North Sea realized his precious pearl was gone. He immediately suspected it had been stolen by Green Dragon.

"Only Green Dragon would be so greedy as to become a thief!" Black Dragon growled. And he ordered his army of stingrays to get his jewel back.

When Green Dragon heard that Black Dragon's army was advancing toward his kingdom, he sent both Silver Eel and Gold Croaker with an army of fish to stop the stingrays at the pass.

The generals and fish fought vigorously, but they were no match for the piercing jabs of the stingrays. They were forced to return home, and the stingrays continued to advance.

"What should I do?" Green Dragon asked, at a loss. He couldn't let Black Dragon's army reach the palace and find the pearl. Not only would he have to give it back, he would have to apologize to Black Dragon, and he hated when he had to do that. All the other Dragon Kings made fun of him.

But the wise advisor Turtle stepped forward with a recommendation.

"Your Majesty," Turtle said, bowing, " Silver Eel and Gold Croaker could not fight Black Dragon's stingrays for they have no armor. You must send one with a hard shell."

"Good idea," Green Dragon replied. "You go."

"I would be honored, Your Majesty," old Turtle said, "but I am too slow."

"Oh, good point," Green Dragon said. "Who should I send, then?"

"Perhaps," Turtle said, "you could release Crab from prison and send him?"

"Ah, yes!" Green Dragon said. "Bring Crab to me!"

Crab, now called Rough-Shelled Crab, was woken up from his nap in prison. He had eaten a pleasant lunch there, which had made him a bit sleepy.

"You can prove your loyalty to me now," Green Dragon said to Rough-Shelled Crab. "Force Black Dragon's army to retreat before they reach the palace."

"Well, I'll need an army, too," Rough-Shelled Crab said. "I can't stop them all just by myself."

"But most of the army is already wounded and injured from the prior battle," Green Dragon said, shrugging. "And the fish soldiers were useless against the stingrays, anyway."

Rough-Shelled Crab considered. "I bet shrimp could be good fighters," he said.

"Shrimp?" Green Dragon said, surprised. Shrimp were the lowly servants of the palace, whose main job was to clean chamber pots and carry away night soil (or poop, as we would call it now).

"They're scrappy and tough," Rough-Shelled Crab said. "Give me an army of them."

"Fine!" Green Dragon agreed. And within minutes, three thousand shrimp were assembled and marched out the palace walls behind Rough-Shelled Crab.

And what a battle raged! Great Rough-Shelled Crab seized stingrays with each of his pincers (his shell protecting him from their stingers) and threw them out of the East Sea over and over again and with such speed that those in the North Sea thought the flying, falling stingrays were a rainstorm. The shrimp, protected by their shells, deluged the other rays with stabbing sticks. There were so many shrimp that rays were overwhelmed and could only fly back to the North Sea, finally defeated.

Green Dragon was, of course, thrilled.

"We won!" he chortled as he saw Black Dragon's army flee. "I guess Crab isn't a traitor."

When victorious Rough-Shelled Crab returned, Green Dragon immediately promoted him to the position of Iron-Armored General. Gold Croaker could not protest, for he was in bed, healing from his wounds.

And the three thousand shrimp? They were also rewarded for their courage. They were all made imperial soldiers, to be under the command of Crab. The shrimp were very honored to be elevated to this position (and happy to give up their prior duties) and immediately accepted.

So, when you eat fried shrimp at a Chinese restaurant, you are eating foot soldiers of the Dragon King! Without doubt, they fought an honorable battle to get onto your plate.

SOUP

湯 的 故 事

INTRODUCTION
緒論

At home, my mother would serve soup at every dinner. Soup was an everyday part of the meal that I took for granted. It was only as I grew older and ate at friends' houses that I realized that this was not common everywhere.

But it is common in China. There is a Chinese saying that goes, "You can eat without meat, but you cannot eat without soup." That is because soup is considered an essential part of a meal in Chinese cuisine. While tea is now poured extensively in Chinese restaurants, traditionally it was soup that was served as the beverage during meals (tea tended to be drunk separately). No feast is served without soup, and it is usually a staple for everyday meals as well. In the Ming Dynasty, during a time of famine, Emperor Zhu Yuanzhang installed a rule that nobles' banquets (which had previously been extravagant and indulgent) could only consist of "four dishes and one soup." This practice quickly passed from the palace to the commoners.

Archaeological evidence of pottery shows that soup could have been boiling in China as far back as twenty thousand years ago. And the oldest soup recipes can also be found in China, perhaps because soup was used as a tonic to treat ailments. It's believed by many that the correct soup can increase strength, fortify the heart, clear the lungs, treat fever, prevent some diseases, and cure others. There are even soups made to help women sustain their beauty!

Generally, Chinese soups are categorized by their composition—thick or thin—or their flavor—sweet or savory. Thin soups are made with a clear broth and tend to be cooked quickly, to accompany heavy or fried foods. Thick soups are cooked longer with more complex textures and tend to be considered a course by itself, instead of a companion dish. Both savory and sweet soups are judged by their aroma as well as their taste and aftertaste.

There are even some soups that can be prepared as sweet *or* savory. Egg Drop Soup (dan hua tang 蛋花湯) is literally translated as Egg Flower Soup because of the way the broken-up egg in the soup looks like flower petals. The Chinese eat a sweet version of it, just like a dessert! But the Egg Drop Soup found in American Chinese restaurants is almost always savory. Personally, I suspect Americans found the idea of a sweet egg soup too strange for their tastes.

Anyway, with such a long history, the Chinese pride themselves on their soup. Most Chinese chefs are careful while making soup. They pay attention to the size they dice their meats and vegetables, and the temperature and amount of the water—for in good Chinese cooking, they do not continually add water; they make sure they put in enough water to make the soup at the start. They also watch as the soup boils, skimming off any foam and calculating the correct time to add any additional ingredients. It's quite different from the style of cooking we have here in America!

In the past, making a slurping sound when eating soup was customary in Chinese culture. Slurping was common because it cooled the noodles or dumplings as you ate, and waiting for the broth to cool might make those elements soggy and less enjoyable. Also, slurping tended to enhance the taste of the soup, bringing out the more subtle flavors. And slurping also showed how much you enjoyed it! However, that doesn't mean you should noisily guzzle your soup down the next time you are in a restaurant! Times are changing, and influenced by Western manners, very loud slurping is frowned upon as rude among some Asians now, too.

Still, some sort of soup is almost always found on a Chinese menu. Soup is the heart of Chinese cuisine, and it has found its way into American hearts as well. To many, a bowl of Wonton or Egg Drop Soup is a comfort food that reminds them of cozy winter evenings of eating Chinese takeout.

But did you know there are stories in those soups? Yes, floating in that broth is a story. Yes, there is a story that you are slurping (quietly) with your spoon. And, yes, they are delicious.

Wonton Soup
餛飩湯

Every Chinese restaurant seems to serve Wonton Soup. For many, me included, it is a comfort soup—like chicken noodle or creamy tomato. It's a soup that is soothing because it is so familiar.

But did you know that Wonton Soup symbolizes the creation of the world?

The word wonton can be traced to two different Chinese words. The first is the Chinese word 雲吞—yutun in Mandarin and wan tan in Cantonese. Since most of the immigrants from China in the nineteenth century were Cantonese speakers from Guangdong, that is most likely where we, in the United States, get the word wonton. This word can be literally translated to "swallowing clouds," which is a very poetic way to think about eating the soup. The soft white dumplings float in the soup, their delicate skins almost transparent—much like clouds in the sky.

However, the other word that wonton can be traced to is from Northern China—the word 餛燉/飩 hundun. This can be literally translated to "mixed confusion." But the characters of those words lead to yet another hundun (pronounced the same but with difference characters) 混沌/渾沌. This hundun refers to primordial chaos or the Daoist creation story of the world. Here is that story.

Long, long ago, before there were people, before there were animals, before there were trees and oceans and land, before there was life or even the world, there was chaos. And only chaos. The universe was much like a soup—simply a swirl of watery, mixed confusion.

But very slowly, the mixture began to congeal and formed a pale, round shape. It had become an egg, but not an egg of any bird. For after eighteen thousand years inside the egg, Pangu woke.

Who was Pangu? He was a giant—a very hairy giant with horns. When he opened his eyes, he saw only the blankness of the inside of the egg. And, by then, Pangu had grown so large that he was starting to feel trapped by the egg and and wanted to come out of it. So, he broke the egg open.

And by breaking the egg, Pangu created heaven and earth. The lighter part of the egg, which he held above him, became the sky. The heavier part of the egg, which he pushed below him, became the earth. Pangu became the pillar of the world, holding the two apart.

So, there Pangu stood, between these two halves. Every day, Pangu grew ten feet, so every day the sky and the land were pushed apart ten feet more—the sky rising higher and the land sinking lower. When Pangu was happy, the sky was clear and full of light. When he was angry, the sky darkened and clouded over. Pangu's sighs would cause the winds to blow; his tears would rain down to create lakes. The blinking of his eyes made lightning streak and his snores made the rumbling of thunder.

This was the world for the next eighteen thousand years. After that, Pangu was so tired that he collapsed to the ground and died from exhaustion. But by then, the two halves of the egg had become so separate that they could never rejoin.

Pangu's body then became parts of the world. His final breaths became the wind and clouds; his voice became thunder, and his sweat became the rain. His left eye became the sun, and his right eye became the moon. His head, arms, and body turned into mountains. His blood made up the oceans and rivers; his flesh was the earth's fertile soil. His teeth and bones became rocks and gemstones, and his beard transformed into the stars of the galaxies. His body hair was the trees and plants. The fleas and lice that had lived in his hair became the animals of the earth and, lastly, his soul dispersed and became people.

And this story is in your Wonton Soup. The hundun or mixed confusion in the name is not about the mixed filling in the dumpling, but the entire soup. Wonton Soup symbolizes the liquid chaos of the world before Pangu, with the dumpling signifying his egg. The dumplings, filled with delicious nourishment, must be broken to be eaten and enjoyed. The sacrifice of the wonton can be likened to Pangu's sacrifice, who sacrificed himself to nourish the world.

Wonton Soup is considered a soup of harmony. It symbolizes the wholeness of the heavens and earth, and all those who live in both. Everyone who eats the soup experiences a sense of fullness. And no wonder! You are eating the creation of the world!

CROSSING THE BRIDGE NOODLE SOUP
過橋米線 (湯)

If you are lucky, you might see Crossing the Bridge Noodle Soup on your Chinese restaurant menu. While it is quite popular in China, it is harder to find—but not impossible—in the United States. I have seen it pop up on Chinese menus here. So, if you do see it, it is worth ordering!

Now, when you order Crossing the Bridge Noodle Soup at a restaurant, you will be served a large bowl of hot, cloudy broth accompanied by a tray of fresh ingredients—raw meats, uncooked egg, finely sliced vegetables and bamboo shoots, and a dish of springy rice noodles. If you look confused, the server might take pity on you and take charge by slipping the ingredients into the hot broth—starting with the meat and ending with noodles. When the soup is finally ready (the server will make you wait a few moments before you dig in), you will be rewarded with the warm, rich—yet fresh—taste of one of the most famous soups of Yunnan Province. This is how the soup got its name.

Long ago, in the charming waterside city of Mengzi in Yunnan, there lived a serious young adult student known as Scholar Yang. Like all student scholars at that time, his entire future depended on passing the imperial exam, which was given one time a year. However, unlike most students, Scholar Yang had a beautiful wife, Jinggu, as well as a young son, Song. Knowing that his wife and child depended on him made Yang even more determined to pass the examination.

Nearby was a large, peaceful lake with water as green as jade. In the middle of this lake was a small, quiet island, connected to land only by a long bridge that stretched across the water like a single chopstick. In order to have no distractions, Scholar Yang decided to seclude himself in the island's pavilion and study there until the exam.

Scholar Yang's wife, Jinggu, was not only lovely but also very loyal. Every day, she cooked her husband's favorite noodle soup for him and then immediately crossed the lengthy bridge to bring it to him. However, by the time she arrived at the pavilion, the soup was cold and the noodles were mushy. Jinggu tried thicker earthenware pots to carry the soup and walked as quickly as she dared, but she was still unable to get any food to him that was warm or appetizing.

Slowly, Jinggu began to notice that her husband was looking weaker and thinner, and she was certain it was because he only picked at the cold, unappealing food she brought him. As a pot of broth heated on the stove, she gazed out the window pondering the problem. She could, perhaps, bring the noodles separately so that they did not get soggy, but how could she keep the broth warm?

Splat! Splat! Splat!

Jinggu whirled around to see Song fling pieces of chicken into the pot from across the room, hot broth splashing as the chicken plopped into it. A mischievous grin stretched across his chubby face.

"I'm helping you cook Ba's soup!" he snickered gleefully.

"Song!" Jinggu began to scold him, but something about the bubbling broth caught her eye. As she examined the soup, she noticed that the cooking chicken had created a coating of fatty oil on top of the broth. She tasted it. The broth tasted good! Rich and savory. And the layer of oil— perhaps it could help keep the broth warm?

Yes, it could! After experimenting a few times, Jinggu realized that she could keep the broth warmer for much longer when the melted fat floated on top to keep the heat in.

The next day, Jinggu filled the heated earthenware pot with boiling broth as she always did. But this time, she covered the broth with the cloudy, chicken fat coating. Then she placed all the other ingredients—the finely sliced vegetables, meat, and noodles—in separate bowls. All of this she carried over the bridge to her husband as quickly as she could.

And it worked perfectly. With her husband sitting in front of her, Jinggu immediately slipped the other ingredients into the piping-hot broth and made him a satisfying soup. The noodles were firm, the vegetables were fresh, the meat was tender, and, most important, the soup was warm. Scholar Yang was delighted and soon finished the entire bowl.

But not as delighted as Jinggu, who watched him eat with great satisfaction. She knew that with this soup, he would now have the strength to pass his exams. Which he did.

On the day Scholar Yang passed his exams, he credited Jinggu—recognizing how her kindness and dedication helped him.

"I could never have done it without the wonderful soup my wife invented and brought me every day," he said to his fellow students.

"I must try this wonderful soup!" one of his friends declared. "What is it called?"

"I don't know," Scholar Yang said. "I shall ask her."

So they called Jinggu out, waved away her modesty, and insisted that she name the soup.

"Very well," she said, blushing, "Let us call it Crossing the Bridge Noodle Soup, as it was the crossing of the bridge that caused me to make it."

And so, Crossing the Bridge Noodle Soup was born. Perhaps if you have a big test in your future, it would be good to have a bowl of it.

HOT AND SOUR SOUP
胡辣湯

For me, Hot and Sour Soup was an acquired taste. The mixture of savory, spicy, and tangy flavors in a soup was surprising, and at first I didn't like it. But that changed one day long ago, just after I had graduated from college and when I was recovering from a particularly nasty cold. My nose was stuffed, and my throat still hurt from the past coughing fits. But I was well enough to meet a friend for lunch at a local Chinese restaurant.

"You should have the Hot and Sour Soup," she told me. "It'll make you feel better."

Why not? I thought, willing to give anything a try.

When the first spoonful of the thick, peppery, and pungent soup filled my mouth—I was transported. The flavors seemed to awaken all my taste buds and, when I swallowed it, seemed to warm and soothe every part of my ailing body. It did make me feel better! And from then on, much like chicken noodle soup has been used to treat illness, Hot and Sour Soup became my own personal soup remedy.

Which is why I chose this Hot and Sour Soup story to share with you today, as you will soon see.

But first, let me tell you a bit about the soup.

Like many foods served in Chinese restaurants here in the United States, your Hot and Sour Soup is unlikely to be the original recipe. It's been adapted from a recipe from Sichuan, a province in southwest China. But, strangely enough, the Sichuan soup is most likely adapted from another recipe—this one from Henan, a province in the central part of China.

The original soup is probably a Henan recipe that would have been called Hot Pepper Soup in English. But in Chinese, it was called Hu La Tang (胡辣湯 or 糊辣湯), with la tang (辣湯) meaning "spicy soup" (the hu part is explained in the story below). But referencing pepper in the English name makes sense, for peppers are an important and distinctive part of the soup.

In the Song dynasty, black peppercorns were imported into China as medicine, not as a spice. These peppercorns were ground into a powder, added to congee (rice porridge), and served to the ill person. As time passed, more pepper medicines were created, and many medicinal congees became more souplike. And these soups began to be eaten not just to treat sickness, but as food. One of the medicinal soups that turned into a common dish was a thick and spicy soup—Hu La Tang!

As people from Henan began to migrate to other provinces, they, of course, brought their recipes with them. So, Hu La Tang found its way to Xian and Sichuan Provinces, where local tastes and ingredients changed the flavors.

In Sichuan—known for its strong flavors—Hu La Tang became much spicier. Also, a distinctive sourness was added, mainly to replace the meat that is in the original recipe. With these new flavors, this version of Hu La Tang was called Suan La Tang (酸辣湯) or Sour Hot Soup.

When Chinese immigrants came to the United States with the Sichuan Sour Hot Soup recipe, it changed again to please the local population, with the flavors becoming a little less spicy. And, eventually, it ended up being called Hot and Sour Soup.

So, that is the long journey of how Hot and Sour Soup was ladled into our American bowls! You can see that Hot and Sour Soup does have a history of healing illness—which is probably why it comforted me all those years ago. That history also includes a legend about healing a Ming dynasty official, as you will see in this story of how Hu La Tang was created.

In the Ming dynasty, there was an official by the name of Yu Qian who was stationed in Henan Province. One year, on what happened to be his birthday, he was conducting a tour of Zhengzhou—Henan's capital—for imperial inspection. During a break from his duties, he decided to celebrate his birthday by trying someplace new to eat. So, when he saw a restaurant called Hu Ji (胡记) Shop, he stopped.

"Hu" was not a Han Chinese last name—and since most people in China were Han Chinese, it meant that the owner must be foreign. In fact, Hu Ji when translated directly meant "memorable Non-Han," so that seemed to indicate this place would have something unusual as well as interesting. Qian entered the restaurant.

"Welcome, welcome," greeted the owner, who was in fact, Hu Ji.

"Hello," Qian said, as he allowed himself to be seated. "It is my birthday, so I want to try something new. What do you suggest?"

"One of our specialties is Hot Soup," Ji said. "I am sure you have never had anything like it before."

Qian ordered it, and he found that Ji was right. The flavors were unlike anything he had ever tasted before, and he couldn't help marveling at its surprising smell and unexpected flavors. Qian was delighted and was generous as he paid his bill and thanked the owner.

"You have truly made this a birthday to remember," Qian said to a gratified Ji as he left.

Not long after, Qian was assigned to a new station in Shanxi Province, and many years passed. But one day, Qian had to visit Henan again and was passing through Zhengzhou. Unfortunately, there were problems with the roads, and Qian found himself staying in Zhengzhou unprepared. Without the proper clothing and personal necessities, Qian caught an unpleasant cold that forced him to stay in bed and delay his journey even longer. When his doctor and attendants urged him to eat, he had little appetite.

As Qian lay sick, he remembered the Hot Soup of the Hu Ji Shop. *That*, he thought, *I could eat.* So, he called for one of his attendants.

"There is a restaurant called the Hu Ji Shop in the middle of Zhengzhou," Qian said. "Go there and get me some of their Hot Soup. The owner, Hu Ji, should be able to make it for you."

The attendant nodded but was puzzled. "How do you know of this place? And of this soup?" he couldn't help asking.

"I ate the Hot Soup at the Hu Ji Shop many years ago," Qian said, "for my birthday."

So, the attendant rushed through the streets of Zhengzhou until he finally found Hu Ji Shop.

"I am here on behalf of Official Yu Qian," the attendant said to Ji. "He requests a bowl of your Hot Soup for me to bring to him."

"I am happy to fulfill the order," Ji said, bowing, "but which hot soup? We serve many kinds here. Could you ask him which one?"

The attendant was at a loss.

"Official Yu Qian is ill, so I do not wish to bother him unless I have to," the attendant faltered. "He said he ate the Hot Soup here before. It was many years ago, for his birthday."

"An official? For his birthday?" Ji raised his head, his eyes brightening with recognition. "I think I remember. He was quite kind....He's sick, you said?"

The attendant nodded. "He can't get out of his bed and has not eaten anything in days."

"I will make the soup." Ji nodded vigorously and hurried away.

In the kitchen, Ji carefully prepared the soup. *If the poor man is sick*, he thought, *I should add some things into the soup to help him get better*....So, deliberately, Ji added extra ground peppers and other healing herbs. And this specially concocted Hot Soup is what he gave to the attendant.

Qian received the soup willingly enough—in his weakened and listless state it was hard for him to be eager about anything. But his fond memories of the soup from before encouraged him to try it again, and before he knew it, he had consumed the entire bowl of Hot Soup.

And what was more, the healing spices and herbs that Ji had put in the Hot Soup worked! Soon after eating the soup, Qian felt such an intense heat throughout his body that it caused profuse sweat, flushing his whole system. Afterward, he slept so well and soundly that when he awoke the next day, he was completely well!

"I feel like I was never sick at all," Qian said, grinning broadly as he jumped out of his bed. He looked at his attendants. "Finally, we can continue with our journey!"

And so they did. But before they left, they stopped at the Hu Ji Shop so that Qian could personally thank Ji for the soup with ten taels of silver.

"Your soup is wonderful," Qian told him. "You should call the soup Hu Hot Soup—Hu La Tang!"

And Hu Ji did!

Because, according to legend, after that the Hot Soup was called Hu La Tang (胡辣湯). The character 胡 (hu) means non-Han Chinese, just like Hu Ji.

However, the soup's name kept changing. As it grew in popularity during the Qing dynasty, the non-Han Chinese, Manchu rulers found the hu (胡) reference alienating and divisive. So a homonym for hu was used—the character 湖—which while still pronounced hu, means paste-like and could refer to the thick congee of the soup's medicinal past instead. And as the soup recipe spread to other parts of the country and beyond, the soup and its name changed as well. Because we now eat a version of this hot pepper soup that is called Hot and Sour.

BIRD'S NEST SOUP
燕窩湯

I was once in a high-end Chinese restaurant and saw a listing for Bird's Nest Soup. I was intrigued by the name but when I saw the price...I was shocked! Why was Bird's Nest Soup so expensive? Is it because the soup was believed to be the secret to preserving youth and increasing energy? Is it because the soup was prized and savored by Chinese emperors? Is it because the soup was made from real birds' nests?

Why, yes, all of those things are true. Yes, even the part about the soup being made from real bird's nests!

Bird's Nest Soup is made with the bowl-shaped nests of swiftlets that would nest in the cracks of steep cliffs. These birds take more than thirty days to create and attach these nests to the stone walls using their own spittle!

In the past, people would climb these rocky cliffs (sometimes falling to their deaths) to poach these nests to make the soup—often hurting the birds. Nowadays, people have taken to nest farming—luring birds to nest in manmade structures and strictly regulating when the nests can be harvested (always after eggs have hatched and the birds have left). If you do decide to order the Bird's Nest Soup, make sure the nest has been ethically farmed—it's worth the extra money!

Still, why would anyone even want to make soup out of a bird's nest, especially one that was so hard to get and created by bird spit, of all things? And how did it become so prized? If you'd like to know, this story may interest you.

During the Ming dynasty, there was a man named Zheng He. Born into a Muslim family, He was only ten when his father was killed during a rebellion in southwest China. He was taken prisoner and was sent to the palace to serve the Yan prince. Smart and resilient, He became friends with the prince, and when the prince was crowned emperor, He became a trusted servant.

He was so trusted, that it was he who was chosen to lead the Treasure Voyages. These were special diplomatic expeditions to show China's greatness and to create ties all over the world. The emperor had hundreds of ships built and filled with Chinese treasures—shimmering silks, delicately painted porcelain, intricately carved jade—all to be used for trade or gifts in faraway, unknown countries. At least, countries not known by He, who had never sailed on a boat before.

But He, with a booming voice and a tall, broad body, was an imposing figure and no one doubted his command. And he was brave. Not only did he sail farther than anyone thought possible, bringing back spices, medicines, dyes, jewels, and even a giraffe (which for many years was believed in China to be a unicorn), but he also battled deadly pirates and incredible storms—including one so fierce and violent that it lit the sky with such glowing electricity that the sailors believed it was a divine light from a goddess.

It was after one of these terrible storms that the fleet was forced to anchor off the coast of Malaysia. Unfortunately, this bare and rocky island was uninhabited by people and, at least at first glance, by any kind of vegetation or wildlife whatsoever. That was bad news to He. Their food supply was low and his crew desperately needed something to eat.

However, He refused to be discouraged. Gathering a small group of men, he led a search for food. As they struggled across the craggy land, with the constantly crashing waves and the ferocious winds surrounding them, He scanned his eyes over the high jagged cliffs. Above, against the highest points, he could see the silhouette of a bird fluttering and then disappearing inside a crack of the rock.

"There!" He said, his voice like a bronze bell. "Go up there and you will find something for us to eat!"

No doubt his men were puzzled, but they made the treacherous climb to the tops of the cliffs and returned with glassy, white, cup-shaped birds' nests.

"Good," He said. "Gather as many as you can and we'll take them back to cook."

When He and the men returned with their load of swiftlets' nests, the awaiting sailors were even more doubtful. But when He stood in front of them like a mountain and bellowed his orders to clean and boil the nests into a soup, all quickly obeyed.

And then they were surprised. For the bird's nest soup was good. Quite good! Not only was it appetizing, but the men felt strong and energized after eating it. The change was so remarkable that He noticed it at once.

Eating the birds' nests have given my men new power, he thought. *I must bring some back to the emperor.*

So, He had more birds' nests retrieved, and when they finally left the island, the nests were carried on the boat alongside all the other treasures that had been collected. Upon his return to China, He presented the bird's nest to the emperor, who then tried the soup. He, too, felt the invigorating power of the soup, and it immediately became a prized delicacy.

And it still is to this day. In fact, it is one of the longest-lasting treasures of all the riches to come from the Treasure Voyages. It is certainly one of the most delicious.

Sizzling Rice Soup
鍋巴湯

I don't call many soups exciting, but Sizzling Rice Soup is an exception. At first, it seems an ordinary soup. It is a simple, aromatic light broth with colorful vegetables and shrimp or chicken swimming around in it; but when the crisp rice is poured onto it, a crackling, sizzling sound fills the air like small firecrackers! And suddenly, the soup doesn't seem so commonplace after all.

This soup (which gets its name from the sound made when the rice is added) has probably existed since ancient times when people would fry their rice to cook it. Frying the rice would cause some grains to burn slightly and stick to the bottom of their pots; and rather than waste food, people would scrape out the bits into soup to soften them.

However, there is one story during the Three Kingdoms period (220–280) that claims the invention of Sizzling Rice Soup. It's attached to the well-known Chinese saying san gu maolu 三顧茅廬, which roughly translates to "three visits to a thatched hut." It is often used to express sincere persistence.

During the time of the Three Kingdoms, the leader Liu Bei was defeated by the warlord Cao Cao. Determined to regain his power, Bei searched for intelligent and talented men who could help advise him and strategize.

Bei soon heard of a recluse by the name of Zhuge Liang, a scholar who, even though he was rumored to be brilliant, lived in poverty. So Bei and his two most loyal generals rode their horses to the mountain of Longzhong to Liang's home.

Liang's place was barely a home—it was a broken-down, crumbling thatched hut where he lived with his wife, Lady Huang.

"I am sorry," Lady Huang said. "My husband is not here."

Disheartened, Bei and his generals returned home.

But three months later, Bei and his generals decided to try again. Unfortunately, just like the first time, Liang was unavailable.

"I am sorry," Lady Huang said again. "My husband is not here."

"When will he return?" Liu Bei asked.

"I do not know. He can wander the mountain for days or even months," she said. "You will have to leave."

Thus, Bei and his generals had no choice but to return home again.

However, months later, Bei decided to try a third time to visit Liang.

"Why?" his generals objected. "It will only be a waste of time and effort."

"We must try again," Bei said. "To fight Cao, I must have the most talented men advising me. I believe Liang is one of them."

So, the three made the journey again to Liang's thatched hut.

"I am sorry," Lady Huang said. "My husband is sleeping and I dare not wake him."

"We will wait," Bei said.

"It may be some time," Lady Huang said. "He was quite tired when he finally arrived home."

"We will wait," Bei repeated.

And Bei and his generals waited. And waited. They stood with their fine horses and rich robes for hours in front of Liang's shabby, dilapidated hut.

Finally, Liang woke up. When his wife told him about Bei and the generals outside, he was quite touched.

"Men as patient and as persistent as they have been," Liang reflected, "will be worth helping." So, he told his wife to welcome them in for dinner.

Lady Huang did, but she was at a loss as to what to serve. There was not even enough rice for dinner for just the two of them, much less three unexpected and obviously high-ranking guests. But Lady Huang had a clever spirit of her own and refused to be daunted. She quickly looked over her kitchen and saw their pot with some remaining grains of rice burned to the bottom.

In an instant, Lady Huang made a soup and poured the leftover seared rice into it, to soften the grains and make them edible. But it was much better than simply edible! The addition of the old rice grains made the soup into a satisfying meal, impressing the men with its aroma and heartiness.

For it was over this reinvigorating soup that Liang agreed to become Bei's counselor. And with Liang's help, Bei was able to defeat Cao and establish the state of Shu.

Who knows what else the soup can do? Perhaps you, too, can plan great deeds over a bowl of Sizzling Rice Soup.

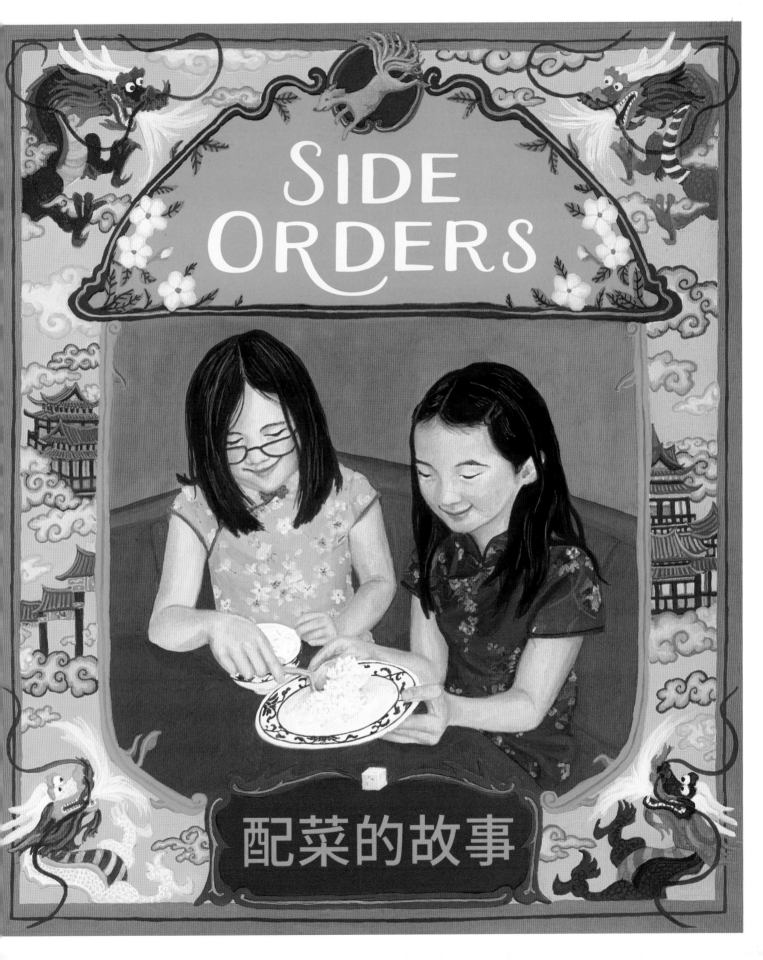

INTRODUCTION
緒論

Yhou could say that every dish on the table at a Chinese dinner is a side order. Or that American Chinese menus have it backward, because what is considered a side order here is really a main dish. At a typical steakhouse in the United States, the server will place the main dish of a steak in front of each person with a baked potato and salad on the side.

This is very different from a typical Chinese restaurant. At a Chinese restaurant, a myriad of different dishes, all to be shared, will be placed on the table, usually atop a lazy Susan, which is a rotating circular platter in the middle of the dining table. Folk legends claim this device was invented by either Americans Thomas Jefferson or Thomas Edison to appease their languid daughters—but it was Elizabeth Howell of Missouri who was given a patent for a "self-waiting table" in 1891. That said, there are records of a "revolving table" in China's *Book of Agriculture* dating from 1313, with attempts by Dr. Wu Lien-Teh in 1915 to popularize a similar "hygienic dining tray." However, it was only in the 1950s, when restaurateur Johnny Kan used a revolving tabletop in his extremely popular Cantonese-style restaurant in San Francisco's Chinatown that the use of the lazy Susan exploded. Other Chinese restaurants quickly copied the idea—and not just in the United States! Lazy Susans are used in Chinese restaurants all over the world—China, Hong Kong, Taiwan, and beyond.

This shared way of eating is now considered a typical Chinese custom. But strangely, eating "family style" is not how the ancient Chinese ate. In fact, it is believed that the Chinese (particularly the nobility) ate almost exclusively at low, individual tables throughout the Qin dynasty.

But China's nomadic northern neighbors had different eating habits. They had high folding chairs that allowed them to sit with their legs dangling, and they would usually all eat together around a warm stove. How their customs slowly creeped into the overall Chinese culture is hard to gauge, but by the Ming dynasty, shared-dish eating with gong-kai (literally translated as "public chopsticks") as the shared serving utensil became the norm. This was all further encouraged by the communist ideas during the Mao era of twentieth-century China.

It's understandable why so many of us welcome this way of eating. Sharing food at the table is a wonderful way to connect with those you eat with, creating a sense of community and collaboration. Also, you get to eat and try a greater variety of food!

Food for a Chinese dinner is usually divided into two categories. First is fan—which literally means "rice," but can stand for any of the starchy staple foods like noodles or grain—and the other is cai (pronounced tsai) which literally means "vegetables," but came to mean vegetable and/or meat dishes. In ancient China, when food was scarce, fan was the main dish and the cai supplemented it.

However, since Westerners were used to the main dish being something meat-heavy, the cai dishes became the focus in Chinese restaurants. That is why the rice (fan) seems to simply be a complement to all the meat and vegetables (cai) dishes.

But why are there no side salads with a Chinese meal?

Well, in ancient China, farmers routinely used manure as fertilizer for their crops and did not trust their water supply (they always boiled their water, which is why tea was so important), so there was an aversion to eating raw vegetables. Therefore, salad or any type of uncooked food was not particularly common.

Thus, the main food of rice and noodles became the side dishes on the American Chinese menu. That is just one of the many ways that Chinese cuisine acquired new identities as it spread through the Western world.

So, give that lazy Susan on your Chinese restaurant table a whirl and try whatever happens to stop in front of you. Whether it is called a side dish or a main course, it is sure to satisfy, and the stories that go with it will, too!

RICE
米飯

At home, we always had rice. Every day the rice cooker would be full of steaming, fluffy white rice that we scooped into our bowls for dinner.

A Chinese restaurant is no different. There is almost always a bowl of snowy-white rice with your meal. Usually it is complimentary with your order.

A staple in Chinese cuisine, rice—alongside fire, oil, salt, soy sauce, vinegar, and tea—was considered one of life's "seven daily necessities" as, for many, it was eaten at almost every meal.

Rice was not only easy to store and cook, but it could also be served in a multitude of ways: sweet or savory, pounded into flour and made into cake or dumplings, or even turned into wine to drink. And leftover cooked rice was quite useful too—fried rice, probably invented as a way to use food scraps in the Sui dynasty (518–618 CE), is said to be much better when rice is already two or three days old!

However, even though rice was constantly and widely eaten, it was not easy to grow. For thousands of years, Chinese people have worked to develop and nurture their land. They created rice paddies and terraces and complicated irrigation systems, all of it sustained by hard, back-breaking physical labor just to grow rice.

That is why rice is so respected in Chinese culture. In ancient China, officials would be paid in sacks of rice, and it was often used in religious rituals as offerings to the gods. Parents would tell children to eat every grain in their bowl or else they would marry someone with a pockmarked face (they really cared about appearance and things like that back then), and if they carelessly wasted their rice, the God of Thunder would come and smash their bed!

But more than that, rice symbolizes the connection between Earth and the Heavens. The traditional Chinese character for rice 米 (pronounced mi) can be found in the Chinese character for spirit 氣 (pronounced qi), showing how rice is actually the foundation for a person's spirit.

So, when you think about it, that is quite a lot for a bowl of rice to hold! And there is even more. Stories and legends about rice abound, perhaps as many as there are grains of rice. Here is one from the Miao (one of the ethnic people) of southern China that tells how rice was brought to the people.

Long, long ago—when the Earth and the Heavens were not so far apart, animals and people were better friends, and the dog had nine tails—the land was bare of all grains. The people foraged for wild plants, but most were prickly leaves and vines, with thorns and spikes. It was only by chance when they were able to find something that was edible and healthy, much less good-tasting. The people could barely survive, dependent on luck for sustenance. If only they could grow their food! But on Earth, there were no seeds to plant.

However, there were seeds in the Heavens. In the majestic, bountiful Heavens, there were storehouses and storehouses of grain seeds—gold, blue, red, white, black, and all twinkling like stars. But it was forbidden to bring even one small seed to Earth. So the people continued to suffer.

Finally, the dog with nine tails could not bear the people's misery any longer.

"I will help them," the dog vowed, each one of his nine furry tails standing straight upward in defiance. "They must be able to grow food for themselves."

So, the dog with nine tails traveled for two months, racing across the sky, until he reached the Heavens. When he finally arrived, he marveled at the glowing azure sky, the jade-colored lake, and magnificent imperial palaces. But even though he was awed, the nine-tailed dog did not let himself get distracted. Quickly, he sniffed out the closest granary.

Now, the nine-tailed dog was not only kind but very clever, for in an instant he was able to get inside. And once inside, the dog very carefully pressed each of his nine bushy tails onto the mountains of seeds. The seeds stuck to his fur. Immediately, the nine-tail dog slipped out of the granary to make his escape.

Oh no! Bad luck! Just as the dog came out the door, one of Heaven's guards caught him.

"HALT!" the guard bellowed. "STOP!"

But the dog knew that if he stopped, all would be lost. So he dashed away, away from the granary and the fine palace, away from the jade lake and the luminous sky and toward Earth.

However, the guard did not give up easily and gave chase. The guard was swift and fierce, but the dog kept running. Seeds flew from the dog's tails, and he could hear them clink against the guard's golden armor like angry rain. When the dog glanced behind him, he could see the guard's black eyes burning. The guard was getting closer. And closer.

But the dog was almost home. He ran with the speed that only desperation can give. He was going to make it....

Slash!

The dog yelped. Just as he was about to make his final leap to Earth, the guard's sword sliced through the air, and with a mighty stroke, the guard cut off the dog's tails!

But not all of them.

As the dog fell to the bare land of Earth, the people saw that one tail remained. And when the dog stood up, finding himself safe at home, they saw a cluster of yellow grains clinging to his last tail. Seeds!

The people gratefully took the seeds and planted them, growing the first rice on Earth. And from that rice, they were able to grow enough food to feed themselves, and that is why rice is eaten today. This is also why the dog only has one tail.

So the next time you eat some rice, give a bit to your dog and say thank you. They deserve it!

RICE CAKE
年糕

"If you want to have a happy life, eat rice every day."

This is the last line of a famous Chinese saying, and one that many in China take to heart. Being an American-born Asian, I don't subscribe to that as much. Don't get me wrong—I like rice, but it's not fundamental to my life!

As we've just heard, rice is fundamental to much of Chinese cuisine. It is so essential that it is even intertwined into Chinese culture itself. One eats rice also on special days, too. Bamboo-wrapped rice (zongzi 粽子) is eaten at the Dragon Boat Festival, in honor of Qu Yuan—the poet who died by suicide by jumping into the river; zongzi was thrown into the river to keep the fish from eating his body. You eat round rice dumplings (tangyuan 湯圓) at the winter solstice because the shape symbolizes unity and completeness. And at the Lunar New Year, you eat a special rice cake called niangao (年糕)—which literally translates to "year cake."

Niangao is not like the rice cakes you buy at American grocery stores—those airy, puffed rice disks that are prepackaged in plastic bags. To make niangao, the rice has been ground to a flour and baked or steamed. Niangao, at first glance, looks more like a thick, dense pancake.

During the Lunar New Year, most people purchase or make niangao to eat at home, or the Chinese restaurant where you are having your new year party will serve it. Eating it means that your year will progress successfully, because the pronunciation of gao (糕) sounds like the word for high or tall, so eating the cake means your year be will higher (or better) than last year!

All this is to say that rice is more than the small bowl you eat on the side. It's a symbol....It's a dumpling....It's a cake....And even more! What more? Well, this story of niangao will show you....

During the Spring and Autumn Period (770–476 BCE), Suzhou was the capital of the Kingdom of Wu. The king of Wu, King Helu, had a trusted advisor, Wu Zixu.

Zixu was brave, virtuous, and wise. He was also very foresighted. During a period of good weather, the kingdom was able to produce a large surplus of rice for several seasons. The king's advisors argued what to do with it.

"We should sell it," said one advisor, "to bring more wealth to the kingdom."

"We should trade it for weapons," said another, "to make our kingdom more powerful."

"Your Majesty," Zixu said, "we should save this rice. Our kingdom will not always be so lucky, and there will be a day when this rice will be needed."

King Helu nodded. "Wu Zixu is correct," he said. "We shall save the rice. Wu Zixu, supervise this matter."

With the other advisors watching disdainfully, Zixu ordered the extra rice to be washed and steamed. Enormous vats and huge steamers were made for all the rice, and hundreds of men shoveled, stirred the grains, and then heated the stoves.

After the rice was steamed, those same men were ordered to mash the grain into a paste—so much paste! Hundreds and hundreds of vats were filled.

"Why?" asked the skeptical advisors. "What will you do with it all?"

"You'll see," Zixu said.

And then Zixu ordered that all the rice paste be shaped into blocks. These blocks hardened into bricks.

"Take these bricks," Zixu ordered the men, "and stack them against the inside of the city wall. After that, build another wall of bricks to cover them."

The other ministers snickered, but the men did as Zixu said. As they finished, Zixu spoke to the workers.

"Remember, if a time of hunger comes to the Kingdom of Wu, you can break down the inner city wall. Tell your children."

Many years passed, and King Helu died and his son Fuchai became king. Unfortunately, Fuchai did not trust Zixu, now old and bent, as much as his father had. Instead, he followed the counsel of his other advisors. So, tempted by power and wealth, King Fuchai invaded the Northern Territories even though Zixu warned against it.

"Your Majesty, you are wasting time and resources acquiring the northern lands," Zixu said. "You should focus on the Kingdom of Yue, which gets stronger every year and looks at our kingdom with greed."

"Don't listen to him," the other advisors told the King. "Wu Zixu is just an old man, afraid of shadows with no vision of a powerful and wealthy Kingdom of Wu."

"Yes," whispered another advisor craftily, who also happened to be taking bribes from the Kingdom of Yue. "And I wouldn't trust him, either. There have been rumors that Wu Zixu may be a spy. He might be trying to sabotage you."

The unwise King Fuchai believed these advisors and soon decided that Zixu was a traitor and had him executed. But Zixu's death marked the beginning of doom for the Kingdom of Wu. For, years later, the Kingdom of Yue—taking advantage of King Fuchai's distraction—did attack the Kingdom of Wu. Only as the armies of the Kingdom of Yue closed around King Fuchai did he realize that Zixu was not a traitor and had, in fact, been speaking the truth. But it was too late.

In shame, the king covered his own head when he died by suicide. "Because I cannot face Wu Zixu in the afterlife," he said, before killing himself with his own sword.

That was the sad end of Wu Zixu and King Fuchai, but for the people of the kingdom, the suffering continued. The battles and the seizure by Yue left the land devastated. Soon, families were facing famine and starvation.

"There is nothing to eat!" they said. "We cannot even eat the bark off the trees!"

"Wait," one man said, thinking hard. "My father told me that Minister Wu Zixu once said that if we were ever hungry, we could eat the wall of the city."

"What?" one of the villagers scoffed. "How are we supposed to eat the wall?"

"No, no," another man said. "I remember this, too. My father said he made rice bricks!"

"Yes," a woman spoke out. "That's right! My father told me that there is a wall of rice inside the city wall!"

So the people rushed to the city wall and, with effort, pried off some of the outer bricks of the wall. Behind them were the blocks of rice that Wu Zixu had ordered so long ago.

"A wall of rice bricks!" the people cried. "It's true!"

"But can we still eat it, after all this time?" one person asked.

"I think they will soften up after we cook it," another said. "And it has got to be better than eating stones!"

They passed out the rice bricks and, miraculously, there was enough for everyone to keep from starving. And when the people sliced up the rice blocks and fried them, they tasted...good! Better than good! Delicious!

"Thank you, Minister Wu Zixu," they all said as they bowed in his memory.

So from then on, every new year, families made bricks of rice paste and ate them in Wu Zixu's honor, in memory of his integrity and wise foresight. Over time, this custom of eating rice bricks became the custom of eating the new year niangao.

NOODLES
麵條

It has been said that people in the West eat potatoes and pasta while people in the East eat rice and noodles. I think that might be true. I know in my family we surely eat a lot of both!

Most Americans associate rice with Chinese cuisine because the majority of Chinese restaurants here were run by people from southern China, where rice was grown in abundance and was a daily staple. Northern China, however, did not have the right climate to grow rice, and instead noodles made from wheat became their commonly eaten food.

And while there have been many debates about whether spaghetti originated in Italy or was really an Italian reinterpretation of Chinese noodles, China can claim to have eaten the noodle first. In 2005, archaeologists discovered a pot at their dig site in Laijia, China. Inside the pot were the remains of four-thousand-year-old noodles! It is the oldest evidence of noodles discovered thus far, so China wins for having noodles first! However, it is possible that the Italians created spaghetti on their own—without Chinese influence—later on.

Just like rice, noodles have long been significant in Chinese culture and cuisine. In ancient times, three days after a baby was born, a tangbing—a type of noodle made by pressing dough into slim pieces—party was given because the long noodles symbolized longevity. Even today at birthdays and new year celebrations, Chinese people eat the long strands of longevity noodles to ensure their long life. While all of this is just a custom done in fun, if Chinese noodles can last for four thousand years, perhaps there is some truth to the superstition after all.

Now, the noodles at an American Chinese restaurant usually fall into two categories: lo mein (捞面) or chow mein (炒面). I used to confuse the two, as the actual noodle used—the egg noodle—is the same. However, there is a difference. Lo mein means tossed noodles, for the noodles are already cooked separately and are then reheated and tossed with vegetables and sauce. Chow mein is stir-fried noodles. For chow mein, the parboiled noodles finish cooking with minimal sauce, allowing the noodles to be more crispy.

That said, both lo mein and chow mein are delicious and difficult to resist. These noodles are even irresistible to mythical dragons, as you will see in this story.

You might recall the Dragon Kings of the Four Seas. Back in ancient China, there was the Black Dragon of the North Sea, the Red Dragon of the South Sea, the Green Dragon of the East Sea, and finally, the White Dragon of the West Sea.

Now, these four Dragon Kings were friends but they were also very competitive. Each was always trying to outdo the other and show off.

"I can crack the clouds like an egg," Red Dragon bragged, "and the rain pours like a waterfall."

"A waterfall!" mocked White Dragon. "Why, your rain is nothing more than spittle!"

"Ha!" said Black Dragon. "Don't make me laugh so hard! My tears are more water than both your rain put together!"

"You might make rain," Green Dragon replied, "but you move your clouds like a sleeping tortoise!"

And so on.

Finally, one day, after a particularly tempestuous argument, the Dragon Kings decided to test one another's skills. On the sixth day of the sixth month of the year, the four would meet over the Yellow River and have a rain and cloud shifting competition. However, when Black Dragon won, the other three demanded a rematch. So, they agreed to meet again the next year at the same time and date. And, of course, when White Dragon won that time, another rematch was made. Soon, it became a yearly tradition. The four Dragon Kings found it great fun.

However, it was not fun at all for the people who lived by the Yellow River. The Dragon Kings' game caused the river to flood dangerously, destroying homes and temples.

"We must have angered the Dragon Kings," the villagers said to each other. "Why else would they cause us such devastation?"

So the villagers built a temple, hoping it would please the Dragon Kings and make them forgive whatever wrong they had done. But, when the sixth day of the sixth month came, the temple was completely unnoticed by the Dragon Kings and was promptly destroyed during their game.

The villagers tried again, with a grander temple. It was also destroyed. They tried again with an even grander temple. That, too, was destroyed.

"It isn't working," the villagers said. "There is nothing we can do to appease the Dragon Kings!"

"Perhaps we should forget about the Dragon Kings," one of the villagers said. "Instead, we should concentrate on the river. I have heard of a village far downstream that created a dam to protect it from the floods. Let us learn from them."

So the people began to make their own dam to protect their village. It was hard work, but all were determined to finish before the sixth day of the sixth month, refusing to return home even to eat. On the fifth day of the sixth month, the men of the village worked through the night determined to work even as day broke. The women, concerned for their husbands, fathers, and sons, also woke before the sun rose to make food for the workers.

One of those women was ShanGu. She was smart, capable, and most of all, observant. Both her father and husband were working on the dam, and she noticed that the bun and cakes that she had brought them earlier had quickly spoiled and had grown mold in the hot, humid weather. She wanted to make something that wouldn't spoil as they worked.

Yet the only thing ShanGu had to cook with was coarse wheat flour. As she stared at it, ShanGu thought that if she made flour into a dough of thin strips and stir-fried it, perhaps that would protect it from spoiling as well as make it easy to reheat. As she tested a small batch, an appetizing aroma wafted from her pan. When she added water, the smell became stronger and even more delectable, and a quick bite told her that it was just as wonderful to taste as well.

ShanGu ran to the other women in the village to tell them about her invention. Soon, all the kitchens were filled with the mouthwatering, enticing smell of ShanGu's noodles.

And what about the Dragon Kings? By this time, the sun had risen, and the four Dragon Kings had assembled to start their game. But a captivating aroma was distracting them.

"What is that smell?" Green Dragon asked.

"I don't know," Red Dragon said, "but it is making me hungry!"

"It smells delicious!" Black Dragon said.

"We cannot begin until we know what smells so good!" White Dragon declared.

All the dragons agreed and began to search for the source of the wondrous smell. They flew up and down the Yellow River, over and through many villages, but they could not find the origin of the smell.

"Where could it be coming from?" Black Dragon moaned, almost in despair. "How can we find out?"

"We will have to ask Jade Emperor," Green Dragon said. "He will know."

The others concurred, and they all quickly flew up to see Jade Emperor at his palace in the Heavens.

"Please," the four Dragon Kings begged, "tell us where that smell is coming from!"

The Jade Emperor readily consented to their request, for he, too, smelled the tempting aroma. Using his divination powers, he deduced that the smell was coming from the kitchen of ShanGu.

"Go to this woman," Jade Emperor said, "and invite her to come here to make this food. I want to try it as well."

When the four Dragon Kings appeared in front of ShanGu, she was extremely surprised. But she was happy to accompany the dragons to Jade Emperor's palace and make her newly invented stir-fried noodles for all the Heavenly Court. As the members of the court, the dragons, and the Jade Emperor himself praised and devoured the noodles, they asked ShanGu about her creation.

"I wanted to make something for my husband and father to eat that would not spoil, since they could not come home to eat," ShanGu said.

"Why could they not come home to eat?" Jade Emperor asked.

"Because they are working nonstop to finish the dam before the sixth of the month," ShanGu replied.

"Why must they finish the dam before the sixth of the month?" Jade Emperor asked.

"Because every sixth day of the sixth month, the Yellow River floods and destroys our village," ShanGu said.

At this, the four Dragon Kings looked at one another in guilt and embarrassment.

"And why," Jade Emperor said, looking directly at the Dragon Kings, "does the Yellow River flood on the sixth day of the sixth month?"

The Dragon Kings gulped.

"That is when we, uh"—Green Dragon bowed his head—"have a little competition with each other."

"I see," Jade Emperor said, his eyes piercing as he looked at each of the Dragon Kings in turn. "I think you should not have this competition anymore, do you agree?"

Each of the dragons nodded, shamefaced.

So, when ShanGu returned to her village, she was delighted to tell everyone that the floods were over. The villagers, of course, were elated and began a jubilant celebration that seemed to never end. Even now, every year on the sixth day of the sixth month, people continue to celebrate by eating ShanGu's stir-fried noodles, known today as chow mein.

Knife Cut Noodles

刀削面

For every kind of pasta you can think of, there is likely a Chinese noodle equivalent. Angel hair pasta can find a relative in the Gold Thread Noodles (Jin Si Mian 金絲面) of Sichuan—which are so thin that they can actually go through the eye of a needle. Italian orecchiette is almost twins with Shanxi's Cat Ear Noodles (Mao Erduo 貓耳朵)—they look very similar, but the cat ear noodle is eaten in a soup. For there are many, many different kinds of noodles in Chinese cuisine. While the wheat flour noodles are most popular, there are also rice noodles and noodles made of mung beans. They can also be thick or thin, hand-pulled or shaved, stir-fried, in a soup, cold, and more. And there are stories for all of them! For example, there are Old Friend Noodles (Laoyou Fen 老友粉), which are noodles that were created to help an old friend recover from his illness. And there are Dragon Whisker Noodles (Long Xu Mian 龍須面) that one eats on February 2 of the Lunar New Year because that date also sounds like the word for dragon head. And there are Sister-in-Law Noodles (Saozi Mian 素臊, a play on words since saozi 臊子 is diced meat and saozi 嫂子 is sister-in-law), which was a dish created for a scholar by his sister-in-law that allowed him to pass his imperial exams; much like the Crossing the Bridge Noodle Soup story in the soup section). These noodles were often renamed Shamed Son Noodles when parents made them for sons that did not pass the exam!

And many of these noodles are finally finding their way to the United States. As American palates have broadened and become more curious, more specialty restaurants are serving these distinctive noodles.

One interesting noodle to try is Dao Xiao Mian (刀削面), a unique noodle from the Shanxi Province. This noodle is not pulled or shaped but actually created by shaving pieces off a block of dough with a knife—Dao Xiao Mian literally translates to "Knife Cut Noodles."

The chef must cut the dough at the right angle, so that the noodle makes the shape of a long willow leaf and is thicker in the middle and thinner on the edges. This allows these thicker noodles to soak up the most amount of broth and spicy oil as possible—giving the diner a fully flavored mouthful.

And just as interesting as the noodle is the story that goes with it. For Dao Xiao Mian has a memorable story that only makes it taste even better!

In 1279, the tribal nomads who ruled the northern territories for decades finally conquered China and ended the Song dynasty. The Yuan dynasty, the dynasty of the Mongols, was now established.

But most of the Chinese people saw the Mongols as invaders, not rulers. The Mongols knew this and were constantly concerned that the Chinese would rise up against them. So, the Mongols took any weapons the Chinese might have, including personal cooking knives! Instead, they only allowed one knife for every ten families.

As you can imagine, ten households sharing one knife made cooking a bit of a challenge. One day, while an old woman was putting a large pot of water on the stove, she called her husband.

"Go and get the knife," she said. "I am making noodles for lunch. By the time you get it, this water should be hot enough."

The old man nodded and went to the neighbors, the Cao family.

"Do you have the knife?" he asked them. "We need it to make noodles for lunch."

"Not us," they replied, "but we're to have it after the Yans. See if they are done and you can have it after us."

So, the old man went to the Yan family's home.

"Do you have the knife?" he asked. "I want to bring it to the Caos so that we can use it after to make noodles for lunch."

"Not us," said the Yan family. "Check with the Changs. We are supposed to get the knife after them, then we'll give it to you to give to the Caos."

So, the old man went to the Chang family home.

"Do you have the knife?" he asked them. "I want to bring it to the Yans, who will then give it to the Caos, so that we can use it to make noodles for lunch."

"Not us," said the Chang family. "Go see the Zhou family. After they are done with the knife, it's our turn."

So, the old man went to the Zhou family home...and you can probably guess what happened there. By the time the old man tracked down the knife at the tenth family's home, he saw it was still in use and would be for quite a while (the Wangs were butchering a cow) and that he and his wife were the last in line to receive it. It would be a long time before they got the knife.

The old man sighed, for he was hungry and now lunch was looking quite far away. But as he trudged back home, he saw a thin piece of iron on the ground. He picked it up. It was not particularly sharp nor fine, but with a bit of imagination one could see it as sort of a blade. At least sharp enough to cut noodle dough.

Maybe my wife could use this? he thought.

So, the old man went home, explained their predicament to his wife, and showed her the found piece of iron. She looked at it doubtfully.

"To make noodles, I need to slice the dough into thin strips," the old woman said. "I don't think I can do that with this."

"Of course you can," the old man replied, whose belly was grumbling with hunger. "Just do it this way."

And he picked up a roundish clump of dough and, using the piece of metal, awkwardly attempted to slice it as if he were slicing a thin piece of apple. His wife laughed, but it gave her an idea.

She reshaped the dough to a blocklike form and held it at an angle over the now very hot, boiling large pot of water (since it had been heating for quite a while). Then, using the same technique she used when peeling cucumbers, she shaved off a long strip of dough with the iron piece. It was not a smooth cut—the strip of dough was jagged and uneven as well as thick—but she let it fall into the boiling water. She did this again and again until the dough was gone and the pot was filled with these oddly cut noodles.

However, even though they were oddly cut, they were also tasty. For when the old woman finally spooned them out with a rich meat sauce, the old man began eating at once. And then could not stop.

"These are so good!" the old man said, his words mumbled as the noodles filled his mouth. "I think I like them even better than the regular ones."

The old woman agreed. "They *are* good," she said. "Something about the shape of them makes them tastier somehow."

"Mmm-hmm." The old man nodded, not wasting words so he could continue eating.

But at that moment, their neighbor Mr. Cao knocked on the door. "I have the knife," he said to them. He sniffed the air. "What are you eating?"

The old man and his wife welcomed him in. "You have to try these new noodles we just invented," the old man said, pushing a bowl toward Mr. Cao.

Mr. Cao tried them and exclaimed in delight. "Let me take some home for my family to try," he said. "How did you make them?"

"I cut them with this knife!" the old woman said, holding up the odd piece of iron with a guffaw of laughter.

Mr. Cao stared at the iron, and then he also began to laugh. "I will tell everyone how you make these wonderful knife-cut noodles!" he said.

So he did. And, then the Yan family tried some, and then the Changs, and then the Zhous.... Soon everyone in the village and beyond was enjoying and making these kinds of noodles—and they still are. Nowadays, chefs can use a real knife to cut the noodles, but they use the same shaving technique that was created in the Yuan dynasty. These Knife Cut Noodles are a way for the Chinese to remember how they found ways to overcome oppression in the past...as well as make a very delicious meal!

TOFU

豆腐

During the hot summers, my mother would serve chilled tofu, sliced into cubes with a slightly sweetened soy sauce dripping over the top—like hot fudge sauce on a sundae. And instead of sprinkles, there would be a scattering of sliced green onions or a Japanese seaweed and sesame seed mixture. While I wouldn't exactly call it a treat—especially when compared to an ice cream sundae—this tofu was a refreshing snack to eat on a hot day.

Tofu—soybeans that have been cooked and pressed into blocks—has been a food enjoyed by Asian people for quite a long time, prepared and used in all different types of dishes. Some say it was the first meat alternative in the world! This may be true, for Buddhist monks in Japan ate it as early as the eighth century to avoid eating meat.

However, for a long time, tofu was relegated to the side in Chinese restaurants as simply a vegetarian option. Many Westerners mistakenly dubbed tofu as "boring" or "bland." However, as people have become more interested in plant-based foods, tofu has found a new popularity. But many Asian people already knew that tofu is a delightful, versatile food.

Originating in China over two thousand years ago, tofu can be seen as a kind of cheese made from soy milk. Like cheese, curds of milk are pressed together to make a block. However, unlike many cheeses, tofu has a very delicate and subtle flavor, odor, and texture.

There are many textures of tofu: silken, regular, firm, extra firm, and super firm; and there are many, many ways to prepare it. From sweet to savory, from deep fried to pudding, from fresh to fermented, tofu is a testament to the creativity of Chinese chefs!

Tofu is simple and inexpensive to make but still highly nutritious and filling, which is perhaps why cooks in China used it so extensively.

It has also woven itself into Chinese culture as well. Tofu is eaten at Lunar New Year as a way to bring happiness to the family because tofu sounds like the word for luck in Chinese. The saying goes "Tofu, tofu, mouthful of 'fu,'" (Doufu doufu mankou doufu 豆腐，豆腐，滿口都福) because fu is the Chinese word for luck. And after a funeral, one eats a tofu meal. This is done due to the influence of Buddhist beliefs that, at least for the day of the funeral, one should eat a vegetarian meal and because the white color of the tofu is the color of death in Chinese tradition (people wear white at Chinese funerals, not black).

During the Qing dynasty, the Empress Dowager Cixi believed that eating tofu would keep her skin looking youthful and insisted on eating it every day. Forty-nine pearl-inlaid steamers were kept to prepare the tofu so that the empress could have her daily tofu.

So, that white cube of tofu you might see is deceptively simple. That humble pressed soybean curd is food that has satisfied the stomachs and spirits of billions of people for hundreds and hundreds of years. And this is the legend of how it was invented.

This story begins two thousand years ago, during the Han dynasty, when Prince Liu An ruled the kingdom of Hu. Even though he was a ruler, Prince An was fascinated by Taoism, a religious and philosophical tradition founded by Laozi. Prince An was especially interested in the Taoist pursuit of immortality. Many Taoists were also experimental chemists, constantly trying to create pills or elixirs that would allow them to ascend to Heaven and live forever.

And Prince An was no different. He, too, continually mixed and boiled and stirred numerous odd plants and crushed minerals in search of an immortality concoction. At one point, Prince An thought he was close to success, so he decided to retreat for a time to Bagong Mountain in Anhui to perfect his brew.

Now, even though Prince An was engrossed in his quest for immortality, he was also a good son. His mother was quite old and one of her biggest grievances was that she had lost all her teeth and could not chew anymore.

"What I miss the most are soybeans," the old woman said mournfully. "Ah! If I could just taste soybeans again."

Prince An nodded. "I will try to help you, Mother," he promised.

So, Prince An took a break from trying to make immortality pills and potions to think of a way to help his mother. She could not chew, but she could drink. Perhaps he could make the soybeans into a juice? Putting his experimental skills to good use, he discovered a way to turn soybeans into a milk.

"Mother, try this," Prince An said as he presented her with a cup of soy milk.

As the old woman drank it, her wrinkled face split into a smile. "My soybeans!" she cried in delight. "I love it!"

Prince An also smiled. "I will make it for you every day," he promised.

So, every morning in his workshop, Prince An would make a fresh batch of soy milk for his mother. Then, after working on his experiments the whole day, he would bring the milk to his mother in the evening.

One day, while working on his immortality elixir, Prince An accidentally knocked some calcium sulfate into his mother's soy milk. Being so fixated by his work, he didn't even notice what he had done.

Now, calcium sulfate does not grant immortality, but it does turn soy milk into a solid. So, at the end of the day, when Prince An went to get his mother's soy milk he found it had turned into a smooth, silky mass. Taoists that sought immortality had no fear of ingesting strange substances, so Prince An tried it and found it glorious! Not as glorious as immortality, of course, but good enough to eat and share.

And, hence, tofu was invented!

Epilogue

Legend has it that Prince Liu An did eventually succeed in making a successful elixir. The moment he drank his potion, he attained immortality and ascended to Heaven—dropping the bottle as he rose. The bottle smashed to pieces on the ground, and some chickens around his workshop pecked at the leftovers and also immediately ascended to Heaven. If all this is true, then Prince An could still be up there now, accompanied by chickens.

INTRODUCTION

緒論

We've reached the main dishes! Are you still hungry? Still have some room?

Well, listen up, because this is where I'll feed your ears! Okay, not literally. But this is the section where I get to tell you why there are dishes named Buddha Jumps Over the Wall and who the empress is of Empress Chicken.

Which usually leads someone to ask me, "Why does Chinese food have all those names, anyway?"

But before I get to that, let me tell you about Chinese food in general. Because, as I mentioned before, what we call Chinese food here in the United States is really just a small glimpse of Chinese cuisine. Almost all the early Chinese restaurants were established by immigrants from the Canton—now called the city of Guangzhou—area of China and served the food from their local area. So for Americans, Cantonese food came to represent all Chinese food.

Now, Guangzhou was the third most populous city in the world during the nineteenth century, but it is only a very small part of China. It's as small as the city of Boston is to the whole of the United States. So, thinking that Cantonese food is the only cuisine of China is like thinking the whole of the United States eats only Boston baked beans and clam chowder. And, of course, that's not even all they eat in Boston, either! Obviously, there is so much more to Chinese food than we know.

The Chinese usually divide their cuisine into eight different types, based on the region: Sichuan, Shandong, Anhui, Cantonese, Fujian, Zhejiang, Jiangsu, and Hunan. Each kind has its distinct characteristics.

But they all share the philosophy of Chinese cuisine. Yes, Chinese food is so important in Chinese culture that it goes beyond just filling your belly—it can be considered an art and even an ideology! Many Chinese philosophers, artists, and scholars wrote whole treatises on food and dining.

8 GREAT REGIONAL CUISINES OF CHINA

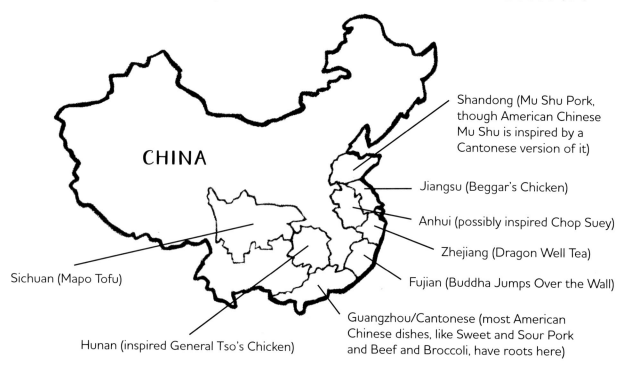

Shandong (Mu Shu Pork, though American Chinese Mu Shu is inspired by a Cantonese version of it)

Jiangsu (Beggar's Chicken)

Anhui (possibly inspired Chop Suey)

Zhejiang (Dragon Well Tea)

Fujian (Buddha Jumps Over the Wall)

Sichuan (Mapo Tofu)

Guangzhou/Cantonese (most American Chinese dishes, like Sweet and Sour Pork and Beef and Broccoli, have roots here)

Hunan (inspired General Tso's Chicken)

In fact, Confucius, China's great philosopher, believed that people should consider ten specific traits in the food they ate. They were: quality, color, taste, smell, shape, time, order, utensils, environment, and mood.

So you can see, Chinese chefs considered every part of the dining experience—from the name of the dish to the color of the plate the food was served on (warm-colored dishes held hot food, while cool-colored dishes held cold—and the colors always complimented the food). Chefs believed a beautiful name would enhance the dish—that an extraordinary name would help make the food extraordinary as well. So this is why Chinese food has all those names!

Tofu would often be renamed White Jade and bean sprouts would be called Dragon's Beard. Dishes also were often named after mythical creatures (see Dragon and Phoenix) or to memorialize important people and create pride (see Kung Pao Chicken). But most of all, the names were meant to connote something enjoyable while giving a hint of the actual dish.

It's a tradition that has continued, even here in American Chinese restaurants—whose main dishes (most of the time) have very little resemblance to any of the food my mother cooked at home when I was a child. But that doesn't mean that I didn't enjoy Chinese restaurant food....I might have enjoyed it even more (but don't tell her!).

CHINESE DISHES WITH FANCY NAMES

phoenix wrapped in green (watermelon chicken)

golden moon that hangs above the silver sea (pigeon egg soup)

dragon's beard (bean sprouts)

lion's head (meat balls)

white jade (tofu)

three pearl soup (chicken meatball, pea, and tomato soup)

So, while American Chinese dishes might not have looked or even tasted like what was found in Asia, they were still given imaginative names. For example, Happy Family. That stir-fry of chicken, shrimp, pork, and vegetables has no Chinese origin but is found in so many Chinese restaurants here in the United States. But the pleasant name implies that the ingredients are in a harmonious mixture—just like the family who will eat it!

But no matter what fancy name the chef calls it, the food has to be delicious. Here are the stories of some of the dishes that have pleased the eyes, ears, noses, mouths, and taste buds of hundreds of thousands of diners for many, many years.

KUNG PAO CHICKEN
宮保雞

My Chinese take-out order usually includes a container of Kung Pao Chicken. And I'm not alone. Kung Pao Chicken is not only one of the most popular and most famous Chinese dishes but it's considered a take-out classic—though, of course, eating it in a restaurant is just as enjoyable.

Believed to have originated from Sichuan—a large province in Southwest China known for its spicy food—it has many characteristics of the cuisine there. Diced chicken is stir-fried with peanuts (a Chinese symbol of happiness because it symbolizes many children) and the famous Sichuan chili peppers. The red-hued dish is aromatic and full of flavor, with the chicken fresh and crisp. If done correctly, Kung Pao Chicken is a delightful balance of spicy, savory, and sweet, and is very, very tasty. Like I said, it's one of my favorites!

And unlike some of the other dishes found on a Chinese menu, you can find this fairly commonly in China—though it will be called Gongbao Chicken (宮爆鸡丁), which contains a homophone of Gongbao (宮保). Kung Pao is just a North American transliteration of gong bao.

Gongbao, when directly translated from Chinese, means "palace guardian." That was also a form of address that was used for those especially distinguished by the emperor—similar to saying Your Highness to royalty in England. Gongbao was also how people addressed the Governor-General of the Sichuan Province during the Qing dynasty; he was a real man whose actual name was Ding Baozhen. And while there are many different variations of the story of Kung Pao Chicken, all of them tie to him.

Ding Baozhen grew up near the Liuchong River in Guizhou Province. Even as a small child, he had to study for the Imperial Examination—the test that would determine if he could get a job for the government. It was crucial for Baozhen to pass this test because his whole future depended on it.

One day, Baozhen wearied of studying. It was a hot day, and he could see young boys his own age playing by the river in the distance. Surely it wouldn't hurt if he took a break?

So, closing his book, Baozhen trotted toward the river. The sun seemed to burn the top of his head, and he felt as if he were a clam being boiled. When he finally reached the river, he could not help but kick off his shoes and dip his feet into the cold water. *Ahh!*

Baozhen knelt and splashed water on his face. Yes, this was much better than studying, Baozhen thought as he waded deeper into the river. Why work and work when he could be here, doing this instead? His feet pressed against the large, smooth rocks as the water rushed around him. He peered into the scurrying waves, and a silvery shadow glinted at him. Was that a fish? With reckless glee, Baozhen lunged at it.

And slipped!

Unfortunately, the river's bottom had a sudden drop, and Baozhen plunged into deep water. And even worse, this part of the river had a strong current and the powerful swells were forcing him under. Baozhen began to panic, for he could not swim. "Help! Help!" he cried in desperation just as the waves yanked him down.

Had anyone heard him? The water closed over him like the lid of a coffin, and his lungs burned as if he had swallowed a searing hot coal. He was dying and drowning, and he knew it— death swirled around him like black ink, blinding him, deafening him....

Then, suddenly, he felt a sharp push on his back. As if he were a bird cracking from an egg, he burst through the surface of the water. He felt himself being pulled, and in the next few moments, he was lying on the river's shore gasping and sputtering.

"All good now?" a boy's voice said over him.

Baozhen opened his eyes and saw a boy, just a bit older than him, also dripping wet, looking at him with concern.

"You saved me!" Baozhen coughed. "Thank you."

"It's fine," the boy said, smiling. "I'm glad you are all right."

"I will never forget you," Baozhen promised.

And Baozhen did not forget—and not just about the boy, but the entire experience. For from then on, whenever he wished to run away from studying, he remembered how he had almost drowned in the river and instead remained to work. And his diligence paid off, for many years later Ding passed the Imperial Exam with distinction and Baozhen was made governor of Sichuan province as well as earning the title of Tutor of the Crown Prince. Such a high-ranking title meant that he was henceforth addressed as Gongbao (Palace Guardian). But before Ding left to govern Sichuan Province, he searched out the boy—who was now a man—who had saved his life in the river.

"The great Ding Gongbao wishes to pay his respect to you and your family before he leaves," the messenger told the man, "in gratitude for the important service you did for him as a child. He will visit you at your home tonight."

The man, who was a simple cook at a local restaurant, was overwhelmed by the honor.

The Great Gongbao, here? he thought in astonishment. "To see me?" He looked around his kitchen in a panic. "I must prepare an exceptional meal for him!" But his food supplies were humble and he was at a loss. The most he had was one piece of chicken breast. "I will have to make do," he told himself.

So, he cut the chicken into small pieces and added peanuts and dried red peppers. He stir-fried it with a sweet flour sauce, vinegar, and spices of his choosing and had just finished cooking when Baozhen and his entourage arrived at his door. He quickly ushered them in and served them dinner.

Baozhen was touched by the man's earnest hospitality, but when he began to eat the spicy diced chicken, he was amazed.

"This is very good!" Baozhen exclaimed. His companions murmured enthusiastic agreements, and they quickly devoured the entire dish.

"I have never had such a wonderful meal," Baozhen said when they had finished.

"I made it in your honor, Gongbao," the cook said, bowing.

"Where do you work now?" Baozhen asked the man.

"I am just a cook at the small local restaurant," the man said.

"No," Baozhen replied. "You are now the head chef at the governor's residence! You must come and cook for me! I want to be able to have this dish whenever I wish!"

And so Baozhen took the cook and his recipe for the delicious diced chicken dish from his hometown to his Governor-General's residence in Sichuan. There, the chef used ingredients local to the area, and it became even more beloved. Whenever Ding Baozhen entertained officials, he always had his chef make the diced chicken dish. Soon, everyone wanted to eat the special Gongbao Chicken and the recipe was imitated all over the country. And it continues to be copied to this very day as Kung Pao Chicken.

Sweet and Sour Pork
糖醋排骨

Have you had Sweet and Sour Pork? If you have, then you already know about those delectable pieces of batter-fried meat—so crispy on the outside but so tender and juicy on the inside. And the bright red coating—sweet and sticky and tangy all at the same time...Yum! It makes my stomach growl just thinking about it! Yours too?

Which might be how the dish got its original Chinese name! Most people agree that Sweet and Sour Pork is an adapted version of Gulou Pork (咕噜肉)— gulu (咕噜) is the sound the Chinese think a stomach makes when it growls! Yes, while Americans say that a growling stomach sounds like gurgle, gurgle, the Chinese say the sound is gulu, gulu! And since stomachs always growled whenever this tantalizing dish was served, it was called Gulou Pork.

The original Gulou Pork had bones in it, so technically it was sweet and sour pork ribs. However, even though European foreigners who were visiting Hong Kong and Guangdong loved the dish, they disliked getting their fingers sticky so they asked for a boneless version instead. One imagines the chefs were probably irritated at this request, but after realizing that they could then charge more for it, they willingly complied! And the boneless version of Gulou Pork was just as tantalizing and caused just as many stomachs to rumble as the original..

Gulou can also be written with the characters 古老, which means "long history" or "ancient story." This is also a fitting name for the dish, as the story of its creation is from a long time ago.

During the Song dynasty, there was an unusual monk known as Ji Gong. He constantly horrified the other monks in the monastery by indulging in wine and meat—two things Buddhist monks abstained from. He also was quite slovenly—his robe was always filthy and tattered—and carefree. He was unconcerned about the serious, strict practices of his fellow monks, and instead of cloistering himself in meditation, he was often found wandering the country, loudly laughing and joking with common folk—with a bottle of wine in one hand and a fan to cool himself in the other.

Yet Ji Gong was a pure soul and a devout Buddhist. He had a kind and compassionate nature and always helped the poor and unfortunate. Despite his eccentricities, his divine spirit gave him powers that amazed all, causing miracles and wonders that were whispered about from province to province. He was said to have stopped an enormous boulder from sliding down a mountain with one hand (his palm print is still in the boulder). Another time, to help construct a temple, he teleported logs from a forest nine hundred miles away (and when one of the monks shouted, "Enough!" Ji Gong was in the middle of teleporting a log, so he dropped it into a well where it remains now—half-submerged). Whenever he encountered struggling craftsmen, he would ask for something nominal—like a shoe or fan—and leave behind a pile of gold coins (and many times the item itself). He brought good luck to whomever he met, and whenever Ji Gong was recognized, people would follow him around. He was well-known as the Mad Monk.

One day, Ji Gong was wandering in the city of Wuxi. After he aimlessly meandered the whole day: *Gulu! Gulu!* His stomach was grumbling. He was hungry. *What should I eat?* he thought. *And where?*

Then he sniffed the air and smiled. Something smelled good!

His nose led him to the outside of the best restaurant in the city, whose specialty was pork ribs. Ji Gong peeked in and saw the owner and his wife furiously preparing for the dinner crowd. Ji Gong grinned. Cheerfully taking his cracked bowl out from his stained and shabby robe, he breezed into the restaurant and addressed the owner.

"Alms for a Buddhist monk?" Ji Gong asked, waving his bowl in front of the man's face. "Surely you could spare a little of whatever smells so good?"

The owner grimaced. His customers would soon be coming and he did not want this unkempt, dirty monk in the middle of his dining room. It would be best to get rid of him as quickly as possible.

"Um, yes," the owner said. Hastily, he grabbed Ji Gong's bowl and threw some pork ribs into it. "Here you go," the man said, shoving the filled bowl back at Ji Gong and pushing him out the door. "Goodbye."

"Blessings to you!" Ji Gong said merrily as he bowed. He sat down right on the ground and began to eat.

When the owner returned inside, his wife stopped him.

"What did you just do?" she asked him.

"I just gave that begging monk some ribs," he said. "I thought that would get him to leave faster."

"You gave a Buddhist monk pork ribs?" the wife said in horror. "Monks do not eat meat! You have probably sullied his begging bowl! He will be unhappy and it will bring us bad luck! Go apologize!"

The owner, realizing his error, ran out to Ji Gong, who was sitting in front of the restaurant.

"So sorry, so sorry," the man said, bowing deeply. "I forgot the pork ribs would not be to your liking."

"On the contrary," Ji Gong said, licking his fingers, "I liked those pork ribs quite a bit. Could I have some more?"

The man stared at Ji Gong as the setting sun created a halo around the monk, making him glow with unearthly brilliance.

"You are the Mad Monk!" the restaurant owner gasped. "The Mad Monk that eats meat and creates miracles."

"Oh yes, they do call me that." Ji Gong beamed. "It's so nice to be famous!"

"Please come in," the owner said. "You are welcome to something else to eat."

"I'd love to have some more ribs!" Ji Gong said as he skipped through the door.

So the owner and his wife sat Ji Gong at a table and served him a fine meal—mainly ribs. And as he ate, the news that the Mad Monk was eating at the restaurant was whispered around the city. Soon the dining room was full, with people waiting at the door—all hoping to catch a glimpse of Ji Gong. It was a busy night for the owner and his wife.

When Ji Gong finished, he did not talk to any of the crowd but instead asked to see the kitchen. As he poked around, accompanied by the wife, he saw the pot the ribs had been cooked in.

"Ah," he said, "the most delicious ribs are in that pot."

At that moment, the wife was called into the dining room. She excused herself and left Ji

Gong unattended in the kitchen. Alone, Ji Gong scraped off a clump of mud from his robe and tore a strand from his palm leaf fan and tossed both items into the pot. Then, smiling, he covered the pot, well pleased with himself.

When the owner's wife returned, Ji Gong was gone.

The next morning, when the restaurant owner opened the pot to cook a new batch of ribs, an amazing aroma wafted out of it. *Gulu! Gulu!* The man heard his stomach growl as he looked inside the pot. There, he saw a fully cooked rack of ribs covered in a succulent red sauce. He pulled a piece out of the pot, and the meat was so tender it almost fell off the bone. It was so enticing that his stomach began to grumble.

"What is that?" the wife said, bursting into the kitchen. *Gulu! Gulu!* Her stomach was growling, too.

"It's ribs," the man said, "but not our usual."

He took a bite and was immediately overwhelmed by the luscious, piquant flavors of sweet and sour. He had to sit down. "The most delicious ribs," he said, licking his lips, "are in that pot!"

The wife gasped. "The Mad Monk!" she said. "That's what he said when he was in the kitchen last night! This must be a blessing from him!"

The man agreed and from then on the restaurant always served pork ribs with the unique sweet and sour sauce left behind by Ji Gong. It became famous far and wide, and other restaurants quickly copied the miraculous dish. For it did seem a bit of a miracle—no matter who ordered it or when, people always felt their stomachs grumble when the Sweet and Sour Pork was placed before them.

Buddha Jumps Over the Wall

佛跳牆

To me, there is no name on a Chinese menu that is as intriguing as Buddha Jumps Over the Wall. While it is usually only found in higher-end Chinese restaurants, I bet many a patron has hesitated in puzzlement when seeing such an odd name on a menu. Why is Buddha jumping over a wall? Why would a dish be called that? What kind of food is this?

Well, Buddha Jumps Over the Wall (also sometimes called Buddha's Temptation) can best be described as a very elaborate, refined, and sophisticated stew. A specialty of the Fujian province, this dish was created in the Qing dynasty and traditionally took more than three days to make. The original recipe calls for over thirty ingredients, including quail eggs, duck, chicken, ham, abalone, sea cucumbers, ginseng, and taro. The dish also used to contain shark fin, but due to environmental concerns most chefs omit that nowadays. But it is still quite decadent, and many restaurants ask that you pre-order a day ahead of time if you'd like to have it.

And it is worth it.

The stew is a harmony of seafood, meat, and wine (don't worry, the cooking makes all the alcohol evaporate)—each retains its own flavor but is enhanced by the others. The fragrant meat seems to melt on your spoon. The seafood is sweet and tender. The wine is intoxicating. Together, the flavors are rich and savory—making an unforgettable meal.

So, how did this meat-based stew get its unusual name? How does a Buddha—when most Buddhists refrain from eating meat—come in? Well, there are many versions of this rather funny story, and this one is as memorable as the dish.

Sometime during the Qing dynasty, a successful scholar wished to reunite with a group of his friends. "Let us all meet in the garden next to the Buddhist temple tomorrow morning," he told them, "and I know, we'll make a stew to eat! Everyone bring something for it." Then he grinned and added, "I'll bring the wine."

His friends agreed. And while they were all friends, it could not be denied that they were also a bit competitive with each other. No one wanted to look less prosperous than the others. So each brought the most choice ingredients they could afford—a whole chicken, the famous dry-cured ham from Jinhua, plump sea cucumbers, juicy abalone, creamy-white-fleshed ginseng, fresh lotus leaves, and more.

As the scholars placed their provisions onto the garden floor, it seemed like the Heavens above had opened up to sing aloud their appreciation of such delicacies. But it was only the monks chanting at the temple next door.

Still, it was quite a sight, and a real chef would have goggled at such lavish ingredients—as well as been exhilarated with all the possibilities that could be created. However, the scholars were much closer to poets than chefs, so they simply placed all the ingredients in the large wine jug (after filling their own bottles and cups) the host scholar had brought. Using the lotus leaves to seal the jar, the scholars placed it on a fire to cook while they talked.

And how they talked! Once they heard about one another's families, they discussed government policies and texts, created and recited poems, and argued about literature. The sun rose and dipped, and if the scholars had been less interested in one another, they would have noticed the monks next door had completed their daily rituals and were now beginning their evening prayers. However, even though the scholars were unaware of the monks, they were aware of their stomachs. Eventually, even poetry could not distract them from the grumbling of their bellies.

"We should eat," one of the scholars declared. "I'm hungry!"

"The stew should be finished," another said, looking at the sun beginning to lower below the horizon. "It's been cooking long enough."

So, the scholars carefully pulled the lotus leaves off the simmering jug. But, oh! When the leaves came off—what an aroma! What a fragrance! The air filled with a bewitching, intoxicating scent of luscious delectability. It was sublime.

However, even before the overwhelmed scholars could even moan in ecstasy, there was a crashing noise all around them. The scholars gaped.

It was the monks! The scholars were now surrounded by the monks from next door! They had all jumped over the wall.

"What is that heavenly smell?" one of the monks asked, almost in a frenzy.

The scholars could not help laughing. "It's just our food," one guffawed, while another, quite inspired, recited a poem:

> *The lid lifts,*
> *and the fragrance spreads to the four cardinal directions,*
> *once the Buddha catches a sniff,*
> *he casts aside his meditation to hop over the wall.*

And thus, this luxurious stew was named Buddha Jumps Over the Wall.

MU SHU PORK
木須肉

Another one of my favorite foods from a Chinese restaurant is Mu Shu Pork (or chicken). This is a dish my mother never made at home, it was not a part of her cooking heritage, so I only ate it in restaurants.

Mu Shu Pork is another Chinese restaurant staple and you can trace its origins all the way to the Shandong region of China, with variations coming from Beijing and southern China. Originally a stir-fried mixture of pork tenderloin, wood ear mushrooms, bamboo shoots, and cucumbers, chefs had to adapt the recipe when they began to cook it in the West. Cabbage and different kinds of mushrooms were sometimes swapped out for the cucumber and wood ear mushrooms, and there were other substitutions as well. As many of the first Chinese chefs in America were Cantonese, they included their southern Chinese adaptation of the pancake wrapper—where diners would scoop up the mu shu mixture into a thin crepelike pancake, brush it with hoisin sauce (a sauce made with fermented soybean paste), and then fold the entire thing in a burrito-like fashion in order to eat it by hand.

Mu Shu Pork (Muxu Rou 木須肉) literally translates to "tree beard meat, and the Cantonese called it Muk See Yuk, which means something like "wood shaved pork." This is most likely because the long, thin, slivered meat strips intermingled with the sliced, barklike wood ear mushrooms gave the appearance of earthy whiskers. The pancakes, in the Cantonese interpretation, represented the earth onto which you placed your forest.

At the end of the Qing dynasty, the government's power was wavering. Not only was the empire losing control of the nation, but they could not control their own palace staff. The emperor's palace was so enormous—consisting of nine hundred eighty buildings and close to nine thousand rooms, with numerous courtyards and gardens—that it was truly a city within itself. It was, in fact, called the Forbidden City, for commoners could not enter, and even the imperial family and government officials had limited access within its walls. Only the emperor himself had complete freedom and reign.

But as the Qing Dynasty began to weaken, so did the restrictions. Fewer guards monitored the servants' movements and one group—the eunuchs—began to take advantage of the greater freedom.

Eunuchs were a special class of servants. They were servants who were born male (usually from poor circumstances with very few options) who decided (or in some terrible cases, were forced) to undergo the horrific operation of castration in order to serve at the palace. The imperial family wanted the eunuchs as servants because castration made it impossible for them to have children. Therefore, eunuchs could not start a competing family line. Because of that, the emperor and the imperial family saw them as less of a threat and trusted them. So, eunuchs often lived among the imperial family, in opulence and extravagance. Many eunuchs, usually to the envy of the rest of the palace staff, were given great privileges and power.

However, even in luxury, the taste of freedom was irresistible. Or at least the taste of non-palace cooking!

Because, during the Qing dynasty, the eunuchs began to sneak out of the palace to go to restaurants. The imperial kitchen staff were not friendly to them, and the cuisine of the common world filled them with insatiable curiosity. And, of course, local restauranteurs welcomed the wealthy patrons who could spend as much on one meal as the chefs made in a week. However, they had to learn quickly how to adapt to this new clientele.

"What is your dinner specialty?" a eunuch asked a chef one day during the early excursions from the palace.

"Ah, you'll love it!" the cook said heartily. "I slice up pork, bamboo shoots, wood ear mushrooms, and cucumbers, and stir-fry it all together with some scrambled egg. It's fantastic—everyone loves it!"

"Sounds interesting," the eunuch said. "What do you call it?"

"Heh, heh," the cook said with an uncouth, clownish laugh. "Well, we call it...." And then he whispered the name into the eunuch's ear.

The eunuch shrank back. "What?" he gasped. "Why such an obscene, horrible name?"

"Well, it's a play on words," the cook said, swallowing his guffaws as he saw that the eunuch did not enjoy the vulgar humor. "You know how huai dan (the Chinese word for broken egg), sounds like the word for bastard....Well, it's ah...ah...I guess it's kind of a joke...."

"A disgusting one!" the eunuch said with disdain. "How could anyone eat something with a name like that?"

"It's really good!" the cook protested. "You should still try it!"

"No, thank you," the eunuch said, and moved on.

But a few days later, a different eunuch stopped by the same restaurant.

"Do you have a special dish you make?" the eunuch asked.

"Oh yes, sir!" the cook said. "It's a stir-fried mix of pork, bamboo shoots, wood ear mushroom, cucumbers, and egg. It's really wonderful!."

"That could be good," the eunuch said, nodding. "What is it called?"

"It's...uh...it's called...uh...," the cook stuttered as he tried to think of a name that wouldn't offend these genteel patrons. It was summer, and a welcoming breeze blew the fragrance from the muxi, the osmanthus bush, near him. The cook glanced at the small pale buds and smiled. "It's called Mu Shu Pork," he said.

"Mu Shu Pork?" the eunuch mused, raising his chin with interest. "What an unusual name."

"Yah," the cook said, pointing toward the bush, "it's because the egg bits in the dish look just like those yellow petals of the muxi flowers."

"Oh, that's lovely," the eunuch said. "I'll try it."

Luckily, the chef had not lied, for no matter what it was called, the dish was delicious. The eunuch loved it and came again and again for it, bringing other eunuchs from the palace with him. Soon, Mu Shu Pork became one of the most popular—and profitable—dishes of all the restaurants, especially since the name was so appetizing!

PEKING DUCK

北京烤鴨

When I was preparing to visit Beijing, China, for the first time, I scoured travel books, magazines, and websites for suggestions of what to see or do while I was there. I remember one of these sources insisted that if you had never been to Beijing before it was absolutely essential that you do these three things:

1. Walk the Great Wall
2. Visit the Forbidden City
3. Eat Peking Duck

Luckily, you do not have to go all the way to Beijing to do number three. While Peking Duck is often considered the national dish of China, it is beloved everywhere. At most sit-down Chinese restaurants in North America, you should be able to find those thin pieces of tender, roasted duck meat and crispy skin—all waiting to be wrapped in a delicate pancake with hoisin sauce.

Perhaps that is because Peking Duck has had such a long time to build its popularity. The dish has quite a history. The practice of roasting duck in China has been around since the Southern and Northern dynasties (420–589), and as early as 1330, there was a written recipe for the dish. Though, of course, it was not called Peking Duck back then—because there was no Peking back then! In fact, technically, there has never been a Peking! Here, let me explain:

This duck dish is named after China's capital city, Beijing. Now, even though this dish was invented during the Northern Song Dynasty (960–1127), it was only during the fifteenth century of the Ming dynasty that the dish came into prominence. This roasted duck became a regular delicacy on the imperial menu and a great favorite of all the nobles.

And it was also during the fifteenth century of the Ming Dynasty that the city of Beiping was transformed into the capital of China and renamed Beijing. So, with both the city and the dish being elevated at the same time, it is easy to see how they became intertwined—with the dish being named after the new capital.

But why do we call it Peking Duck and not Beijing Duck? Unfortunately, that is part of the history of transliteration mistakes between the east and west. In the past, Westerners commonly misspelled Beijing as "Peking." That is because early European traders interacted with those in the southern ports of China who usually spoke Cantonese. In Cantonese, Beijing is pronounced something like "bak king"—with a hard "k" sound. So, when those Europeans romanized the name, they interpreted it as "Peking." The Peking transliteration became accepted as the common name of China's capital in the Western world—until China finally corrected everyone in 1979. But by then, the famous duck dish named after the capital city was known as Peking Duck—and that name stuck!

Regardless of the name's spelling, Peking Duck has served many purposes besides delightfully filling one's belly. Though it does do that very well—during my trip to Beijing, I ordered it twice because I loved eating it so much. However, my love for Peking Duck is nothing compared to the Qianlong emperor who was recorded eating it eight times in two weeks in 1761!

But as I was saying, Peking Duck was used for more than just food. Manchu nobles during the Qing dynasty would give each other ducks as a symbol of their generosity. In the 1970s, Peking Duck was credited with helping to win over Secretary of State Henry Kissinger during his secret trip to China, which led to President Richard Nixon's landmark public trip there—historically changing international relations between the two countries. That is why serving Peking Duck is sometimes dubbed duck diplomacy.

So, making Peking Duck is worth the effort. But it is quite a lot of effort. First, one must have a special "Pekin" duck (yes, a Pekin duck is used to make Peking Duck—one is a breed of bird, and the other is the dish we eat, so try not to get them confused! I suspect but can't confirm *that the Pekin duck is named so because of the dish. However, it does seem to be too much of a coincidence for it not to be, right?) The duck must be fed a special food so that it is fattened correctly. After the duck is butchered and plucked, it must be blown up—like a balloon! This separates the skin from the meat and fat to give the roasted duck a crispy skin—an extremely important characteristic of Peking Duck.*

After boiling in water, the duck is soaked in a maltose syrup, which colors it a rich mahogany red, and then hung on a hook to dry for four to five hours. Then the duck might be marinated with a special sauce and, depending on the chef, roasted in an oven or over an open fire.

When the meat is juicy, and the skin is crispy, reddish-golden, and glistening, the duck is done. Now it just needs to be served.

And this is the part that I always have a hard time being patient with. The thin, round pancake on my plate. The small dishes of slivered spring onion, cucumber, and hoisin sauce in front of me on the lazy Susan. My dinner companions and I (because it is rare to eat Peking Duck by yourself!) sitting quietly. All of us and everything waiting in anticipation.

Except for the chef. The expert chef—who has taken years to master the traditional skill of carving Peking Duck—is gracefully and neatly slicing that shiny, glazed duck into exactly 108 pieces.

Why 108 pieces?

Well, that involves a story about a troop of soldiers—though some stories claim it was a group of Buddhist monks or bandits. Whatever type of group it was, they determined the fate of how one cuts Peking Duck—and subsequently, how we eat it!

During the Song Dynasty, the imperial army was sent repeatedly to fend off Mongol invaders. There were constant attacks along the borders, both northern and southern, and the Song soldiers had to fight valiantly. It was after one of these battles that a troop of 108 soldiers decided to cut through the Dabie Mountains to get back to their home of Hangzhou, the capital city of Song.

Now, cutting through the mountain pass was faster—the other way was a long route through Wuhan—but it was much less populated. The troop passed very few villages and cities, which meant there were few places for them to stop and get something to eat!

So the soldiers were quite hungry when they finally came across a remote mountain village.

"Where do we get something to eat?" the troop commander demanded to a passing villager child. "Where are the restaurants?"

The child gulped, awed by the battle-scarred and rugged warriors. "We only have one restaurant," she said, and pointed a single finger down the street.

The commander gazed in the direction of her finger and saw a small building with a single duck hanging in its window. He nodded.

"Forward, men!" he ordered. "Dinner awaits!"

However, as the 108 men tramped toward the restaurant, the restaurant owner—who was also the chef—was horrified.

"They are ALL coming here!" he gasped, his eyes as wide as teacups. "I am not used to serving so many people! What do I have that can serve all of them?"

In a mad frenzy, the owner rummaged through his kitchen. Wheat flour. Spring onions. There were also cucumbers in the garden. Maybe he could make some sort of pancake for the soldiers?

Just then, the soldiers arrived—the commander booming at the door like thunder. The owner scurried to greet them.

"I'm so happy to serve you," the owner babbled, "but since I was not aware that you were coming, I have only wheat pancakes to offer all of you."

The commander frowned. He pointed at the one solitary roast duck hanging in the window. "What about that?" he said.

"You are welcome to the duck," the owner said, "but I only have that one."

The commander grunted. "I have one hundred eight hungry men," he said, "including me. If we don't eat soon, it could get unpleasant. We'll take your pancakes and the duck, too."

The owner nodded, and as he set his wife to making the pancakes, he took down the duck. He brought it to the kitchen and stared at it as his mind raced. One hundred eight hungry men who could become unpleasant. If only some received duck and others did not...that could be another reason for them to become unpleasant. He had to make sure that every soldier got a piece.

Now, the owner—despite living in a remote area with a humble restaurant and being easily cowed by imperial soldiers—was, in fact, a master chef. As he grasped his knife in his hand, he nodded to himself. Yes, he could cut this duck into 108 pieces.

And he did. Carefully and skillfully, he cut the duck so that each piece was about the same thickness and size, the skin still attached to the tender, roundish slices. The chef did not waste one single bit, for when he was done, the skeleton of the duck was as neat and clean as an empty rice bowl.

With the pancakes, every soldier received a slice of duck meat. And how they enjoyed it! They longed for more, but all agreed that the one slice they tasted was incredible! And as the 108 men marched home, they licked their lips to savor the leftover flavor and looked forward to eating the duck again.

And ever since then, whenever that duck—the one we now call *Peking Duck*—is served, we make sure that not one single bit of it is wasted by carving it into 108 slices. And each slice is delicious!

Beef and Broccoli

芥藍炒牛肉

I always know that I can't go wrong when I order Beef and Broccoli. The tender, marinated slices of beef flank stir-fried with emerald-green broccoli, both swimming in a rich brown sauce, are a reliable crowd-pleaser as well as reliably tasty. Beef and Broccoli is also on almost every Chinese menu, from fast-food mall joints to high-end restaurants.

And why not? It's so simple and so delicious! But is it Chinese?

Yes, it is—though with a few caveats. It's believed that the Beef and Broccoli served in America's Chinese restaurants is an adapted version of Jielan Chao Niurou (芥蘭炒牛肉), a fairly well-known Cantonese dish. Literally translated, Jielan Chao Niurou means "stir-fried beef with broccoli." So, the connection between the two dishes is fairly straightforward!

However, if you were to order Jielan Chao Niurou in China, you would not get the Beef and Broccoli you see in America. That is because the vegetable we call broccoli is not a vegetable found in China.

But there is a Chinese broccoli called jielan. It is a plant that is grown in Guangdong, as well as other warmer regions in China such as Guangxi and Fujian. Unlike the treelike structure and flowering heads of the broccoli we are used to eating in the United States, jielan is leafy with glossy leaves and thick stems. Yet, jielan is most certainly the vegetable that the original Chinese Stir-Fried Beef with Broccoli dish is referring to—the broccoli found in American Beef and Broccoli is originally from Italy!

The Cantonese approach to cooking is to use fresh ingredients and to adapt with seasons, environments, and the palates of diners. So, you do not have to stretch your imagination much to picture a Chinese chef in North America, wrestling with the inconveniences of cooking in a foreign land, unable to find any jielan. But refusing to be baffled by a single vegetable, he simply decided to substitute with this less bitter but similar-tasting Italian broccolo. And after realizing that the locals liked it this way, he decided to continue with it. Hence, Beef and Broccoli was born.

However, one has to wonder if this chef was ever wistful for the jielan of his home country. For the Chinese, broccoli jielan has long been interwoven with longing.

You might remember the Qianlong emperor, who was the sixth emperor of the Qing dynasty. He would occasionally travel China in disguise. Not only did that allow him freedom from the formality of the palace, it also gave him a chance to see how commoners lived.

For one of these incognito excursions, the Qianlong emperor decided to visit Peach Mountain, a village in Guangdong Province. However, when he finally arrived at Peach Mountain it was dusk, and he found himself standing in front of a home's large red gateway, pondering what to do. Fortunately, the owner of the home noticed him.

Now, the owner had no idea that this was the emperor, but he was a keen observer. The owner could tell the man's clothes (despite being a disguise) were finer than those of an average villager and that the stranger's companions treated him with deference. The owner quickly concluded that the man standing in front of his gate was of some importance, and so waved him in.

"We are looking for a place to spend the night," the emperor said to the homeowner. "Is there an inn nearby?"

"Don't worry about an inn," the man replied, seeing a shimmer of silk gleam from under the emperor's plain robes. "You are welcome to stay here."

And with that, the homeowner ushered the emperor and his men into his house.

The next morning, before the rest of his officials had awoken, the emperor went outside to view the countryside. However, he had only gone a few feet when the lush green garden of the house seemed to envelop him. It was a lovely sight. The graceful stalks swayed gently in the breeze like fans, and the morning sun made the glossy, blue-green leaves shine. As the emperor peered closer, he saw that the entire garden was growing the Chinese broccoli jielan, and he was filled with surprise and wonder. He had never thought a field of broccoli could be so lovely; it was as if he were walking in the Heavens.

Just then, the emperor heard a lilting laugh. When he turned, he saw a beautiful woman in a window.

The emperor felt himself gasp. A shaft of golden light fell over her, bathing her in a soft glow. Every curve of her face seemed carved of ivory, every strand of her hair a silk thread. The leaves of jielan bowed and stretched before her like a carpet of jade. She was exquisite. Was she a fairy? Perhaps she was the Goddess Nuwa!

At that moment, the woman caught sight of him. She was horrified that a strange man was staring at her. "Who are you?" she screeched. "Go away!" And in her irritation, she picked up a bowl of water she had used to wash her face in and threw it at the emperor.

Luckily, she had a horrible aim and the bowl crashed to the ground in front of him. Only one drop of water flew up and landed on the emperor's face. But the one drop was enough to wake the emperor from his dream. He quickly saw that this was no fairy or goddess, just a young girl from the village who powdered her face.

The emperor continued to gape, though now in surprise instead of awe, when a waft of perfumed powder tickled his nose. He glanced at the bed of broccoli and saw it had been dusted with the girl's makeup that had spilled as she threw the bowl. He shook his head and smiled, laughing inwardly at his own foolish daydreams. He composed a short poem:

> *The mountain village girl has the beauty of a goddess,*
> *Tempting me to stay.*
> *But she cares more for the Chinese broccoli,*
> *For she blesses that with her fragrant powder.*

The emperor soon left but shared his poem afterward. The emperor's poem immediately brought attention and interest to the village's broccoli, and it became renowned for its extraordinary flavor and scent. And while dishes using the broccoli became quite popular throughout the land and the palace, the emperor probably never ate it without a wistful sigh.

EMPRESS CHICKEN
貴妃雞

Many restaurants have Empress Chicken as a selection on their menu. However, if I were to order Empress Chicken from each restaurant and line up the food on a table, you would probably be surprised at what you see. For it is likely that there would be a row of very different dishes. You might see chicken wings in a spicy sauce. Or tangy nuggets of deep-fried, breaded chicken. There might be a poached chicken, elegantly carved and sliced, or even a casserole.

That is because Empress Chicken is probably the dish that has been the most changed from its traditional roots than any other on a Chinese menu. Even the name has evolved.

Most people believe the original Empress Chicken was Yang Guifei Chicken (Yang Guifei Ji 楊貴妃雞), named after a famously beautiful concubine of a Tang emperor. Of course, as Chinese restaurants opened in North America, Yang Guifei was unknown to customers here, so chefs called it Concubine Chicken. However, the concept of concubines—unmarried female companions of an emperor—was foreign and, when explained, distasteful to those same customers. So, proprietors again changed the name—this time to Empress Chicken. As the most favored concubines often acted as the empress, and an empress was something easily understood by Westerners, this name stuck.

But changes to the actual dish seem endless. For alongside the name transformation came alterations to the preparation, cooking, and flavor. It is thought that the original Empress Chicken recipe was made from boiling and then immediately chilling (in an ice bath) a whole, *tender young chicken that was stuffed with fragrant vegetables and herbs. Then, after numerous other cooking steps, the white meat was then artistically sliced, arranged on a plate, and covered in a thin sauce with vegetables.*

However, as the dish traveled, it was adapted to fit modern and Western tastes in a variety of ways. Sometimes the dish used only wings; sometimes the white meat was cut into bite-size pieces. The sauce became thicker—sometimes spicier and sometimes sweeter. As the popularity of General Tso's Chicken rose, Empress Chicken followed many of the same preparations of being deep-fried and breaded. These days, any dish featuring the white meat of a chicken can be called Empress Chicken.

White chicken meat was an important part of the original recipe—at least according to legend. That said, even the legend has dubious origins, as some believe Yang Guifei Chicken was a French recipe brought to China in the nineteenth century! Still, this story is interesting to think of as the beginning of the ever-evolving Empress Chicken.

In the records and stories of ancient China, there are many mentions of the Four Great Beauties. These are the four women whose beauty was so captivating that they changed the course of history. There was Xi Shi, who lived during the seventh century, Wang Zhaojun of the Western Han dynasty, Diaochan of the Three Kingdoms, and lastly Yang Guifei of the Tang dynasty. Guifei was said to be so beautiful that when she walked in the gardens, the flowers bowed their blossoms in shame for they could not compete with such loveliness.

There was one person who completely agreed that no flower could be as captivating as Guifei. And that one person was very important. He was, in fact, Emperor Xuanzong—the seventh emperor and ruler of China during the Tang dynasty.

Now, Emperor Xuanzong adored Guifei. He loved her with such passion that it would eventually cause his downfall. However, he was for a time blithely unaware of this and doted on Guifei with famed fervor—vowing his eternal love for her under the crescent moon.

Emperor Xuanzong made Guifei his imperial consort and spared no expense or inconvenience to please her. Her family was given choice positions, seven hundred workers were designated just to sew her clothes, and he even used the imperial courier system—the exclusive messenger system supposedly reserved for urgent communication that consisted of horses galloping at top speed through the night—to obtain fresh lychees for her to eat. Anything Guifei wished, Emperor Xuanzong would command.

One day, during a time of bliss—before the whispers of rebellion or tragic calamities— Guifei and Emperor Xuanzong were enjoying each other's company in the palace garden, sipping wine and listening to music. Guifei, who tended toward overindulgence, was a bit tipsy and woozy from drinking too much wine. But she was enchanted by the music and as the song began to finish, she whispered in an unintelligible murmur to the emperor, "I wish I could fly to Heaven...."

However, the emperor thought she said, "I wish I could eat Flying Heaven...."

So, never missing an opportunity to please his beloved, the next day Emperor Xuanzong made a command to the chefs of the imperial kitchen.

"Yang Guifei said she wishes to eat Flying Heaven," the emperor said. "Make that for her dinner tonight."

The chefs nodded but looked at one another furtively, each hoping the other would know what dish Flying Heaven was. But as soon as the emperor left, it was clear none had any idea.

"How can we make a dish when we do not even know what it is?" they asked one another in desperation. But they shuddered to think of what would happen if they did not follow the emperor's command. "What do we do?"

Finally, one of the cooks—a chef from Jiangsu—stepped forward.

"Perhaps," he said, "Yang Guifei meant this as some sort of riddle. We need to think of what kind of food Flying Heaven would be."

"Well, it must be something that flies," one chef piped up. "So, it must be a kind of bird."

"Yang Guifei is very fond of chicken," another chef offered. "A chicken dish would please her."

"Very well," the chef from Jiangsu said. "We'll make it a chicken dish. But how could it be like heaven?"

The other chefs continued to gape, at a loss. But the chef from Jiangsu refused to be defeated.

"The chicken breast is the purest part of the chicken," he mused. "Pure like Heaven! And perhaps since the chicken can fly, eating the white meat of the chicken breast would be like eating Heaven that could fly."

The other chefs' brows began to furrow and their lips pursed in doubt. Now that they thought about it, chickens did fly, but they did not fly very high. They were not likely to fly to the heights of Heaven. And the white breast meat tasting like Flying Heaven? That also seemed questionable.

"Unless anyone else has another idea?" the chef from Jiangsu said.

The chefs looked at one another again and shrugged. They did not have any other ideas. One by one, stymied by their own lack of imagination, they nodded at the chef from Jiangu. Flying Heaven would be white chicken breast!

So, without wasting any more time, they quickly put the Jiangsu chef's idea into action. They took the plumpest rooster, slaughtered it, and stewed it with mushrooms, vegetables, bamboo shoots, and other spices—taking great pains and using every cooking method they knew to make the meat as exquisite and tender as possible. Then, placing only the daintiest pieces of white meat on the plate, they carefully and beautifully arranged the dish with jewel-colored vegetables and bathed it with an elegant, light sauce to ensure its delicacy. When they were finished, the dish was a gorgeous, mouthwatering masterpiece, with a fragrance sure to entice Guifei. At least they hoped so.

"As you requested," the chef said as they presented the dish before the imperial consort. "Flying Heaven."

Guifei's eyebrows furrowed in confusion, as she had no memory of requesting such a dish. However, the tempting aroma stifled any questions as she hurried to taste it. And as Yang Guifei placed one of the luscious pieces of chicken in her mouth, she could not help calling out.

"This is heavenly!" she cried.

Emperor Xuanzong sat up, interested. "Let me try," he said.

And when the emperor ate a piece of the succulent chicken he, too, cried out. "Yes, heavenly," he agreed.

"That is why this dish is Flying Heaven," the chef said eagerly. "We thought a dish with such a name should have unmatched tenderness, color, and fragrance."

"Well, unmatched tenderness, color, and fragrance sounds just like me," Guifei said to the emperor, with a kittenish smile. "Maybe we should call it Yang Guifei Chicken instead."

"Yes, yes, you are all that," the emperor replied, returning her smile with equal flirtation. "I agree."

Then he turned to the chef. "We shall call this dish Yang Guifei Chicken from now on."

And so it was. Flying Heaven became Yang Guifei Chicken, and as time passed and the dish spread, the name—and the recipe—changed again and again and again, becoming what we now call Empress Chicken.

General Tso's Chicken
左宗棠雞

If you've ever eaten Chinese food in the United States, you most likely have tried General Tso's Chicken. Can you picture a plate of sticky, breaded, crispy chicken bites—sweet, savory, spicy, and tangy all at once? It's easily one of the most popular, if not the most popular, Chinese foods in the United States. But while I have eaten General Tso's Chicken, I have wondered just as many times about General Tso himself. Was he a real person? Did he invent this chicken recipe?

Well, yes and no.

There really was a General Tso. His full name was Tso Tsun-t'ang (later romanized to Zuo Zongtang); he lived during the Qing dynasty, and he hailed from Hunan province. General Tso was a scholar, a minister, a governor, and most famously, a general. Born to a wealthy family, he was at first a tutor to the local governor-general's family and lived a quiet life cultivating silkworms and writing books.

However, in 1850 the civil war called the Taiping Rebellion erupted—the bloodiest civil war in China's history. Suddenly, Tsun-t'ang, the quiet silkworm farmer, showed himself to be a ferocious fighter, ruthless to his enemies and a gifted leader to his troops. Within two years of the war, Tsun-t'ang was given command of the military of his province.

And he led them to victory. General Tso drove the rebellion out of Hunan. And especially because he was from the area, he became quite a local hero. The Hunan province still proudly heralds his achievements to this day.

So, did he make General Tso's Chicken?

No.

General Tso actually had nothing to do with the General Tso's Chicken that we all know. General Tso never ate it, and he never knew there was a chicken dish named after him.

That's because General Tso's Chicken was invented more than sixty years after he died.

There have been many debates about the origins of General Tso's Chicken. Eileen Yin-Fei Lo, author of The Chinese Kitchen, *says that in Hunan the dish is called Chong Ton Gai 宗堂雞, which translates to "Ancestral Meeting Place chicken." Such a name would hint at an ancient origin. However, Chong Ton Gai, when spoken aloud, sounds quite a bit like General Tso's full name (Tso Tsun-t'ang) so it's been argued that those in China just reinterpreted the name.*

Most agree that General Tso's Chicken was not created in mainland China. It wasn't created in the United States, either (though it was adapted and adopted there). General Tso's Chicken was, by most accounts, invented in Taiwan. But it's still not that straightforward! There are different stories about its creation, with many contradicting the others. For example, one story says General Tso's Chicken was an invention to appease a late-night request of Taiwan's premier. Another story says General Tso's Chicken is really a variation of a dish called General Ching's Chicken—though no one seems to know who General Ching was. And yet even another says the cut-up chicken dish was just given that name because that was how General Tso cut up his enemies!

But the tale I am going to tell you now is the one that is most commonly accepted as true. It's complicated, with twists and turns, but it's fascinating, too! So, while you are eating your first or second order of General Tso's Chicken, here is a good story to chew with it.

Peng Zhangui was born in 1919. He was born and raised in Hunan Province and grew up to become an extraordinary chef. He was so exceptional that he became a chef for the ruling Nationalist Party of China, serving all the government's important leaders. China's civil war caused those in the Nationalist government (including their chefs) to flee mainland China for the island of Taiwan. So, in 1949 Chef Peng Zhangui found himself in Taiwan.

Chef Peng Zhangui, like most of those who had fled to Taiwan, yearned for the day he could return to China and held the memories of his home close to his heart. However, the Nationalist government continued to operate, now governing Taiwan instead of China and renaming themselves the Nationalist Republic of China (as the leaders hoped to return and reclaim mainland China in the future). So, Chef Peng continued to cook and serve officials and government leaders.

During the Taiwan Strait Crisis of 1954—an armed struggle between the Communist People's Republic of China (PRC) and Taiwan—numerous leaders and politicians from the United States, who were determined to stop the growth of Communism, came to Taiwan to offer aid. Taiwan's government welcomed them and hosted a state banquet. Chef Peng, wishing to make a good impression on these foreign officials, decided to create a special new dish for the event.

Influenced heavily by his hometown Chinese roots, Chef Peng devised a boned-chicken dish that he described as "typically Hunanese—heavy, sour, hot, and salty[1]." (But not sweet like the dish we know—that was to come later.)

What should he name it? This was a state banquet, and this new dish needed to have a name worthy of such an occasion. It was a Hunan-inspired dish, Chef Peng thought, so it should have a Hunan-inspired name. He thought fondly of his hometown and the heroes of it.

And that is when he remembered General Tso, Hunan's most famous champion. Mighty, fierce, honorable General Tso—yes, he decided, General Tso's Chicken was a good name. It was dignified. Powerful.

Thus, the dish was created.

But how did General Tso's Chicken come to the United States? That was due to the efforts of another chef: Enter Chef Tsung Ting Wang.

In the 1970s, Tsung Ting Wang was the chef of the well-known Chinese restaurant Shun Lee in New York City. But he wanted to open his own Hunan-inspired restaurant. So, in preparation, he went to Taiwan to sample the cuisine of Hunan chefs.

By this time, Chef Peng had opened up his own restaurant in Taipei, Taiwan, where he served his General Tso's Chicken. Chef Wang, after savoring Chef Peng's creation, was impressed. Yes, something like this might work for his restaurant in New York.

1: From *The New York Times Magazine* article "Hunan Resources," by Fuchsia Dunlop.
https://www.nytimes.com/2007/02/04/magazine/04food.t.html?_r=1&scp=1&sq=fuchsia%20dunlop&st=cse

However, Chef Wang knew his clientele. To make this chicken dish appeal to Americans, he knew he would have to adapt it. When he returned to New York City, Chef Wang experimented with his own version of the dish—deep-frying pieces of battered, boneless chicken and covering it with a sweet, sticky sauce. This, he felt sure, would make General Tso's Chicken popular with Americans.

And he was correct. Very correct.

Because Chef Wang's version of General Tso's Chicken became a Chinese-food phenomenon. People gobbled it up and ordered it over and over again. Chinese restaurants all over the country began to copy it and served their own imitations. Everyone loved General Tso's Chicken.

Well, everyone except for one person: the original creator, Chef Peng.

When he was shown photos of the General Tso's Chicken that is now served in North America—deep-fried, battered chicken nuggets drenched in a candy-red-colored sauce and garnished with broccoli—Chef Peng could not hide his disgust. "This is all crazy nonsense,"[2] he declared.

Nonsense or not, General Tso's Chicken became a craze that no one—not even its creator—could control. Nowadays, you can find General Tso's Chicken at almost every Chinese restaurant in North America—from food-court cafeterias to sit-down dining rooms. And strangely enough, because it is so popular with tourists, General Tso's Chicken can now even be found in mainland China. The Americanized version is acknowledged as a Hunanese dish, included in culinary publications and cooked by chefs in Hunan!

So, when you think about it, General Tso's Chicken—a Chinese dish that was never created in China or even eaten by the real General Tso himself—found its own way back home. And that in itself is rather legendary.

2: From the documentary *The Search for General Tso* by Ian Cheney. New York: Wicked Delicate Films, 2014.

MAPO TOFU

麻婆豆腐

Sichuan cuisine—food originating from Sichuan Province of Western China—is perhaps one of the most distinctive and popular of the cuisines in China. In general, Sichuan cuisine is known for eight specific characteristics: numbing (ma 麻), spicy (la 辣), hot (tang 燙), fragrant (xiang 香), crispy (su 酥), tender (nen 嫩), fresh (xian 鮮), and lively (huo 活).

Mapo Tofu, considered a classic Sichuan dish, has all eight.

It is also one of the few dishes on an American Chinese menu that one could find home-cooked for dinner in an East Asian person's home (it is also a common dish in both Korean and Japanese cuisine). I have many friends who said they ate Mapo Tofu as a child and make it at home now. Unfortunately, I cannot claim the same. My mother never made it—her cooking repertoire had very little Sichuan influence, and when I was young, I had an aversion to spicy food anyway. If a plate of Mapo Tofu was placed in front of me, I would have pushed it immediately away. So, it is a dish I never tasted as a child.

How can I be so sure? Well, no matter what age you are, if you have had Mapo Tofu, you would not forget it. Soft, silky cubes of tofu bathed in a fiery, bright, vermillion meat sauce, with Sichuan peppercorns and dried chilies often swimming in the oil. One bite makes a circus of flavors on your tongue—each spice racing, flying, and jumping acrobatically over your tastebuds with an exploding finale of the famous Sichuan mala sensation—the numbing and hot feeling left over in your mouth. For those who love spice, it is a dish not to be missed.

However, even though Mapo Tofu is popular in Chinese restaurants all over the world, one can only get the true fierce spiciness of the original in Sichuan. Everywhere else, modifications have been made to the level of heat—for not everyone can manage it! Like most cuisines, Mapo Tofu has been adapted to suit the tastes of the local diners.

But while the amount of spice is usually adjusted, the piquant and tangy flavors of the original have remained the same—as has the name. Mapo Tofu (mapo doufu 麻婆豆腐) literally translates as "Pockmarked Grandma's Tofu," which is an acknowledgment of its maker. For while the story of its creation has a number of variations, they all feature her.

Over one hundred and fifty years ago, there was a woman by the name of Wen Qiaoqiao. She was good-hearted, hardworking, smart, loyal, and a marvelous cook. Matchmakers would have lined up at her door with potential suitors, if not for her face. Unfortunately, as a child, she was afflicted with smallpox. Qiaoqiao survived but her face was cratered with scars from her illness, and most (because people cared a lot about appearance imperfections back then, probably even more than they do today!) turned away when they saw her.

But not all. A poor (and smart) man named Chen Chunfu decided he cared more for what was under the skin than the damage done to it and married her. And with that marriage, Wen Qiaoqiao became Lady Chen.

Now, Chunfu was poor in gold, but he was rich in ideas. "I know how we can make our fortune," he told his wife. "You are such a wonderful cook—we'll open a restaurant!" And so they did.

The couple opened a restaurant near the Bridge of Ten Thousand Blessings in Chengdu, the capital of Sichuan, and for a while, it did seem as if blessings had come to them. Their restaurant was a success. Lady Chen worked in the kitchen, choosing to hide from view, while Chunfu worked in the dining area, welcoming customers and serving them. And so many came! Lady Chen's food was very good.

But then after many years, bad luck fell. Chunfu fell ill and died. Lady Chen was heartbroken, and worse yet, she found that not only had she lost her husband but the customers of the restaurant, too. Because without her husband, she could no longer hide in the kitchen—and when people saw her, they refused to eat at the restaurant.

"That is Lady Chen?" a man, simpleminded and thoughtless, said in horror when he glimpsed her scarred face. "I never saw her before!"

"I'm not eating here anymore," said a vain, silly girl. "If I do, I might end up scary-looking like her."

"Yes," a fussy, unkind woman agreed. "I don't want to see someone like that when I'm eating."

Soon, Lady Chen—once the co-owner of a thriving business—found herself almost destitute. But she would not give up. Every day, even though her hair had turned white from worry and her steps moved slowly with sadness, she opened her restaurant with the hopes that someone would come.

And one day, someone did. A hungry merchant of cooking oil entered the restaurant. Unlike many of those in the village, the merchant was well traveled and familiar with unusual appearances. What was more, through his many experiences, he knew that the way one looked rarely showed one's character. So, when Lady Chen crept out of the kitchen to greet him, he barely noticed her scarred face. He was more concerned about getting something to eat.

"See here," he said to Lady Chen, "I'm on my way to sell my cooking oil, so I don't have any money right now. Do you think you could cook something for me—it doesn't have to be anything grand—and I'll pay you in oil?"

Lady Chen agreed. She used some of his oil to make a dish with tofu and minced pork and brought it to him. As the stranger breathed in the piquant aroma, he smiled.

But when he tasted it, he was exhilarated!

The flavors of the dish exploded in his mouth like joyful fireworks—the tenderness of tofu, the hot spice of the peppers, the richness of the pork—it was a delectable dance in his mouth.

"I have never had anything so wonderful before!" the man gasped.

"Just a little tofu dish," Lady Chen said modestly.

"No, no," the man insisted, "I have traveled to many places and eaten many things—this is by far the best and most exciting dish I have ever eaten! I will tell everyone I meet to come here and eat this!"

And he did. When he went to the village, he told everyone about the amazing tofu dish he had at the restaurant.

"But the lady who cooks there is all scarred and ugly," one of the small-minded villagers said. "Her face scares us."

"Bah!" the oil merchant scoffed. "You are being silly. What are some scars? She's a nice pock-marked grandma!"

And his words made the villagers begin to see Lady Chen—and themselves—in a different way. Had they been unfair to Lady Chen? Yes, they had not found her face attractive but that did not mean she was not a good person. And even scarred, she was an elder who deserved respect. The villagers started to feel ashamed…and they wanted to try this wonderful dish that the merchant raved about. Soon, a few ventured to try it and returned with praises.

"The merchant was right!" they cried. "The tofu is delicious!"

So, before long, everyone was clamoring for the dish. Lady Chen's restaurant was booming again! The villagers lost their baseless fear of Lady Chen and realized her true nature—and began to affectionately call her Pockmarked Grandma, the nickname the merchant had given her. They called the tofu dish Pockmarked Grandma's Tofu—which became famous beyond her dreams. Lady Chen embraced the name that was now said with love and even renamed her restaurant to Pockmarked Grandma Chen's Tofu (Chen Ma Po Doufu 陳麻婆豆腐) so all would know where to get her dish they loved so much.

Of course, nowadays, you can get Pockmarked Grandma's Tofu or Mapo Tofu at almost any Chinese restaurant in the world. But if you happen to be in Chengdu, China, and pass the Bridge of Ten Thousand Blessings you may yet see Pockmarked Grandma's Tofu restaurant—and the owners will tell you that it is the same restaurant where Lady Chen first made her dish! Yes, there is a real Pockmarked Grandma's Tofu restaurant! But don't count on seeing Lady Chen, for the Pockmarked Grandma left us long ago. However, the original flavors of her tofu are still with us.

CHOP SUEY

雜碎

Perhaps no food has had a greater rise and fall in Chinese American cuisine than Chop Suey—an assortment of meat and eggs that is stir-fried with vegetables in a thick, light-colored sauce. In 1886, journalist Allan Forman heralded Chop Suey as "a toothsome stew," but by 2009, Chop Suey was scorned as "strangely flavorless, with no redeeming qualities" by author Andrew Coe in his book Chop Suey: A Cultural History of Chinese Food in the United States.

Regardless of different opinions about its taste, Chop Suey is intertwined with the history of the Chinese in America. Like many immigrants, the Chinese chased fortune during the Gold Rush starting in 1848, sailing the sea to come to America. However, once here, they faced many hardships. Due to the language barrier, most Chinese miners found themselves working for mining firms (and later the railroads) in groups or "gangs"—which also meant they were paid less than Westerners who negotiated their pay individually. So, because the gangs were cheaper, companies preferred to hire Chinese workers—causing a lot of resentment from European miners. This, as well as racial discrimination, persecution, and harsh working conditions, forced the Chinese people to navigate much hostility and frightening violence. However, the Chinese found ways to survive and even thrive as merchants, railroad workers, farmers, laundrymen, as well as restauranteurs who used yellow flags to signal that their restaurants were open.

But the anti-Chinese sentiment grew so fervid that in 1882 the Chinese Exclusion Act— the first and only government legislation to exclude immigrants solely because of race—was passed, making it almost impossible for Chinese people to immigrate and work in the United

States. However, one of the few loopholes in the Chinese Exclusion Act was a special merchant visa for certain types of businesses...including restaurants.

Hence, there was a boom in Chinese restaurants as cooking food continued to be one of the few ways in which Chinese people could survive in the United States. For while many Americans were distrustful of the Chinese, they were willing to risk eating their food.

In 1896, the Qing dynasty Viceroy Li Hongzhang came to visit the United States, and Chop Suey was reported (falsely) as the "national dish of China." This brought the dish to prominence, and people were eager to try the food of the "Chinese Prince"—which is what they erroneously called Hongzhang (who was not a prince, just a politician). But Chinese restaurant owners didn't care that all this interest was based on false reporting. They were just delighted to have these new customers and were eager to oblige and create Prince Li's Chop Suey.

By 1943, the Chinese Exclusion Act was repealed (after sixty-one years), showing a decrease in the open hostility to the Chinese. Even so, Chinese people were still not wholly embraced. However, Chop Suey was! It became the dish of choice for almost everyone—it was as popular as hot dogs and pie! Chinese restaurants were referred to as Chop Suey Houses, and eating there showed one's worldly sophistication. So, Chop Suey, regardless of its origin, allowed the Chinese immigrant community to flourish even amongst the deep anti-Asian sentiment of the country.

However, by the 1970s, Chop Suey's popularity had plummeted. With people from China now legally allowed to immigrate to the United States, Americans were exposed to a more complete picture of Chinese culture. They then realized that Chop Suey offered a poor imitation of what Chinese cuisine actually could be and that it was not an exact recipe from China. Soon, Chop Suey was ridiculed for not being "really Chinese."

But perhaps it is. Many believe that Chop Suey is the American translation of zasui (雜碎), a peasant food from Taishan (also known as Toisan in Cantonese), a county in the province of Guangdong, China. The Chinese characters refer to animal entrails (intestines and organs), a primary ingredient in traditional zasui. If this is the case, Chop Suey actually has a very long history in Chinese culture—even mentioned in the Journey to the West, a sixteenth-century Chinese classic novel, when the Monkey King fights a demon, proclaiming, "I bought a pot for cooking zasui—so I'll delight in eating your liver, entrails, and lungs!"

Given many Americans' distaste for entrails, it's not likely that any modern Chop Suey now includes it. But perhaps the first dish of Chop Suey in America did and (like all cuisine) was adapted over time. And myths were created to fit the food. Because even though the actual Chinese characters of zasui indicated entrails, when the words are spoken aloud (especially when using the Toisanese dialect: tsap seui) it sounds like one is saying "odd scraps." And that could explain this long-believed legend of the origin of America's Chop Suey. Admittedly, historians agree that this legend is very unlikely, but I have to confess, deep down, I hope it's true!

Golden Mountain. That was what the people of China were told. In America, there was a mountain of gold just waiting for people to take. Yes, they would have to leave their homes and cross the ocean on a long and treacherous journey, but the Golden Mountain would be waiting for them.

So, dreaming of fortune, many of them decided to go. By the mid-1850s, tens of thousands of Chinese people had taken journeys on ships to America. But there was no Golden Mountain waiting for them.

Instead, they found a foreign land where they were unwelcome, and opportunities for survival, much less fortune, were scarce. And with that, they also found they could not return home. They were stranded in a strange land, alone.

"We must find another way to make gold," they said to one another.

And so, with only what they carried with them across the ocean, the Chinese immigrants found one way—with restaurants! Every day, the people from all countries poured into the ports of California and disappointed miners returned from the gold fields, and all were hungry. *We can earn money by feeding them*, the Chinese immigrants realized.

So, their gold became the triangular yellow flags they hung outside their buildings to show people it was an eatery. However, it was hard-earned gold. In order to persuade customers to try their food, the Chinese people charged extremely low prices. Miners could get an all-you-can-eat meal for as little as a dollar—which was less than half the price of other places that served a single paltry portion.

But it worked. Hungry diners were willing to eat at a Chinese "chow chow'" restaurant for the satisfaction of a full stomach. The Chinese in America had not found fortune, but they had found a way to survive.

But it was a tenuous survival. Opportunities became scarcer and scarcer as mines dried up and many blamed foreigners. It was especially easy to attack the non-European-looking Chinese. Often, Chinese people were helpless victims of violent attacks.

Which might have been why one night, a Chinese chef let a group of miners into his restaurant even though he had already taken down the yellow flag. It was late, and the chef, tired from a hard day's work of cooking and serving, had just finished cleaning up the kitchen.

However, none of that mattered to these miners.

"We're hungry! Feed us!" one of the men growled. His words were slurred, and he smelled of alcohol.

"Yeah!" said another, who stank even worse. He pointed his dirty, hairy finger at the cook—his hand as large as a shovel. "We want some of that chow chow!"

The chef knew better than to anger a group of rough, drunk miners. Without a doubt, one slight annoyance would fire them into a violent rage, and the chef knew he would bear the brunt of it.

"Yes, yes," the cook said. "Come in."

As they sat down, the chef felt an inner panic. Did he even have any food for these men? The food shipment was expected tomorrow morning, but that would be too late for the miners...and too late for him.

"Well, give us what you got!" the man ordered, much louder than needed.

The chef nodded. "One moment, while I go cook it," he said, bowing, and hurried away.

In the kitchen, the chef looked over his supplies in a frenzy. The vegetable basin was empty. The meat tin was empty. The shelves were empty. What could he do?

"Hey! Didn't you hear?" a miner bellowed. "We're hungry! Do we need to hurry you up?"

The chef gulped. In desperation, he looked into his scrap can. That was not empty. It was full of fragments of cabbage, oddments of chicken and entrails, stumps of celery—all leftover bits from today's meals.

Another menacing shout echoed from the dining room.

"One moment, one moment," the chef called.

So, the chef dumped the contents of the can into his pan and began to stir-fry the miscellaneous scraps. While it fried, he quickly threw in a starchy sauce and seasonings. Then he flung everything onto some plates and brought them out to the miners.

And they loved it!

"Hey, this is good," one mumbled.

"Yah," the other agreed.

"Hey, chow-chow cook!" another yelled. "What do you call this?"

The chef looked at their rude, drunken faces and thought how they had hectored and threatened him; a sudden rebellion flared within him. Invisibly to them, a wicked grin was bubbling secretly. The food was just leftover scraps! Garbage! And they didn't know it.

"Tsap Seui," the chef told them, knowing that they would have no idea that the word meant "odd scraps" in his Taishan dialect.

"Chop Suey," the man repeated, incorrectly. "Good. Make sure I get it next time, too."

The Chinese chef did not bother to correct him. And he was happy to serve the miner odd scraps anytime it was ordered.

BEGGAR'S CHICKEN
叫花雞

Beggar's Chicken (Jiao Hua Ji, 叫化鸡 yes, literally Beggar's Chicken) is one of the most well-known dishes of China. That said, it is a dish that is difficult to find in any restaurant, even in China. It is a special dish and is only now finding its way to exclusive Chinese restaurants here in the United States. If by chance, you happen to be in one of these special restaurants and see it on a menu, you might wonder if it is called Beggar's Chicken because the price will make you into a beggar!

That is because Beggar's Chicken (cheekily nicknamed by many as "Wealthy Chicken," but at times formally referred to as "Rich and Noble Chicken" when the word Beggar is found demeaning) is also known for being very difficult and time-consuming to make. It takes up to six hours to prepare! At Jiang Nan Spring, a Chinese restaurant in Los Angeles, California, diners must order the dish at least twenty-four hours ahead of time. Due to all these restraints, I admit, I have never eaten it. But I really want to!

Because I have heard that this elaborate and luxurious dish requires a hammer to serve it. Yes, you heard me right. A hammer.

Beggar's Chicken begins with a whole chicken stuffed with onion, ginger, mushrooms, and vegetables. Then, after being wrapped in large lotus leaves, the chicken is packed in mud. Traditionally, six pounds of mud.

Then it is slow baked for hours and hours. When it is ready, the chef will present the now-hardened mud lump to his guests and take out his hammer.

Thump!

The first whack of the chef's hammer will crack the shell of mud, and a wonderful aroma will waft from it and fill the air. Guests will be tempted to close their eyes in delight—but if they do, they will miss what is next.

Because—Thump! Thump! The chef will hit the hardened lump again, and this time the shell will shatter into pieces, like a broken sheet of ice. The chef, carefully and gingerly brushing away the small fragments, will pull off the largest segments, opening the shell. And that gaping opening will reveal the most succulent and supple chicken meat one can imagine.

That is what makes Beggar's Chicken worth the cost, work, and wait. When done correctly, it is said to be a chicken baked to perfection with no equal.

Which probably should be expected when you realize that this is a recipe that has been exalted for over 250 years—or perhaps longer. For, of course with a name like Beggar's Chicken, this dish has an interesting legend! Nowadays, people who tell this story usually set it during the transition between the Ming and Qing dynasties (1618–1683). However, some say the recipe is over one-thousand years old! If that is the case, then this legend—if true—took place much earlier.

It is said that there once was a beggar who lived in Changsu in the Jiangsu Province. One early morning on a hot day, he was especially hungry. He was, in fact, starving. He was so desperate for food that when he came across a farm and saw chickens pecking along the ground, he grabbed one and wrung its neck.

Unfortunately, the beggar did not realize that this was an imperial farm—one of the many farms designated to produce food just for the emperor—and thus well guarded. So when the rest of the chickens squawked and screeched madly, not one but a whole troop of men rushed out to investigate.

"Halt!" a guard shouted from a distance. "What are you doing?"

The beggar was terrified. Clutching the dead chicken, he ran away—the guards charging after him. By hurtling through brush and trees with the speed fear gave him, the beggar was able to lose them. Finally, he found himself alone along the banks of the river. But he was still frightened. And hungry. He looked at the stolen chicken in his hands.

I have nothing to cook this with, he thought. *And if I make a fire out in the open, the smoke might attract the guards. But I must find a way.*

As he looked at the lotus flowers floating on the river, he had an idea. *I'll steam it under a fire!* he thought. So the beggar fished some lotus leaves from the river and wrapped the chicken in it. Then he dug a hole in the ground, placed the chicken in it, covered it with a layer of mud, and lit a fire over it.

But even a fire in a hole causes smoke, for just as the fire was at a steady burn, the beggar heard the clamor of the guards.

"I think he's over there!" The beggar heard one shout.

The beggar had no choice but to run again, leaving his cooking chicken behind.

Luckily, with his head start, the beggar was able to lose the guards again. This time, he found a hiding spot in the village— an abandoned alley off the main street. The beggar hid there for hours, not daring to show himself in the open. Only when the sun began to sink downward did he feel it was safe. Then carefully he crept back to the river where he had left his chicken.

By this time, the fire was out, but the coals were still warm. As the beggar dug out his chicken, he found that the heat from the fire had hardened the mud around the entire bird—like a clay cocoon. But before he could even wonder about it, he heard the crack of a tree branch. Were the guards still here? Quickly, with the mud-encased chicken under his arm, the beggar darted back to his hiding place in the village.

Once back in his alley, the beggar took a closer look at his chicken. It was a curious creation, but he was hungry and needed to find a way to eat it. Using a stone, the beggar cracked the hard-mud shell open.

Immediately, a wondrous smell enveloped him. The beggar gasped in joy and began to pull open the chicken's mud shell.

Oddly, this day was the same day that the emperor toured his imperial farms. He had just finished and was now in the village, looking for something to eat. His carriage had stopped on the main street, and the emperor and his entourage were walking along to see what interested him.

And what interested him was an alluring aroma coming from the alleyway. What was it? It was so fragrant, so enticing....The emperor followed the scent into the alleyway to the beggar, who was now devouring the chicken as if he could not stop.

"What are you eating?" the emperor demanded.

The beggar looked up at him, his fingers and lips shining from the succulent juices of his meal. The food was so heavenly that the beggar could not even feel fear at the emperor staring down at him.

"Beggar's Chicken!" he replied with a grin.

The emperor pulled a piece of chicken from the beggar's hands and placed it in his mouth. His eyes widened.

"Add this chicken dish to the court's menu," he ordered his attendants. "I want some Beggar's Chicken of my own!"

With that, the meal of a beggar became the dish of an emperor...and of many hundreds and thousands of people throughout history and today. Perhaps it will even be yours! If it is, I beg you to share it with me, and we can each eat like a beggar and a king.

Dragon and Phoenix
龍鳳配

Soon after I first learned to read, I remember studying a Chinese menu at a restaurant. I was excited that I could read the menu on my own, but I was even more exhilarated when I saw a listing for "Dragon and Phoenix" (Longfeng Pei 龍鳳配, literally "Dragon and Phoenix Match"). Wow! I was enchanted. What kind of dish was this? It sounded magical.

"Can we get this?" I asked my mother, pointing at it.

She nodded, and I spent the whole beginning of the meal in eager anticipation. I was sure it would be some sort of otherworldly dish that would fill me with awe.

But when the waiter placed the dish on the table, announcing nonchalantly, "Dragon and Phoenix!" I was surprised. And disappointed.

It was just a plate of chicken and shrimp.

It was a fine plate of food, with the shrimp on one side and chicken on the other, each in its own pleasant sauce (though many restaurants often serve the dish with shrimp and chicken stir-fried together). But after imagining something much more mythical, it was a bit of a letdown. I mean, why didn't they just call it Shrimp and Chicken? How was this Dragon and Phoenix?

Well, as I've mentioned, Chinese cuisine has a long history of fanciful names (if you have not noticed from this book!). Because in the Chinese tradition, eating and dining were not simply something to fill one's belly, but almost a ritualistic experience to savor and remember. And they also often used cultural symbols in the names of their dishes to help achieve that.

In Chinese culture, the dragon is a legendary creature of enormous importance. There are many legends of the Dragon Kings who ruled the Four Seas, as well as other numerous dragon stories. Unlike the European dragon, which is usually portrayed as a vicious, fire-breathing beast, the Chinese dragon symbolizes nobility, wisdom, and good fortune. Historically, the Chinese dragon was associated with the emperor and imperial power—in the Ming and Qing Dynasty, only the emperor could wear the dragon motif.

So, because the dragons ruled the sea—and they had long, sinuous bodies—whenever seafood such as lobster, eels, or prawns were used in a dish, those foods were often dubbed "dragon." In America, with its less varied taste in seafood, dragon on a Chinese menu usually means shrimp—hence dragon in the name of the shrimp and chicken dish.

But what about the chicken?

Well, if the dragon symbolized the emperor, the Chinese phoenix—a mythical, majestic, multicolored feathered bird—was used to symbolize the empress. Like the Chinese dragon, the Chinese phoenix is also different from the European version. While the European or Greek phoenix is more eagle- or hawklike, the Chinese phoenix is closer to a mix of a pheasant and a peacock. And the Chinese phoenix lives forever, unlike the European phoenix, which dies by bursting into flames and then rebirths itself from its own ashes. That said, many recent Chinese stories have been happy to claim those powers for the Chinese phoenix as well. But traditionally the Chinese phoenix was a symbol of virtue, loyalty, refinement, and beauty. The empress would wear a phoenix crown, an elaborate headdress of kingfisher feathers, gold, pearls, and jewels.

And since the phoenix was a bird, whenever Chinese chefs used duck, squab, or chicken they often called it phoenix. Since chicken is the most common and popular poultry in the United States, phoenix here is chicken.

However, there is more to Dragon and Phoenix than a colorful renaming of shrimp and chicken. With a dragon symbolizing the emperor, it is also supposed to represent masculine qualities or the sun—while the phoenix represents feminine qualities or the moon. When the dragon and phoenix are joined—shared on the same plate—it's to symbolize the balance and harmony between male and female characteristics—the sun and moon. Both are important and needed for the dish, just as both are important and needed for life and the earth. And when they are together in balanced concert, they create a delicious dish (and a healthy human existence!).

That is why at many Chinese weddings, a Dragon and Phoenix dish is often served (with higher-end receptions opting to use lobster instead of shrimp). The dragon and phoenix motif has a long, poetic association with many Chinese romances and fairy tales, as you will see from this story.

During the Spring and Autumn Period in the Qin Kingdom, Duke Mu reigned over the kingdom and doted on his youngest daughter. Even before she could walk, she loved jade. She always reached for anything jade that happened to be around and, if allowed, would amuse herself with it for hours. Because of this, the duke named her Nongyu (弄玉) which means "gather jade."

As Nongyu grew older, her love of jade did not lessen. The duke knew that he only needed to buy her a jade trinket to please her. Little jade birds, jade hairpins, jade bracelets and necklaces—all made her clap her hands in glee. When one day the duke presented Nongyu with a jade flute, she was enchanted. Nothing the duke had ever given her before filled her with such delight. Immediately, she began to play it.

And Nongyu did not stop playing it, practicing night and day. She carried it everywhere she went and soon became quite skilled. Her favorite place to play was the Phoenix Pavilion. Surrounded by garden greenery and flowers, this small, brilliantly colored building with its swooping arched roof was as beautiful as the bird it was named after. Nongyu adored coaxing magical melodies from her flute there.

At daybreak, Nongyu would steal off to the Phoenix Pavilion with her jade flute. She would play softly so she did not disturb anyone. But at the sound of her first notes, the birds would quietly join in chorus, and together, they seemed to wake the world. During the day, when Nongyu played loudly, the sun seemed to shine brighter with her song, beaming a cascade of gold upon the Phoenix Pavilion. And at night, before Nongyu parted for bed, her wistful melody seemed to draw the moon up into the sky, which thanked her with a silvery path home.

With such charms, when Nongyu grew to marrying age, Duke Mu felt it would be easy to betroth her to a prince or some such aristocrat. But whenever he suggested any such meetings to Nongyu, she always begged away to play her jade flute. And since she was his youngest daughter and his favorite, the duke indulged her, and Nongyu remained unmarried.

But one night, as Nongyu played the moon into the sky, she heard something that almost made her drop her jade flute. It was the sound of another flute!

The music was faint, but Nongyu could feel the message in the song. The notes seemed to be calling to her. "Are you there?" they said. "Are you there?"

Nongyu's eyes widened. She brought her flute to her lips and played her loudest and strongest, wanting to make sure her song could reach the other flute. "I am here!" her flute thundered back, like the roar of a dragon.

And the song that returned to her was like a delighted trill of a phoenix!

"Then, let's play!" the sound cajoled.

Nongyu grinned in merriment. Together, she and the unknown musician began to make music that no one in the world had ever heard before. The birds fell silent. The dogs stopped howling. The babies stopped crying. All the people hushed and tiptoed to their windows, straining to hear each magical note. Duke Mu stood on the balcony of his palace and, as the music enveloped him, was unashamed of the tears that streamed down his face. The two flutes were making the most beautiful sound ever heard throughout the Kingdom of Qin, and beyond.

The next morning, the entire kingdom was chattering about the marvelous music. The duke, still immensely moved by it, called upon his daughter.

"Who were you playing the flute with last night?" the duke asked her.

"I do not know, Father," Nongyu replied. "But I would like to."

"As would I," the duke said, stroking his beard. "Where was the sound coming from?"

"Far away," Nongyu said. "But I think...I think it was coming from Hua Mountain."

So Duke Mu sent his best men to Hua Mountain to find the unknown flute player.

When Duke Mu's men reached Hua Mountain, they knew they had come to the correct place. For as they approached, they could hear a melody floating in the wind—drifting from above like a feather falling. They climbed the mountain and when they reached Star Cliff, they saw a young man piping on a flute.

"Are you the musician that played the music with Nongyu?"one of the men demanded.

The young man, of course, was quite surprised—and a little intimidated—to see a group of high-ranking ministers and soldiers show up at his hut on the mountain.

"I don't know anyone named Nongyu!" the man sputtered. "I am Xiao Shi, and I am just a woodcutter who plays the flute when my work is done."

The duke's men looked at one another.

"You had best come back to the palace with us," one of them said. "Bring your flute." And Shi had no choice but to obey.

When Shi was brought before Nongyu and the Duke, Nongyu felt immediately drawn to him. And Xiao Shi, of course, felt the same. Without saying a word, they each knew that the other was the harmony to their melody. Nongyu realized that without knowing it, she had been playing dragon sounds to call her own dragon— and that dragon was Shi. And Shi now saw that his phoenix song had been his way to find Nongyu.

Duke Mu was no fool. He saw that somehow, within seconds of being in each other's company, the two were deeply in love. He frowned, not sure if he wished his beloved daughter to be with a poor commoner.

"This is the one who played the music the other night, Your Majesty," one of the ministers said, pushing Shi forward and out of his lovestruck stupor.

"You are a musician?" the duke asked.

"No—yes—" Shi stammered. "I do play the flute."

"Let me see it," the duke demanded.

Shi carefully placed his flute, his most prized possession, into the duke's hand.

The duke's eyes widened. Could it be? Yes, this man's flute was also made of jade! The same color and grain as Nongyu's—almost as if they were both carved from the same stone. The duke nodded to himself, resigned. This was fate.

"Very well," he said, handing the flute back to Shi. "Then, let's hear you play."

Shi brought the flute to his lips, his eyes on Nongyu. As the first notes flew from his flute, Nongyu could not resist reaching for hers. Together, they began to play. It was the music of a phoenix and dragon dancing and frolicking in perfect tandem. Again, the world stood still to listen in enchanted awe. Only when the song came to an end did anyone breathe.

"What heavenly music!" a minister gasped. The court murmured in agreement. The duke smiled. "You two," he said, looking at his daughter fondly, "are obviously meant to be together."

So Nongyu and Shi were married. They played their flutes together endlessly. Nongyu taught Shi how to play like a dragon, and Shi taught Nongyu how to play like a phoenix. Soon, they each mastered the other's songs so well that they switched: Shi's signature song became that of the dragon and Nongyu's the phoenix. And their music, if possible, only became more marvelous and beloved. Duke Mu had a platform built high above for them to play so that everyone could hear their songs. All of the Qin kingdom enjoyed their constant music.

Until one day, after playing constantly for many years, their skills had reached perfection. Nongyu had learned to make the music of a phoenix and Shi the music of a dragon so flawlessly that a real phoenix and dragon swooped down from the sky!

The legendary creatures landed in front of the musicians and bowed, the phoenix in front of Nongyu and the dragon in front of Shi. And then, the bird and beast waited.

"Shi," Nongyu whispered to her husband, "I think they want us to go with them."

He nodded, and they both smiled at each other with a happiness beyond rapture.

"Let us go, then," he said.

So, they climbed onto the phoenix and dragon, and they flew up into the sky, higher and higher until five-colored clouds—the auspicious clouds that showed the will of Heaven—formed and hid them from view.

"The Jade Emperor must want them to play for him in Heaven," the people of Xin whispered to one another as the silhouettes of Nongyu and Shi disappeared, "and has made them immortals!"

And, since then, the Dragon and Phoenix is often used to symbolize happy couples, a pairing so perfect that even the Heavens must acknowledge it. And with its balance of seafood and poultry, the Dragon and Phoenix dish is considered a perfect pairing as well—though not one acknowledged by immortals in Heaven, but by diners in restaurants instead!

Buddha's Delight
羅漢齋

With all the imaginative names on a Chinese menu, sometimes vegetarians have a difficult time choosing which dishes they can eat. However, most know that Buddha's Delight is a safe choice—as long as they don't get it mixed up with Buddha's Temptation or Buddha Jumps Over the Wall! Either of those (they are actually two different names for the same dish) will be full of meat—and maybe even shark fin—and all kinds of ingredients that vegetarians and Buddhists might want to stay away from; though crafty proprietors have always been happy to encourage Buddhists to break their vows—hence the name "Buddha's Temptation"!

But a true Buddhist meal is vegetarian. One of the teachings in Buddhism is not eating meat because all life is sacred, including the lives of animals (Buddhists usually do eat eggs and milk, since the animal is not harmed). So, Buddha's Delight (Luohan zhai 羅漢齋, literally Buddha's Fast—"fast" in this case meaning "diet" or "intake of food")—a medley of vegetables stir-fried until tender in a savory brown sauce with no meat—is the perfect dish for a vegetarian.

However, it's a delightful dish for nonvegetarians as well. I am not a vegetarian, but Buddha's Delight is often included in my take-out order—because I love it! And I'm not the only one. Buddha's Delight is popular all over the world, finding its way into American Chinese restaurants in the 1960s and now served daily. However, in China, Buddha's Delight is often eaten on the first day of Lunar New Year—one of the most important celebrations in many Asian countries.

The Chinese tradition of Lunar New Year has a multitude of customs and superstitions (such as don't wash your hair for the day or else you might wash away your luck!). So, some eat

Buddha's Delight for good luck—because eating a dish that has not harmed a living being is a virtuous way to start the year, and such virtue will hopefully be rewarded! Others eat Buddha's Delight as a way to return to healthier eating—after the rich, decadent feasting of Lunar New Year's Eve, a dish of all vegetables is pretty good for your digestion. And of course, a lot of people eat Buddha's Delight on Lunar New Year for both reasons!

There are many variations of Buddha's Delight. At Lunar New Year, people make sure they include symbolic vegetables like bamboo shoots (representing new beginnings) or noodles (for long life). And nowadays, to make things easier, most people just have nine or ten ingredients. But the traditional recipe for Buddha's Delight calls very specifically for eighteen ingredients. Why? Well, it's all explained by how Buddha's Delight was created.

During the Song Dynasty, around 1120 CE, there was a Buddhist monastery in the city of Guangzhou. The Buddhist monks at this monastery were very devout and followed a strict schedule of meditation, prayer, work, and begging for alms.

Now, begging for alms—asking for donations of food—is an important part of being a Buddhist monk. Not only do the monks need food to survive but the monks believe their begging gives people a chance to do good deeds. And by doing good deeds, the monks believe that the givers will earn merit and will be blessed. To Buddhist monks, begging for alms is thought of as a circle of kindness.

So, one day, as according to their practice, the monks of the monastery dispersed to beg for alms. Six of the monks went east, toward the city. Another six monks went west, toward the village. The last six went south, toward the farmlands. But eventually all eighteen of them separated and walked alone, each carrying their begging bowls quietly.

The monks returned just as the sun began to arch overhead. While none of the bowls were empty, none of the bowls were full, either.

"In the city," one of the monks who went east said, "we were given bamboo, bean threads, pressed tofu, fried wheat dumplings, dried black mushrooms, and pickled radish. But only a little of each."

"In the village," one of the monks who went west said, "we were given wood ear mushrooms, lotus root, golden needles, gingko nuts, bamboo shoots, and water chestnuts. But also, only a little of each."

"The farmers gave us many things...," said one of the monks who had gone south, "bean sprouts, celery, broccoli, peas, corn, and some cabbage. But, like all of you, a small amount of each."

"Venerable friends," another monk said, "it is obvious that none of us were given enough to make a meal for ourselves alone. However, if we combine what we were given, we may be able to make a dish that we can all share."

The other monks quickly nodded in agreement. Together, they worked to slice and peel the vegetables, soak the dried food, and start the cooking fire. When all was ready, each put their collected food—all eighteen ingredients—into a heated pan with a little oil. As their food was cooking, one of the monks found some soy sauce and sesame oil to add as well.

And then it was done. As one of the monks let the mixture slide onto a large plate, all the monks breathed in the enticing, warm aroma—their eyes widening in surprised pleasure. In a matter of moments, the monks were devouring their portion like hungry oxen. When they finally finished, each looked up from their bowls at one another.

"That was delicious!" a monk exclaimed. "What good fortune that none of us were given enough to eat—it caused us to share our food and create this dish!"

The other monks smiled and laughed in agreement.

"Yes," another monk said. "From now on, we shall always do this. We will put our donations together to make and share this delight!"

So they did. The dish became a daily meal at the monastery and soon other monasteries began to do the same. And not long after, the recipe found its way out into the villages, cities, and farms and all began to make and share this divine Buddha's Delight.

DESSERT

甜點的故事

INTRODUCTION
緒論

Y ou may have noticed that there is usually a scant offering of desserts on a Chinese menu— usually there is not even a dessert section! It's something I have always regarded with disappointment. Having a huge sweet tooth, dessert is my favorite part of a meal. I always have room for a slice of red velvet cake or a bite (usually many bites) of crème brûlée. But there is nothing like that after you eat Chinese food. There's no Chinese tiramisu equivalent, no Chinese truffle cheesecake substitute—there's just no fancy dessert ever served at the end of a typical Chinese meal.

That is because there is not a dessert course in Chinese cuisine.

This is not to say that there are no sweet foods in Chinese cuisine. There are plenty of them— take a walk down a major Chinese city and you will be inundated with sweet street food offerings like candied haws, a type of berry skewered on a stick (tanghulu) or dragon beard candy, similar to cotton candy (long xu su). There are also specialty bakeries and shaved ice shops.

However, these treats are considered snacks or even appetizers. They are eaten between or before or well after a meal—rarely as part of it. At the end of the meal, there might be a soup— which could be sweet or savory. And after the dishes are cleared, maybe a plate of fruit to help cleanse the palate. But there is no Chinese tradition of eating an elaborate, prepared sweet dish after dinner. There is no dessert.

In fact, there is no exact traditional Chinese word for dessert. The word used nowadays, tian dian 甜點, originally only referred to the sweet snacks in dim sum (a meal consisting of a mixture of light snacks, both sweet and savory). However, with the Western desire for dessert and no direct translation, the meaning of tian dian has been expanded.

CHINESE SWEET TREATS

sweet rice balls
(tang yuan)

mooncake
(yue bing)

candied haws
(tang hulu)

egg tarts
(dahn taht)

sesame seed balls
(jian dui)

mango sago
(yang zhi ganlu)

But, of course, Chinese immigrants in the United States sensed Americans' desire for dessert. So, when they opened their restaurants, why didn't they turn one of their sweet snacks into a fancy, lavish dessert? They took numerous savory snacks and made them into appetizers. Why not do the same with dessert? Chinese restaurateurs were nothing if not ingeniously adaptable.

That might have something to do with the bottom line. As author A. Zee says in his book *Swallowing Clouds*, "...many traditional desserts require a great deal of work to make....Most restaurateurs are simply unwilling to go to the trouble, particularly since the profit margin on desserts is generally smaller than that on the main dishes."

So, considering how much work the cooks had to do just to make main dishes, Chinese restaurant owners probably decided adding complicated desserts to their menu was just not worth the effort. Instead, Chinese restaurateurs relied on shortcuts to satisfy the sweet tooth of their customers—shortcuts that became the minimal desserts of Chinese food. But even these small treats have sweet stories to share that are perfect to finish a meal.

ORANGES
橙子

When I was a child, whenever we finished our meal at our local Chinese restaurant, the owner, bowing gratefully, would place a small tray with the bill on our table. Along with that tray, he always placed a small dish of sliced oranges. These, my sisters and I always quickly gobbled up. For some reason, these complimentary orange slices always tasted sweeter than the oranges we had elsewhere. When I said this to my mother, she replied, "Chinese people always know how to pick the sweetest oranges."

Whether this was true or even if she included us in having that skill, I'll never know. (Even though both my parents are from Taiwan, during my childhood they identified as Chinese, not Taiwanese.) But I do know that many people think that it is the sweetness of those oranges that have made them a common Chinese restaurant dessert substitute.

However, they are much more than a dessert consolation prize. You may notice around Lunar New Year an abundance of oranges—displays of oranges in entryways of Chinese restaurants, images of tangerines hanging on the doors of businesses in Chinatown, or even a big bowl full of them in the home of an Asian family. That is because in Chinese culture, this citrus fruit symbolizes luck, gold, and success—all things you want when a new year begins!

Oranges represent this good fortune for many reasons. The brilliant color connotes happiness, and its roundness signifies wholeness and unity. But even more so, the word for orange in Chinese is a homophone. When one says the word orange (cheng 橙) in Mandarin, it also sounds like the word for success (cheng 成 is success, while the word for large tangerine (ji 吉) sounds like the word for luck (juzi 桔子). In Cantonese, the word for orange (or large tangerine) is pronounced ganzi (柑子), which sounds like how one would say the word gold, gamzi (金子).

So, when a restaurant offers you slices of oranges, they are not just giving you a refreshing end to your meal, but they are thanking you with a wish of good luck and gold! This reverence of oranges has a long history in Chinese culture, with one of the oldest legends as follows.

In the Western world, Guanyin is simply called the Goddess of Mercy, but in the Eastern world, her name means "the One Who Sees and Hears the Cries of the Human World." For Guanyin is the embodiment of mercy, compassion, love, and kindness. In Chinese Buddhism, they consider her a bodhisattva, similar to what Christians would call a saint. For Guanyin had become so pure and enlightened that she could have ascended to Heaven but decided not to so that she could help others.

Instead of Heaven, Guanyin went to a bamboo grove on the rocky island of Mount Putuo in Zhejiang Province. As she arrived, a sacred lotus platform—an elaborate seat rather like a multi-petaled, flower-shaped cushion—bloomed from the hard stone. And there, sitting on the lotus platform, Guanyin would listen and help and teach.

However, when the platform sprouted from the earth, a pebble got caught in its expanding lotus-shaped petals. As the platform continued to expand, its petals slightly arched upward and the pebble rolled down toward the center. It stopped right at the edge of the seat—right in front of where Guanyin sat cross-legged—and remained.

There, every day on the lotus platform, the small stone sat in front of Guanyin. It soaked up the dew of the sky, the light of the sun and moon, and the wind of Heaven and Earth. It felt Guanyin's breath, the vibrations of her beating heart, and the tears that she shed as she heard of suffering. It heard every word of her teachings, every one of her lessons of kindness, and every story she spoke.

After the stone experienced this for thirty thousand years, a curious thing happened. It began to think and feel and...move! For after so long with such a pure being, the rock had gained a spirit and had turned into a stone child.

This stone child sat in front of Guanyin for many more years—but now thinking their own thoughts and dreaming their own dreams. One day, Guanyin was called by the gods of Heaven to an event. The stone child watched as Guanyin floated up to the top of Mount Tai to the Heavenly Gates. As she passed through, the leaves of a divine tree fluttered above her, its branches arching over the gate. The stone child stared at the tree's branches, for they were laden with fruit a color as bright as the sun and as round as the moon, and all seemed to glow with an ethereal light.

Then the stone child looked down at the earth, bare of these golden fruit trees but full of people suffering from sickness and hunger. For the first time, the stone child frowned.

When Guanyin returned, the stone child moved from their place on the lotus platform and climbed onto Guanyin's knee.

"Hello, child," Guanyin said, welcoming the stone. "What do you wish for?"

"I wish to take a golden fruit from the tree outside the Heavenly Gate," the stone child replied, "grow it on Earth, and bring it to the people to help cure their sickness and ease suffering."

Guanyin smiled, well pleased. "You have learned well," Guanyin said. "Go and do so, with my blessing."

The stone child floated to the top of Mount Tai to the Heavenly Gates. As the golden fruits hovered above, the stone child hesitated—awed by the unearthly splendor. But remembering Guanyin's approval, the stone child moved forward and plucked a fruit from the tree.

As soon as the fruit was in hand, the stone child transformed into a man. The man felt his weather-beaten but clean-shaven face and looked at his calloused hands in surprise, but smiled.

"Guanyin has given me the power to change my form," said the stone child—now transformed into a poor, young farmer. "This will make my task much easier!"

So, the farmer gave himself the name Shi Ren (Stone Man) and made his way down to earth with the fruit in his hand.

Shi Ren decided to go to Huangyuan, to the bottom of Lotus Peak. Guanyin had once lived in that area, so he felt it would be auspicious. Once there, Shi Ren found clear water and flourishing greenery with mild weather. *Yes*, Shi Ren thought, *this is where I will begin.*

Accordingly, Shi Ren built himself a hut. Then, using mud, he created a mound six feet high. In the center of this mound, he planted the golden fruit and watered it.

Every day, Shi Ren tended the mound—watching, watering, waiting. Finally, after six months, a vibrant green shoot sprouted. Shi Ren whooped with joy.

He nurtured the plant, protecting it from animals and insects as well as any harmful wind or weather. With his care, the sprout quickly grew and, in another six months, became a great tree. This tree bloomed with a wilderness of small white flowers and, when the petals fell, created a beautiful blanket of white.

"The color of Guanyin's robe," Shi Ren whispered. "I hope she is pleased."

Guanyin must have been pleased, for soon after, small round fruits began to form on the tree. As they grew larger, they began to get brighter as well. First they were green, then greenish-yellow, then yellow, then orange...until finally they were the same vibrant golden color as the fruit from the Heavenly Gates. Shi Ren had done it! He had grown golden fruit on earth!

But now he needed to bring it to the people. Shi Ren collected the fruit and went to the banks of the nearby River Chengjiang. There he found a crowd of people clustering around an unconscious girl.

"She's fainted, she's fainted!" a woman was saying as she gently shook the girl. "Wake up!"

"It's because she hasn't had enough to eat," someone said. "She needs something to eat."

"We all need something to eat," another in the crowd responded. "I've been so tired and weak; my mother's teeth are falling out, and my uncle has bruises all over his legs."

"I can help!" Shi Ren cried, running to the crowd. He dropped his bag onto the ground and pulled out one of the golden fruits. As the people gaped in surprise and curiosity, he quickly peeled the fruit open and squeezed some of the juice into the unconscious girl's mouth.

The girl stirred, licking her mouth with her tongue. "What is that?" she murmured. "It's good."

Shi Ren let more juice drip into her mouth, and soon the girl was sitting up. He broke off a section of the fruit for her to eat. As she smiled and swallowed, the other villagers clamored around Shi Ren.

"What is that?"

"Where did you get it?"

"Can I have some, too?"

Shi Ren nodded happily, quickly sharing the rest of the fruit with all. As each person bit into a piece of the fruit, they all cried out in joy at its luscious sweetness.

"This is wonderful!" they all said. "How do we get more of this gold fruit?"

"You must grow it," Shi Ren told them. "I will show you how."

Soon, with Shi Ren's help, everyone was growing a gold fruit tree—usually many of them. Around homes, in pots, and around the river, gold fruit trees sprouted and blossomed. During the harvesting season, the landscape of the riverbank was green jade adorned lavishly with gold—the vivid gold of the fruit that flourished in their trees.

And as well as having sweet fruit, the people of the area rarely were ill again. Gone were complaints of weakness or bruising or falling out teeth—they, in fact, lived long and healthy lives. The gold fruit that Shi Ren brought had helped cure them, and not only eased their suffering, but brought them joy.

Which has only continued to this day. Even now, the gold fruit is considered a symbol of good fortune and is celebrated as an auspicious sign—which is quite an honor for our familiar, ordinary orange.

Red Bean Soup
紅豆湯

The only times I have been served dessert in a Chinese restaurant is during a Chinese banquet—at a big holiday celebration or life event such as a wedding. At such occasions, after eight lavish courses (yes, eight! Because in Chinese the word for eight sounds like the word for fortune, so eight courses is a dinner of good fortune!), the banquet is usually finished off with tangshui (糖水), a light and sweet Red Bean Soup.

It is a simple recipe—usually only calling for three ingredients: red beans (or adzuki beans), sugar, and orange peel. But its simplicity is part of its elegance. For sweet Red Bean Soup is not only served after an extravagant banquet, where its color denotes good luck, but as an everyday appetizer or even as a snack. It can be served hot or cold, or even frozen!

For non-Asian Americans, it may seem strange to have beans as an ingredient in a dessert. But red beans have been used in desserts for hundreds and hundreds of years in Asian cuisine. As early as the seventh century, Buddhist priests, intrigued by the meat-filled dumplings and buns of the common folk, searched for a vegetarian filling for these snacks. With a bit of ingenuity, they turned to red beans and, over time, began sweetening it. And by sweetening it, the red bean became an inspiration and mainstay for a plethora of treats enjoyed by Buddhists and non-Buddhists alike.

However, even before that, red beans were used for something other than food—something that might surprise you! Red beans were actually first used as medicine! Yes, what we eat now for dessert was first a medicine. If only all our medicines could turn out this sweet....

One morning in the spring during the Song dynasty, Emperor Renzong (1022–1063) woke with a terrible soreness on both sides of his face. As his fingers touched his face, he realized his cheeks were swollen and inflamed. He immediately summoned the imperial doctor.

The doctor looked at the emperor and then announced, "An evil wind has entered His Majesty through his nose and mouth. I suggest His Majesty spread cool gold about his face to reduce the swelling and keep other evil winds from attacking."

So the emperor swathed his face in gold, but unfortunately his condition only worsened. Three days later, his face had swollen to where he could barely speak and could not eat—only able to sip on liquids. The royal doctors were at a loss, but each tried to show authority.

"His Majesty must have a knot of evil in his blood," one declared. "We should find a medicine to unblock his qi."

"His Majesty has ingested some poison," another said. "We must flush out the toxin."

"I still believe it is the evil wind," the third said, "but now we must clear the heat that is causing the attack."

Regrettably, all the remedies the doctors attempted failed and only made the emperor's suffering worse. As the doctors argued, the emperor lost his patience and complained bitterly, "It takes a thousand days to build an army, but only one second to use it. You doctors have used a thousand medicines, but I have not had one second of relief!"

At his words, the doctors turned white and threw themselves on the ground, begging for forgiveness. And soon after, an official declaration flew from the doors of the capital, describing the emperor's illness.

"Anyone who can cure the emperor will be rewarded handsomely," the declaration stated in bold letters.

But no one stepped forward.

All the famous doctors in the city looked at one another and shook their heads. "We dare not," they said. "It would be like accompanying a tiger—much too dangerous if we fail!"

Since no one answered the appeal, the call spread farther and farther until finally it reached a small rural village. There lived a family doctor by the name of Fu. Now, this small-time doctor had been working on a medicine of his own—grinding and mixing adzuki beans and adding water to make it taste better. He called his medicine the Ointment of a Thousand Uses.

I wonder if my ointment could help the emperor, he thought.

So Fu packed up his medicine and went to the palace. Since he was the only one who answered the appeal, he was immediately ushered in.

"Can you help me?" the emperor demanded, his face now so swollen that his words were barely understandable.

Fu nodded and quickly unveiled his concoction. The rich, earthy smell of the beans filled the air.

"Spread this on your face, Your Majesty," Fu said.

The emperor did as suggested and, to his surprise, instantly began to feel better. He could feel the swelling begin to subside and sighed in relief. "Now if I could only eat something," the emperor said.

"You can eat this," Fu replied, motioning toward his medicine. Noticing that the emperor had trouble swallowing, he asked for some hot water and put his red bean mixture into it—creating a soup.

The emperor quickly gulped it down. "Delicious!" he said in between mouthfuls.

And in three days, the emperor's swelling had disappeared. Soon he was completely well, and the kingdom was amazed. Fu was heralded as a miracle doctor, and all flocked to him, regardless of their ailment, to receive his miracle cure made of adzuki beans.

Of course, Fu was not sure if it was placing the paste on the skin or eating the soup that cured the emperor. But as the Red Bean Soup was quite tasty and wearing bean paste on one's face tended to be inconvenient, most chose the soup option. Soon, people were eating Red Bean Soup not just for good health but for pleasure as well.

And we still do! For it's much easier to eat your dessert of sweet Red Bean Soup when you know it's good for you, too.

ICE CREAM
冰淇淋

As I mentioned earlier, there is rarely a dessert section on a Chinese menu, but if there is one, you will probably see ice cream listed. Whenever I saw that, I used to inwardly laugh. It seemed like such a random—and slightly lazy—option for a Chinese restaurant's dessert. Ice cream was the foundation of American banana splits and hot fudge sundaes, the sibling to Italian gelato and spumoni! Surely, I thought, ice cream has no ties to Chinese food.

I was wrong.

Because even though it's not quite known who came up with the idea to use shaved ice to make a sweet treat (the Chinese and Persians and Romans will have to figure out the answer among themselves), it is known that as early as the Zhou dynasty (1046–256 BCE) the Chinese were using ice for their food. In fact, there were people called icemen (bing ren 凌人) whose sole task was to store ice in a way to keep it from melting. Around the end of the Tang dynasty, the Chinese discovered a way to make ice using saltpeter (a chemical that is used in gunpowder that was discovered by Chinese monks looking to create immortality potions), but ice was still quite precious. For in the Song dynasty, a block of ice was valued as much as jade or gold.

However, the ice cream we are used to—the kind bought in grocery stores, scooped at ice cream parlors, and served in Chinese restaurants—is considered an Italian creation. Which is probably true. However, the idea for ice cream could have come to Italy from China.

How? Well, have a scoop of your favorite flavor, and I'll tell you.

During the Yuan dynasty, when the Mongols ruled China, they brought their own customs—including their own preferences for food (such as cheese, as we've discovered).

Before their successful invasion, the Mongols had a nomadic way of life. They foraged for fruits and vegetables, hunted wild game, and herded sheep and goats (and at high elevations, yaks). Their animals were used for more than meat—they used their animals' wool for clothing and tents, their dung for fuel, and most important, their milk for butter, yogurt, cheese, and drinks.

This was different from the Chinese, who tended to use their cattle for plowing fields and to eat for meat, not for milking. Milk products, in general, were rare and unfamiliar to most Chinese.

But not by the Mongols. Kublai Khan, the leader of the Mongols and the new emperor of China, especially enjoyed having milk. But that was a problem when he settled in China's capital of Beijing.

"PLLLAH!" Kublai Khan, now Emperor Shizu of Yuan, sputtered as he threw his cup to the ground. "The milk is spoiled! Again!"

"So sorry, so sorry, Your Majesty," said the servant, shaking with fear as he kowtowed. He knew if he got out of this with his life, he would be lucky. "I promise….I swear….It was fresh this morning…."

"If it was fresh just this morning," the emperor roared, "then why isn't it fresh now?! It's the same every day!"

"It's the heat," one of his advisors, a fellow Mongol, chimed in, feeling pity for the cowering servant on the floor. "Out on the Northern steppes, the cold air would keep the milk fresh for days. Here, where it's warm, the milk curdles in a few hours."

"Well, then find a way to cool it!" the emperor demanded.

"Kublai," said another Mongol advisor, one who had known the emperor since youth and had no fear of speaking to him so informally, "be reasonable. It is the middle of summer. What do you expect this poor fellow to do? Find a frozen lake and chop some ice to cool it for you?"

At those words, the Chinese servant twitched. He poked up his head, a fearful hope lighting his eyes. "Your Majesty, we…I…I am able to cool water to make ice," he stammered. "Perhaps…"

"What?!" the emperor sputtered. "You can make ice?"

The Mongol advisors all sat up in attention, all intrigued.

"Yes, yes." The servant nodded eagerly. "I can show you!"

The emperor nodded, and the servant ran from the room. In an instant, the servant returned, bringing out the ice-making device. Hands trembling, the servant demonstrated to the Mongols the way the Chinese had been making ice for more than a hundred years.

First, the servant placed a metal basin with water inside a larger wooden bowl. Then he filled the larger wooden bowl with water. When that was done, the servant lifted the lid of a small, ornate bronze vessel and carefully spooned from it a special powder (which we now call saltpeter) and added it to the water. Then he spun the smaller metal basin until it became cold. When the servant deemed that the metal basin was cold enough, the bowl was stilled, and water turned to ice.

"Amazing," the emperor said. His anger had drained away and was replaced by awe. The Chinese had so many innovations—ones that the Mongols would never have even dreamed of—that he could not even try to hide his wonder. The emperor touched the ice in the metal basin. "Can you do this with milk?"

"I can try," the servant said, relief washing over him. He looked at the ice maker that had given him his escape from punishment and silently thanked it.

And the servant thanked it again after he froze the milk. Because when he brought the result to the emperor, Kublai Khan tasted it and smiled.

"Ahh!" the Emperor said. "That is good!" He turned to his Mongol advisors. "Try it!"

His fellow Mongols murmured their agreement enthusiastically.

"I think it might be even better if it was sweeter," one of them said. "Maybe with some fruit on it?"

"I can do that," the servant said quickly, bowing as he hurried to fulfill the Mongol rulers' wishes.

Thus, Iced Milk (Nai Bing 奶冰) was created and immediately became a favorite in the palace. So, when one day a foreigner from another land—a stranger with light-colored hair named Marco Polo—came to see the emperor, he was offered some. And when Marco Polo finally returned home to that country he called Italy, he took the memory of iced milk with him...which may have led to what we all now eat, enjoy, love, and call ice cream.

FORTUNE COOKIES

簽語餅

There may be no truer Asian American food than the fortune cookie. Here in the United States, the fortune cookie is always associated with Chinese food—thrown into the take-out bag or placed on the tray with the bill.

But when I ate in restaurants in China, Hong Kong, and Taiwan, no such cookie would ever appear. In fact, once I dared to ask for a fortune cookie, and the server looked at me in confusion.

"Never mind," said my native-to-the-area dinner companion, actively trying to ease the server's distress, "she means an American cookie. They don't have them here."

Fortune cookies can only be found easily in the United States (in China, at some tourist areas, restaurants now occasionally have them because they're so often requested!). It is an American invention, created sometime in the early twentieth century. Now, where in America and by whom? Well, that's up for debate. In fact, in 1983, San Francisco's City Hall held a trial to determine the birthplace of the fortune cookie.

Los Angeles claimed that David Jung—a Chinese immigrant and founder of Los Angeles' Hong Kong Noodle Factory—was the fortune cookie inventor. The claim is that Jung, also a minister, created the cookie around 1918 with inspirational bits of scripture enclosed inside to give to the poor.

But San Francisco claimed that Japanese immigrant Makoto Hagiwara invented the fortune cookie earlier in 1914. He created it as a snack, with thank-you notes inside, for the Japanese Tea Garden in San Francisco.

Who won? Well, with the hometown advantage and a dramatic unveiling of iron grills by San Francisco city employee Sally Osaki—who claimed the irons were the original ones used by Hagiwara to make the cookies—Los Angeles did not really have much of a chance. San Francisco City Hall ruled that San Francisco was the birthplace of the fortune cookie.

So, does that mean the fortune cookie actually has Japanese roots? Probably. The Japanese have a new year custom of receiving good fortunes in a light, flat cracker called the tsujiura senbei (辻占せんべい), which translates to "fortune cracker," according to Jennifer 8. Lee, author of the Fortune Cookie Chronicles. So that is a very direct connection to the fortune cookie! The senbei, however, is not sweet and is made with sesame and miso. But it is easy for the Japanese to claim that butter and vanilla were used as substitutes to appeal to Americans' sweet tooth.

Then how is the fortune cookie connected to Chinese food? For without doubt, it is now linked to American Chinese cuisine.

Well, in the 1940s, Chinese restaurateurs were eager to please American customers and increase their business. American customers, however, were used to having something sweet to eat after their meal—and, as discussed before, since a dessert course was not a part of Chinese cuisine, restaurateurs in San Francisco were left scrambling. This unfortunately coincided with the Japanese Internment during World War II, when the American government incarcerated all people of Japanese descent in the United States—even children who had even never even been in Japan—out of misplaced and racist fear after the Japanese bombing of Pearl Harbor. So, it's likely that since the Japanese Americans were unable to make their fortune cookies, Chinese-owned businesses in San Francisco took over Hagiwara's Japanese invention and sold it as their own cookie. Which then became the cookie of Chinese restaurants in the United States!

How did it become so popular? Well, San Francisco was a port city for soldiers serving in World War II, and those soldiers would often eat at a Chinese restaurant on their way in or out of the United States—and at San Francisco Chinese restaurants (remember, San Francisco is the "birthplace" of the fortune cookie) they would receive the cookie.

And the fortune cookie is nothing if not memorable! Because before long, returning soldiers were asking Chinese restaurants in their hometowns in the Midwest and back East for the cookies. Of course, those Chinese restaurants hurriedly obliged—giving Chinese food in the United States a Japanese dessert.

But maybe it's not actually a Japanese dessert? Could the fortune cookie trace roots to Chinese culture as well? Possibly!

It's unclear exactly when the messages in fortune cookies began to be actual fortunes and not thank-you notes or inspirational scripture. In ancient times, Japanese senbei did include new year wishes in them, but there is also an ancient story in China that couples messages and pastry. This legend involves the mooncake—the traditional round cake eaten at the Mid-Autumn Festival—and a message of destiny. (You might be wondering if there's a story about the creation of mooncakes as well, but it would be extremely rare to find mooncakes on a Chinese menu, so that story will have to wait for another book.) This story might be the beginning of our fateful, famous fortune cookie; read on to see if you agree....

We learned that in 1279, the Mongols finally succeeded in taking over the kingdom and ruled China. It was, however, a precarious rule. Their armies were made up of Mongols and several other Turkic nomadic tribes, so the Han Chinese often called them Tartar invaders with much anger and resentment. The Mongols knew that the Chinese could rebel at any time. This fear made the Mongols impose harsh and unmerciful rules upon the Chinese people—from mutilating all boys' thumbs at birth so they could not use a bow to allowing only one knife per ten households. This, of course, only made the Chinese more resentful—which in turn made the Mongols even stricter. By 1368, to prevent uprisings, the Mongols did not allow people to meet in groups, and a Mongol soldier was stationed at each home.

But that only made the Chinese more resolute. A young man named Zhu Yuanzhang was determined to lead a rebellion. Luckily, he also had a good friend Liu Bowen who was wise with strategy.

"We must organize to strike the Mongols together at the same time," Bowen told Yuanzhang. "We must fight in unison, or it will be in vain."

"But how?" Yuanzhang asked. "Those Tartar invaders will not even let us speak to each other."

And as if on cue, a Mongol soldier yelled from a distance. "Hey!" he shouted as he rushed toward them. "What are you doing?"

"I have an idea," Bowen said quickly, and then in a louder voice so that the approaching soldier could hear, he said, "Yes, I hope you have a happy Mid-Autumn Festival next week."

Bowen's last words to Yuanzhang were not mere subterfuge. He knew the Mid-Autumn Festival, an important and traditional celebration in Chinese culture, was an opportunity. Every Chinese family would eat a mooncake that evening in honor of the festival while the Mongols—disdainful of local food and customs—would not. Bowen decided to use that to his advantage.

So, in secret, Bowen went to every pastry shop in his area and spoke to every owner. He sent men to the pastry shops of every Chinese territory under Mongol rule. They ordered thousands and thousands of mooncakes, each to be delivered to every Chinese family. And in every mooncake, a slip of paper was baked into it. A slip of paper that said:

At the third watch tonight, attack the Tartars.
Let us kill the housekeeping masters together.

And the Chinese got the message. At the third watch on the evening of the Moon Festival, every family attacked the Mongol soldier stationed in their household and then brought their fight into the street and country—the start of the end of the Mongol rule. That same year, Yuanzhang would become emperor, and the Ming dynasty would begin.

The message in the mooncake is a legend long cherished by the Chinese—so much so that in the late nineteenth century when Chinese immigrants came to the United States to work on the railroad, they celebrated the Mid-Autumn Festival with that tradition. Since they did not have mooncakes, the immigrants baked slips of paper with words of encouragement into biscuits and gave them to each other.

And from biscuits, it is easy to see how the jump to cookies—fortune cookies—could have happened.

But is that what happened? Was the fortune cookie inspired by the mooncake legend? We will probably never know, but we can at least be grateful that we have the good fortune to enjoy the delightful, sweet treat of the fortune cookie.

AUTHOR'S NOTE

Dear Reader,

I had the idea for this Chinese menu "story feast" many years ago. Back in 2004, I wrote and illustrated a picture book called *Fortune Cookie Fortunes* (which was a follow-up to my picture book *Dim Sum for Everyone!*). Upon researching the origin of the fortune cookie, I learned that even though it was always associated with Chinese food, it was a completely American invention.

And when I mentioned this to people, many of them exclaimed, "Oh, so, fortune cookies aren't *really* Chinese?"

This was always said in a tone of disdain, sometimes disgust. And this bothered me. For, as an American-born Asian person who struggled to find connection with her heritage, I could easily see the same words said about me. Maybe, I thought, I should do a whole book on American Chinese restaurant food—a book that would give American Chinese food some respect.

But it took over fifteen years for me to make the attempt. I'm not exactly sure why I waited, but I am glad I did. Writing novels such as *Where the Mountain Meets the Moon* and *When the Sea Turned to Silver* have given me confidence in my identity that I did not have years ago. In those books, I adapted Chinese folktales to fit my own narrative—balancing the original spirit of the stories with my own Asian American storytelling. And by doing that, I found a way to truly connect to my cultural heritage. I found that adapting the folktales with my own voice gave me the power to claim the Asian part of my Asian American identity and to do it with pride.

Which is what I hope this book does for my readers as well. Because American Chinese food is not something to be ashamed of or to scorn. Yes, every Chinese dish served in an American restaurant has been adapted and changed. Yes, many do not have the flavors of traditional Chinese cuisine and are unlike what you would find in China. But Chinese American cuisine is the flavor of resilience, the flavor of adaptability, the flavor of persistence and triumph. Above anything, this food is the flavor of America.

Because right upon their arrival in the United States during the Gold Rush (see the Chop Suey story), Chinese immigrants faced racism, violence, and almost never-ending hardship. But they used their cuisine—their cuisine with its rich and wonderful histories and myths—to survive. They constantly adapted and changed their recipes to use the ingredients that were locally available and to woo non-Asian customers. By doing so, they created a new branch of Chinese cuisine—the Chinese cuisine of the diaspora. And this creation allowed Chinese immigrants not only to survive but eventually to thrive.

However, Chinese immigrants had to make sacrifices. In order to compete and coax non-Asian diners to their restaurants, Chinese restaurateurs offered their food for an extremely low cost. So, even though it takes as much time and skill to prepare as something like French food, the stigma of Chinese cuisine being "cheap" food remains.

Which I hope this book helps to dispel.

Chinese food has a rich and wondrous history and culture. Every mouthful you eat from a Chinese take-out box was born of centuries of ingenuity, myths, and legend. I hope after reading this book, every time you take a bite of Chinese food, you think of these stories. And hopefully it makes you appreciate what you are eating that much more.

Because unfortunately, the hardships have continued.

I revisited this book idea in 2020, when the COVID-19 pandemic began to refuel anti-Asian hate. Because when the COVID virus first started spreading in China, many blamed anyone and anything Asian—even Asian Americans—for the suffering the pandemic caused. Asian elders were violently attacked. Chinatowns were boycotted. And Chinese restaurants were avoided. All of this was unfair and unjustified.

The food served at these restaurants is not foreign, it is American. It is a part of the history of the United States. American Chinese food is a part of American culture, so any

American can claim it as part of their inheritance. But first we must acknowledge it. And we must appreciate it.

I hope that by creating this book, retelling the old stories and myths of these foods, it helps give all readers a new respect for a part of their own culture. The stories in this book, like all my books, have been adapted through my own Asian American lens. Sometimes, when a dish had multiple origin stories, I combined them into one. And sometimes, I added details where there were none. For example, the dialogue between characters—even real historical characters—is mostly from my own imagination (unless sources are cited). But even with all this embellishment, I tried as much as I could to stay true to the original spirit of all the stories. Much like the actual Chinese dishes themselves, the stories I have served here have been modified but the essence and flavor are the same. And just like the food, these adapted and reinterpreted stories are for all of us to claim as part of our American heritage with pride.

So, I hope you enjoyed your meal! I truly enjoyed making it for you and hope you will come back again soon.

Best,

Grace 林

My Mother's Scallion Pancake Recipe

INGREDIENTS

4 cups all-purpose flour

6 pieces green onions

1½ cups warm water

½ tsp white pepper

1½ tsp salt

1½ tsp sugar

6 tsp cooking oil

2 tsp sesame oil

TO MAKE:

1. Mince the green onions, add white pepper, ⅓ tsp salt and sesame oil, then stir. Do not over-stir; do not allow the mixture to become too liquid-like.

2. Pour flour into a big bowl, add ½ tsp salt, and 1½ tsp sugar. Add the warm water a little at a time, mixing all the while.

3. Knead the mixture into a smooth ball. Make a depression in the center and add 2 tsp oil. Knead again until very smooth. Cover for 15 minutes.

4. Cut this dough into three equal pieces, and roll one piece into a thin square flat layer.

5. Spread approx a third of the remaining salt onto the square, pressing the salt into dough with your hands. Then, spread approx 4 tbsp of the green onions on the flat dough.

6. From the edge of the dough, roll the dough into a long, snake-like cylinder. Then curl into spiral shape (like a cinnamon bun).

7. Cover for another 10 minutes.

8. On a clean countertop, spread a little oil, then put the dough on it. Use a rolling pin to roll the dough into a flat round shape.

9. Repeat steps 5–8 for the remaining two pieces of dough. Afterward, you can freeze and save them for future use within a couple of weeks, or fry them immediately.

TO COOK:

1. Spread 2 tsp of oil in a hot wok, then place one flat pancake into it. Holding the wok over medium heat, move wok in a circular motion, allowing the pancake to move around. Every 30 seconds flip the pancake over.

2. When both sides of the pancake are a light brown color, take the pan out of the heat and continue to flip the pancake in the cooling pan. This will show the layers of the pancake.

3. Leaving the pancake in the pan, add 1 tsp oil around the pancake. Turn the pancake over one last time.

4. Now, place pan over low heat and cover for 1 minute.

5. The pancake is ready to be eaten.

This recipe makes three pancakes, which can serve three people or one— depending on how hungry you are!

ENDNOTES

CHOPSTICKS

Yu the Great Invents Chopsticks: There are many wonderful, fanciful details that I left out of this story of Yu the Great, for the sake of simplicity. In one story that I did not use, Yu the Great is helped by a Chinese dragon and an enormous turtle to dredge ditches. I suggest looking up Yu the Great to read more.

Daji Invents Chopsticks: In the versions of this story I read, Daiji doesn't test the emperor's food to save chefs because she misses her favorite dishes. In fact, no reason is given. But considering that all the stories about Daji portray her as incredibly selfish and heartless, I can't imagine she was helping the chefs out of kindness!

How Chopsticks Prevent Poisoning: In the stories I read, there is not really a reason Ziya's wife tries to poison him; she is just portrayed as kind of an "evil shrew." I felt this was very biased and sexist, so I tried to give her a bit more humanity—even though trying to murder your husband is a bad thing to do!

Also, Ziya's wife's name is actually Shen Jiang, I used her last name (clan name) to refer to her in the story. While it is just a coincidence that her first name is Jiang and she married a man whose last name is the same, I thought trying to explain that her name was Jiang Jiang and referring to her as Jiang with her husband being the other important character in the story was just too confusing! Off topic, this confusion is something that I have a personal connection with—my mother's name is Lin-Lin, and she married my father Jer-Shang Lin...now her name is Lin-Lin Lin. It was always a bit of a muddle trying to explain this to people.

TEA

Dragon Well Tea: Here I combined two stories—the story of Dragon Well Village and the story of Dragon Well Tea—into one. In my version it is hinted that the mysterious stranger might actually be the dragon guardian in disguise, but in the original story there is no mention of that.

Jasmine Tea: In some stories, the girl who Chen Guqiu helps is a tea fairy. Other stories say that she is an immortal in disguise who repays kindness. I decided to follow the version that allows the reader to assume that she is a normal, mortal girl.

Oolong Tea: One version of this story portrays Oolong as a lazy ne'er-do-well who lets his tea leaves wilt. Another version says he shoots the deer by a mysterious statue of Guanyin—hinting that the discovery of this tea has a supernatural origin. But this version is the one most commonly shared....And it's the one I liked best as well!

White Hair Silver Needle Tea: In the original stories, while the old man is acknowledged as probably an immortal, and the tea does get its name from him, it is never said that he is the tea fairy of White Hair Silver Needle Tea. But I felt sure it must have been something that would've crossed Zhi Yu's mind! Also, the idea of using the rice cakes in Zhi Yu's ears is sometimes attributed as only Zhi Yu's idea with no hint from the old man. However, it felt right in my version to have him give her a little extra help.

Also, I'd like to point out that this story of an evil Chinese dragon is an anomaly. In most stories, Chinese dragons are noble or godlike (with godlike flaws, much like the Greek gods). This is one of the very few stories where a Chinese dragon is portrayed as an evil beast.

The Origin of Tea: Da Mo is also the celebrated monk the Japanese daruma doll—a good luck figurine with no legs or arms—is fashioned after. That is because during Da Mo's nine years of meditating without moving, his arms and legs are supposed to have atrophied and fallen off! I suppose that happened during year eight or nine, as year seven is when he sliced his eyelids—he obviously still had arms then!

APPETIZERS

Dumplings: There is another story about the invention of dumplings that involves a dangerous beast that is killed at Lunar New Year; the villagers butcher it and use its meat for dumplings. While that version is quite exciting, I could not find many details on it, and this story of Zhang Zhongjing is the story that most share and believe.

Egg Rolls and Spring Rolls: This is one of the many legends I came across where the wife is (annoyingly) nameless. There are no official records of Cai Fuyi's wife's name, even though she is obviously an important character in this story! However, after much searching, my assistant

Izabelle Brande did find a Chinese video that gave Cai Fuyi's wife the name Li. We were unable to determine if that was historical or a fabrication but, in case it was true, I decided to use the same. Also, in the original versions of the story, Cai Fuyi does not offer to demonstrate his skill in court and is never asked to. I don't know why, as it seems an easy way to prove his innocence! So, I added the addition of one of the ministers saying that anyone could write with two hands for a short amount of time so the story would make more sense...though, I don't think anyone can write with two hands easily for even just a few minutes. I tried. It's hard!

Scallion Pancakes: *There is a lot of debate about* The Travels of Marco Polo. *Many believe that the book is a work of fiction, that Marco Polo only repeated stories he heard from others and fabricated his adventures. It was cowritten with romance writer Rustichello da Risa, so it is probable that Rusticello "spiced" things up to make things more interesting. That said, no one can deny that his book sparked an unparalleled interest in the East, inspiring many explorers—including Christopher Columbus.*

Fried Shrimp: *While this is a real myth, I admit I added many details of this story from my imagination. For example, the actual myth makes no mention of the shrimps' prior job, only that they eagerly became soldiers. I added the chamber pot detail because I imagined one would be eager to be anything else if that was their job! And also, I thought it was funny.*

SOUP

Wonton Soup: *Some stories do not have humans come with Pangu, instead telling a different human creation story with the goddess Nuwa. However, there are even other versions of the Pangu story that say that the fleas of his hair became the animals, and the lice became the humans! Gross, right? You can decide which version you like best!*

Crossing the Bridge Noodle Soup: *While the scholar's surname of Yang is found in many stories (and only Yang, without a second name), the wife and son were (as so often in these stories) nameless. So, while I left Yang with only his surname, I have taken artistic license and gave the wife and son names appropriate to the area and time period.*

Hot and Sour Soup: *Another version of this story is that the soup was created as an immortality elixir for the emperor during the Ming dynasty. But I felt I had already written about immortality tonics in the tofu section, and we didn't need another story about that. Also, Yu Qian was* an official that seemed to have lived an unfortunate life—he was later falsely imprisoned twice and then executed—so I felt he deserved to be remembered a bit.

Bird's Nest Soup: For simplicity's sake, I declined to mention in this story that Zheng He was also a eunuch—and that he was forced to become one when he was taken prisoner as a child. But it shows what a powerful and admirable person he was, to overcome so much trauma and become such a heroic leader.

Sizzling Rice Soup: Lady Huang's name is fictional. In the original stories, Zhuge's wife is described as smart as he is but ugly, and it is a bit of an ongoing joke among the villagers. I deleted those mentions as I didn't think it was needed as well as being very outdated!

SIDE ORDERS

Rice: This story also has many versions—in some the dog never had nine tails, in others there is no mention of the dog's adventure in Heaven, just that he shows up with seeds on his tails and saves all the humans from starving.

Rice Cakes: The politics in this story are even more melodramatic than what I portrayed here. In one version of this story, Wu Zixu—whose entire life is extremely sensational—is ordered to commit suicide as a traitor, and before he does so, Wu Zixu asks that his eyes be cut out from his corpse afterward and hung on the city gates so he can watch the Yue army capture the kingdom of Wu. In Taiwan, Wu Zuxi is worshipped by Taoists as one of the Water Gods.

Noodles: The 六月六節 Gugu Festival (not quite the right translation as there doesn't seem to be an official English translation of it)—that day that people eat Shan Gu's noodles—is celebrated by many tribes in China. The Han and Buyi consider it a day of blessing, to thank the Heavens for being healthy. The Miao people celebrate it as an ancestral holiday, to show thanks to your family—especially your mother! Some see it as Yu the Great's birthday and celebrate it as such, while others—which is more in keeping with the story I shared—see it as a day where the Jade Emperor opens the gates of Heaven to bestow blessings upon the Chinese people.

As a side note, ShanGu is not really a proper first name; it means "Benevolent Auntie" and is probably only the remembered nickname of the real woman.

Knife Cut Noodles: This story had many different versions but none quite explained why the noodles are called "knife cut noodles" when they were created without a real knife! I had to make *the inference that the name was a bit of a joke among the villagers. Also, while the story of the old man having to wait for the knife is true to the legend, I added the details of the villagers' names and created the repetitive story structure.*

Tofu: *The epilogue I included, where Prince Liu An ascends to Heaven with his chickens, is actually the source of the Chinese idiom:* 人得道,雞犬升天 *"Once a man achieves the Tao, his chickens and dogs will rise to Heaven," which is to mean that one person's success causes all his friends to have success as well. It is not used positively; it's meant to show how unworthy people get unfair advantages because of who they know!*

CHEF'S SPECIALS

Kung Pao Chicken: *This is another story that is a compilation of many, many legends put together. Some say Ding saved a childhood friend and was served this chicken dish as a thank-you. Other legends say Ding loved this chicken dish so much that he insisted that his chef accompany him everywhere to make it. And there were even more....I did my best to try to honor all of them by telling this version.*

Sweet and Sour Pork: *In my version of this tale, I added the wife character and emphasized the (true) "Gulu" onomatopoeia of stomach growling...artistic license! There is also a completely different story told by the* South China Post *where foreigners would cry out "Good!" when they ate Sweet and Sour Pork, which the chefs interpreted to "Gulu!" and hence called the dish "Gulou" pork. But I liked the Ji Gong story better!*

Buddha Jumps Over the Wall: *This dish was also called* 福壽全 *"Full of Happiness and Longevity," with completely different stories—one involving a chef trying to imitate a dish he only tasted once to a wife who did not know how to cook.*

The story I told (which is quite well-known) includes the lines an unknown poet wrote: 壇啓 葷香飄四鄰,佛聞棄禅跳牆來. *The translation I put in the story was done by my research assistant, Izabelle Brande.*

Mu Shu Pork: *It's not exactly known what offensive name Mu Shu Pork had before it was changed to please the more discriminating sensibilities of the eunuchs. But eggs and chicken in slang can mean anything from prostitutes to testicles—nothing a highly cultured eunuch would enjoy hearing about, much less want to eat!*

Peking Duck: Every version of this story that I found was extremely brief; I was unable to find many details. With research, I was able to make some educated guesses on when and where this story might have happened, but most of the small details—such as the village having only one restaurant—are my fabrication.

Beef and Broccoli: I adapted the Chinese poem of the emperor in this story so that it would be easier to understand in English. The more literal translation (done by my research assistant, Izabelle Brande) would be more like:

"The mountain village girl surpasses the beauty of a goddess,
My emotions tempt me to stay longer
I envy that the Chinese broccoli has better luck with her
and has been blessed with the fragrance of her powder."

山僻村姑賽天仙, 惹朕情牽意流連。
堪羨芥藍多豔福, 得沾美人脂粉香。

Empress Chicken: Some believe that this dish was created in the late 1930s by a chef working at Meilongzhen (a restaurant in Shanghai), with the Chinese opera The Drunken Beauty as its inspiration. But the real Yang Guifei lived during the Tang dynasty, so with the whimsical notion that this story might be true, I put the creation of Empress Chicken during her lifetime in the timeline.

General Tso's Chicken: This tale is so twisted that I had to leave out some of the odder details so as not to get too sidetracked. But one fascinating detail is that after General Tso's Chicken became so popular, Chef Peng came to the United States to open his own restaurant and show Americans "real" General Tso's Chicken. While it was not hated, almost everyone preferred Chef Wang's copycat version!

Mapo Tofu: There is a Mapo Tofu restaurant in China in Sichuan near the Bridge of Ten Thousand Blessings that claims to be the original restaurant of Lady Chen. However, there are also a couple of other restaurants in the area—and also not in the area—that claim the same thing. Which is the real one? Are any of them the real one? I don't know! Part of the reason why I don't *know is because the story I shared is a compilation of the many different versions of the Mapo Tofu legend. But while discerning the "real" one is beyond my detective skills, my bet is that you would not be disappointed by the food at any of them.*

Chop Suey: The original legend of this story is only a few sentences, mainly passed on orally. While I did add how the name was an act of secret rebellion on the part of the Chinese chef, I am willing to wager—if the story is true—that it is not that much of an embellishment.

Beggar's Chicken: This dish also has many, many versions of similar stories. The most different version tells of a group of beggars cooking the chicken for a sick friend without any mention of stealing. Another variation has a savvy restaurateur smelling the fragrant beggar's food and making the beggar a chef. I put together a couple of the more popular versions to make the one I shared.

Dragon and Phoenix: In the original versions of this story, the flutes that Nongyu and Xiao Shi play are actually two different instruments. Nongyu plays a sheng while Xiao Shi plays a xiao. These are specialized Chinese wind instruments. The sheng is a reed instrument with many pipes that I have a hard time finding an American comparison for. However, the xiao is a bit like a recorder. Regardless, my story does not differ from original stories in that both the instruments are made of jade, which convinces Duke Mu that Nongyu and Xiao Shi are destined for each other.

Buddha's Delight: This is another story that has been told many times but with very few details, so again I was forced to add my own. In my version, the attitude of the monks is very much inspired by the poem by Buddhist nun Rengetsu, who thanked the people who refused her lodging, for it allowed her to see the beauty of a cherry tree in full bloom in the moonlight. That spirit of gratitude, I felt, is what would make a Buddha delight.

DESSERT

Oranges: "When the stone child turns into a farmer"—original versions of this story describe him as 石人 (Stone Man), and they do not specify if he is still made of stone. I decided to interpret that as meaning that he had named himself Shi Ren (Stone Man) even though he was now human. Also, while the stories did say Shi Ren did bring oranges, it is never really explained why he chose this particular deed to do—I embellished and had him observe the orange trees in Heaven.

I also afflicted the people of earth with a scurvy-like illness that could be cured by the vitamin C of oranges!

Red Bean Soup: The emperor was probably afflicted with what we now know as mumps. It is more likely that by the time Fu came with his red bean remedy, the emperor was finally recovering from the mumps than the red beans being a cure. But timing is everything, and Fu was brave enough to make the attempt to try to help, so I think he deserved his reward. Also, while the original story focused more on the red bean paste as an ointment than an eaten remedy, I emphasized the edible alternative to show more of the direct connection to Red Bean Soup.

Also, I changed what the emperor yells at his doctors when they are unable to help him. In the original story he uses a fairly famous idiom and says, "It takes a thousand days to build an army, but only a second to use it; you doctors are all talking about internal ailments when my sickness is on my skin!" The army idiom is about how extensive preparation is the true secret to success. While I appreciated the idiom, I didn't really see how it fitted in this situation—at least to modern-day American audiences—so I adjusted the emperor's words.

Ice Cream: It is unknown if Marco Polo really did see and enjoy "Iced Milk" during his time in China, but it really is possible! The Mongols did not trust the Chinese they ruled over and instead gave many foreigners high positions, trusting them more. Marco Polo was, most likely, one of these favored foreigners.

Fortune Cookies: The evidence of the ethnic origin of the fortune cookie is so nebulous that even at the mock trial in San Francisco the judge declined to state whether it was Japanese or Chinese immigrants who created the cookie. According to Jennifer 8. Lee's book, The Fortune Cookie Chronicles (page 39), when it came to this matter the judge said, "Matters of the East, we should leave to the East."

ABOUT ME

People may be wondering about my specific ethnicity, as I mention that my parents are from Taiwan, and this is a book that focuses mainly on food that originates from China. My parents are most likely of Han Chinese descent, but my verifiable ancestors were those living on the island of Taiwan before the Nationalist Government of China fled there in 1949. When the Nationalist Government arrived, my parents were still young, so they grew up in Taiwan while it was called the Nationalist Republic of China. Because of that, my parents were taught how to write and speak in Mandarin Chinese, and also learned Chinese traditions and customs. Both my parents immigrated to the United States in the late 1960s. At that time, the United States government recognized Taiwan as the Republic of China. I was born here in the United States and throughout my childhood, my parents identified as Chinese—so I did as well.

But when the United States no longer recognized Taiwan as China and acknowledged mainland China as the Republic of China; my parents felt that they needed to make adjustments to their identity. It was only when I was in college that my family began to forcefully identify as Taiwanese American, which is how I identify now. That said, I can still see the rich overlap of Chinese culture in my heritage just as much as the American interweaving. As I said in my author's note, I feel that I can claim it all with pride.

ABOUT THE USE OF TRADITIONAL CHINESE CHARACTERS

Those who read Chinese know that there are two types of Chinese characters used these days—Simplified and Traditional. Simplified characters are now the norm in mainland China but they were not popularized until the 1950s. The majority of the stories in this book took place way before that; and for many of the stories it was the written characters of the food's name that pointed us in the direction of its history. And, of course, those names were in traditional characters. So it felt right to use traditional characters consistently throughout this book as well.

ABOUT AMERICAN CHINESE RESTAURANTS VS.
CHINESE AMERICAN RESTAURANTS

Under the advisement of my fact checker and copyeditor, Jennifer So, this book refers to the food and restaurants as American Chinese, not Chinese American. That is because in some areas of the United States, Chinese American restaurants serve Chinese versions of typical "American" food—steak and potatoes, pork chops, beef stew, etc.—while American Chinese restaurants serve Americanized versions of Chinese food: Sweet and Sour Pork, Mu Shu, Egg Drop Soup—the food featured in this book. It's a slight distinction but a notable one. Ah, America! We are truly cross-cultural and it's wonderful!

BIBLIOGRAPHY

GENERAL SOURCES

Andrews, Evan. "11 Things You May Not Know about Marco Polo." History. A&E Television Networks. March 12, 2013. https://www.history.com/news/11-things-you-may-not-know-about-marco-polo.

Bawden, C. R. "Kublai Khan." In *Encyclopedia Britannica*, January 1, 2022. https://www.britannica.com/biography/Kublai-Khan.

Brille, Ann, trans. *The Classic of Mountains and Seas*. London: Penguin Books, 1999.

Carnivore Girl. "Cat's Ear Noodles (Mao Er Duo 貓耳朵)." *Veggies for Carnivores* (blog). June 3, 2010. http://veggiesforcarnivores.blogspot.com/2010/06/cats-ear-noodles-mao-er-duo.html.

Coe, Andrew. *Chop Suey: A Cultural History of Chinese Food in the United States*. New York: Oxford University Press, 2009.

Earthstoriez. "Proverbs and Wise Sayings in Relation to Rice from China." October 20, 2021. https://www.earthstoriez.com/china-rice-sayings/.

Eating China. "Chinese Food Quotations." April 16, 2021. https://www.eatingchina.com/articles/quotes.htm.

Economist. "Confined in Prison, Marco Polo Roamed across the World." *Economist*, May 23, 2020. https://www.economist.com/books-and-arts/2020/05/23/confined-in-prison-marco-polo-roamed-across-the-world.

Fan, Xiao. "The Legend behind Zongzi." *Artifacts Journal*, April 2014. https://artifactsjournal.missouri.edu/2014/03/the-legend-behind-zongzi/.

Fu, Shelley. *Chinese Myths and Legends: The Monkey King and Other Adventures*. Illustrated by Patrick Yee. North Clarendon, VT: Tuttle. 2018.

Gavin. "Top 10 Most Popular Chinese Desserts." China's Most Popular Desserts and Sweet Foods. August 4, 2022. https://www.chinahighlights.com/travelguide/article-chinese-desserts.htm.

Gong, Rosemary. *Good Luck Life: The Essential Guide to Chinese American Celebrations and Culture*. New York: HarperResource, 2005.

Gross, Daniel A. "The Lazy Susan, the Classic Centerpiece of Chinese Restaurants, Is Neither Classic nor Chinese." *Smithsonian Magazine*, February 21, 2014. https://www.smithsonianmag.com/arts-culture/lazy-susan-classic-centerpiece-chinese-restaurants-neither-classic-nor-chinese-180949844/.

Han, Y. N., trans. *Essence of Traditional Chinese Medicine*. Illustrated Chunjiang Fu. Singapore: Asiapac Books, 2003.

Hanes, Phillis. "No Chinese Meal Can Be Complete without Soup." *The Christian Science Monitor*, June 26, 1980. https://www.csmonitor.com/1980/0626/062607.html.

Hong, Qin Yao, trans. *Origins of Chinese Cuisine*. Illustrated by Chunjiang Fu. Singapore: Asiapac Books, 2003.

———. *Origins of Chinese Food Culture*. Illustrated by Chunjiang Fu. Singapore: Asiapac Books, 2003.

———. *Origins of Chinese Tea and Wine*. Illustrated by Chunjiang Fu. Singapore: Asiapac Books, 2004.

Hui, Ann. *Chop Suey Nation: The Legion Café and Other Stories from Canada's Chinese Restaurants*. Madeira Park, BC: Douglas & McIntyre, 2013.

Jurafsky, Dan. "Why the Chinese Don't Have Dessert?" Adapted by Leopold Costa. *Stravaganza* (blog). November 28, 2014. https://stravaganzastravaganza.blogspot.com/2014/11/why-chinese-dont-have-dessert.html.

Keats School. "The Soup Culture in China." Keats Chinese: Learn Chinese in China. https://keatschinese.com/china-culture-resources/the-soup-culture-in-china/.

Krull, Kathleen. *Kublai Khan: The Emperor of Everything.* Illustrated by Robert Byrd. New York: Viking, 2010.

Lee, Jennifer 8. *The Fortune Cookie Chronicles: Adventures in the World of Chinese Food.* New York: Twelve, 2008.

Li Wenrui. "Essential Foods for Chinese New Year's Eve." *China Daily News*, February 8, 2021. https://www.chinadaily.com.cn/a/202102/08/WS6020a51ca31024ad0baa8004_13.html.

Liu, Haiming. *From Canton to Panda Express: A History of Chinese Food in the United States.* New Brunswick, NJ: Rutgers University Press, 2015.

Lo, Eileen Yin-Fei. *The Chinese Kitchen: Recipes, Techniques, Ingredients, History and Memories from America's Leading Authority on Chinese Cooking.* New York: William Morrow, 1999.

Maraini, Fosco and Edward Peters. "Marco Polo: Compilation of Il milione," In *Encyclopedia Britannica*, April 11, 2022. https://www.britannica.com/biography/Marco-Polo/Sojourn-in-China#ref140161.

"Marco Polo and His Travels: Who Was Marco Polo?" Silk Road: History of the Silk Road. March 27, 2019. http://www.silk-road.com/artl/marcopolo.shtml.

Martin, Rafe, and Manuela Soares. *One Hand Clapping: Zen Stories for All Ages.* Illustrated by Junko Morimoto. New York: Rizzoli, 1995.

McCawley, James D. *The Eater's Guide to Chinese Characters.* Chicago: University of Chicago Press, 1984.

Mooey, S. C. *Chinese Feasts & Festivals: A Cookbook.* Illustrated by S. C. Mooey. Singapore: Periplus, 2006.

Rawarin, Narongsak. "Notion of Rice in Isan Local Literature." Research Institute of Northeastern Art and Culture (RINAC). Mahasarakham University. Accessed February 2022. https://rinac.msu.ac.th/articles/V-Notion-of-Rice-in-Isan-Local-Literature.pdf.

Roberts, Moss. *Chinese Fairy Tales and Fantasies.* With the assistance of C. N. Toy. New York: Pantheon Books, 1979.

Rothman, Julia. *Food Anatomy: The Curious Parts & Pieces of Our Edible World.* North Adams, MA: Storey, 2016.

Sanders, Tao Tao Liu. *Dragons, Gods & Spirits from Chinese Mythology.* Illustrated by Johnny Pau London: Peter Lowe, 1980.

Sima, Qian 司马迁. *Lishi* 历史 [Records of a Grand Historian]. Chinese Text Project.

Song, Candice. "Chinese Soup: Lists, Varieties and Menu." China Highlights. March 4, 2021. https://www.chinahighlights.com/travelguide/menu/soup-menu.htm.

Tang, Wilson. *The Nom Wah Cookbook: Recipes and Stories from 100 Years at New York City's Iconic Dim Sum Restaurant.* With Joshua David Stein. New York: Ecco, 2020.

Tian, Hengyu, comp. *Infamous Chinese Emperors: Tales of Tyranny and Misrule.* Illustrated by Hengyu Tian. Singapore: Asiapac Books, 2006.

Wan, Kwoklyn. *Chinese Takeout Cookbook.* London: Quadrille, 2019.

Wei, Clarissa. "The Chinese Noodle That's Thin as a Thread." Goldthread. September 15, 2020. https://www.goldthread2.com/food/chinese-noodle-thats-thin-thread/article/3101630.

———. "The Special 'Gold' Chinese Noodle That's Thin as a Thread." *South China Morning Post*, September 16, 2020. https://www.scmp.com/lifestyle/food-drink/article/3101665/special-gold-chinese-noodle-thats-thin-thread.

Wu, Cathy. "Explainer: Everything You Need to Know about Qingming." That's Online. April 1, 2021. https://www.thatsmags.com/china/post/12915/explainer-the-story-behind-qingming-festival.

Xu, Shitao, comp. *Origins of Chinese Cuisine*. Translated by Jingyu Wu. Illustrated by Chunjiang Fu. Singapore: Asiapac Books, 2000.

Zee, A. *Swallowing Clouds: A Playful Journey through Chinese Culture, Language and Cuisine*. Seattle: University of Washington Press, 2002.

VIDEOS/DOCUMENTARIES

Cheney, Ian. *The Search for General Tso*. Brooklyn, New York: Wicked Delicate Films, 2014.

Cushing, Christine. Confucius Was a Foodie, Season 1 & 2. Toronto, ON: Lofty Sky Entertainment. https://confuciuswasafoodie.com.

Wei, Clarissa. *Eat China*. Season 1. Goldthread. Hong Kong: South China Morning Post, 2020. https://www.goldthread2.com/series/eat-china-season-1/3099238.

———. *Eat China: Noodle Edition*. Season 2. Goldthread. Hong Kong: South China Morning Post, 2018. https://www.goldthread2.com/series/eat-china-noodle-edition-season-2/3127744.

WEBSITES

Chenxi. "Enjoy Interesting Stories Behind Traditional Chinese Cuisines". *Global Times*, August 8, 2019. https://www.globaltimes.cn/content/1161394.shtml.

Debczak, Michele. "How American Chinese Food Became Its Own Cuisine." Mental Floss. Jan 26, 2022. https://www.mentalfloss.com/article/654741/american-chinese-food-history.

Johnson, Bryan R. "Let's Eat Chinese Tonight." *American Heritage*. December 1987. https://www.americanheritage.com/lets-eat-chinese-tonight#1.

Pun, Raymond. "Chinese American Food: Stories of Odds and Ends." *What's on the Menu? Food for Thought* (blog). New York Public Library. November 15, 2012. https://wayback.archive-it.org/18689/20220313120120/https://www.nypl.org/blog/2012/11/15/chinese-american-food-odds-and-ends.

Travel China Guide. "Yu the Great, Dayu: The Founder of the Xia Dynasty." Nov. 12, 2022. https://www.travelchinaguide.com/intro/history/prehistoric/great_yu.htm.

CHOPSTICKS

Chinese Knife Culture 中国刀文化. "Kuaizi yu Jiang Ziya de gushi ni zhidao ma?" 筷子与姜子牙的故事，你们知道了吗？[Did you know of the story of chopsticks and Jiang Ziya?]. Sohu. June 12, 2019. https://www.sohu.com/a/358680436_100131621.

Chinese Text Project. "*Gui cang*" 归藏 [Return to the hidden]. Accessed February 2022.

Deason, Rachel. "Why Do Chinese People Eat with Chopsticks?" Culture Trip. December 20, 2017. https://theculturetrip.com/asia/china/articles/why-do-chinese-people-eat-with-chopsticks/.

Global Volunteers. "Cultures and Traditions of China: The Invention of Chopsticks." November 25, 2016. https://globalvolunteers.org/the-invention-of-chopsticks/.

Huasheng Online 华声在线. "Dao cha qiyuan Zhongguo, Da Yu famingle kuaizi canju beihou de lishi he wenhua "刀叉起源中国，大禹发明了筷子 餐具背后的历史和文化" [Origin of knives and forks in China, Yu the Great invents chopsticks, and the history and culture of cutlery]. *San xiang dushi bao* 三湘都市报. Accessed February 2022. https://epaper.voc.com.cn/sxdsb/html/2016-02/18/content_1064775.htm.

Interesting History Network Shanghai 趣历史. "'Kuaizi; qiyuan yu shenme shihou? 'kuaizi' jingran shi Daji faming de?" '筷子' 起源于什么时候?'筷子' 竟然是妲己发明的? [When did "chopsticks" originate? Are "chopsticks" really Daji's invention?]. January 6, 2020. http://www.qulishi.com/article/202001/385978.html.

sbar.com.cn. "Jiang Ziya yu kuaizi de gushi" 姜子牙与筷子的故事" [The story of Jiangzi Ya and chopsticks]. December 26, 2007. http://www.sbar.com.cn/caipu/24053.

Xu Zhonglin 许仲琳. *Feng shen yanyi* 封神演义 [Creation of the Gods]. Translated by Zhizhong Gu. Beijing: Xinshijie chubanshe, 2000.

Zhou Huixin 周慧心. "Jiang Ziya Daji Da Yu kuaizi de chuanshuo yu shei you guan?　姜子牙妲己大禹 筷子的傳說與誰有關?"[How are Jiang Ziya, Daji, and Yu the Great related to the story of chopsticks?]. *Da jiyuan* 大紀元. October 3, 2014. https://www.epochtimes.com/b5/14/10/3/n4263478.htm.

TEA

Apple. "Molihua cha de gushi" 茉莉花茶的故事 [The story of jasmine tea]. December 15, 2012. https://www.puercn.com/cwh/cdcs/42489.html.

Bai Hao Yinzhen. "Silver Needle White Tea: Bai Hao Yinzhen." Vicony Tea Directory. September 2016. http://www.vicony-teas.com/directory/tea-encyclopedia/bai-hao-yinzhen.html.

Benn, James A. "The Early History of Tea: Myth and Reality." In *Tea in China: A Religious and Cultural History*, 21–41. University of Hawai'i Press, 2015. http://www.jstor.org/stable/j.ctt13x1kn2.6.

The Chairman's Bao. "Not for All the Tea in China…10 Surprising Facts about Chinese Tea!" April 9, 2018. https://www.thechairmansbao.com/10-facts-tea-in-china/.

Chinese Text Project. "Shennong bencao jing" 神农本草经 [Treatise on food].

Destination Tea. "Tea Story: —the History of Afternoon Tea." March 21, 2022. https://destinationtea.com/teastory/.

Forrest, Florence. "The Ancestor of Tea: Chinese Folktale." *Crackle Mountain* (blog). January 1, 1970. http://cracklemountain.blogspot.com/2006/06/ancestor-of-tea-chinese-folktale.html.

Guo, Sally. "Chinese Tea Culture." China Travel. July 22, 2021. https://www.chinatravel.com/culture/chinese-tea/culture.

———. "History of Tea Drinking in China." China Travel. June 23, 2021. https://www.chinatravel.com/culture/chinese-tea/history.

Imperial Tea Garden. "Compressed Tea Bricks." *Imperial Tea Garden* (blog). April 12, 2018. https://www.imperialteagarden.com/blogs/tea/tea-money.

Jiang, Fercility. "Chinese Tea Facts (10 Interesting Things)." China Highlights. October 13, 2021. https://www.chinahighlights.com/travelguide/chinese-tea/interesting-things-to-learn-about-tea.htm.

Jin Junmei 金骏眉. "Baihao yin zhen de lishi yu chuanshuo gushi" 白毫银针的历史与传說故事 [The history and legends of white hair silver needle tea]. October 27, 2018. https://www.egoll.com/baihaoyinzhen/baicha_1620.html.

———. "Guanyu wulongcha de liang ge chuanshuo gushi de zhengli" 关于乌龙茶的两个传说故事的整理 [Setting straight the two legends of oolong tea]. January. 11, 2014. https://www.egoll.com/wulongcha/tea_1566.html.

Kong Yao 孔瑶. "wulong cha de laili yu chuanshuo, shuoshuo shenme shi wulong cha乌龙茶的

Lu Yu 陆羽. Huang, Michelle, De, Wu (trans.). "Chajing" 茶经 [The tea classic]. *Global Tea Hut: Tea and Tao Magazine*, no. 44 (September 2015).

Maguire, Jack. *Essential Buddhism: A Complete Guide to Beliefs and Practices.* New York: Pocket Books, 2001.

Mukun Xiaobao 木坤小宝. "Baihao yin zhen chuanshuo" 白毫银针传说 [The legend of white hair silver needle tea]. January 21, 2019. https://www.puercn.com/baicha/bccs/154044.html.

Oolong tea's origins and legends, a discussion on what is oolong tea. 来历与传说，说说什么是乌龙茶" Xiao xian huishi jiankang wang shipin guanli bu 小县惠氏健康网食品管理部 November 13, 2017. https://www.haocai777.com/Article/zix-un/15389.html.

Ray-Murray, Fergus. "Oolong Tea." May 14, 2005. https://oolong.co.uk/tea/.

Shaolin Monk Corps. "About Shaolin Temple." Shaolin Temple 少林寺. July 3, 2021. http://www.shaolin.org.cn/newsin-fo/217/226/345/22757.html.

Sohu 搜狐."Liaoliao longjing cha de chuanshuo" 聊聊龙井茶的传说 [Speaking of the legend of dragon well tea]. March 18, 2020. https://www.sohu.com/a/381062716_120592457.

Story 365 故事."Longjing cha de chuanshuo" 龙井茶的传说 [The legend of dragon well tea]. November 8,2019. https://www.gushi365.com/info/8654.html.

Teasenz. "The Legend of Silver Needle Tea: The Origin of Bai Hao Yin Zhen." Chinese Tea Culture & History. September 19, 2019. https://www.teasenz.com/chinese-tea/legend-silver-needle-bai-hao-yin-zhen-story-origin.html.

Umi Tea Sets. "The Legend of How Oolong Tea Began." *Umi Tea Sets* (blog). July 30, 2021. https://www.umiteasets.com/blogs/umi-tea-sets-blog/the-legend-of-how-oolong-tea-began.

Ya Liuzhin. "Wulongcha chuanshuo jieshao" 龙茶传说介绍 [Introducing the legend of oolong tea]. August 28, 2020. https://www.puercn.com/wulongcha/wenhua/223305.html.

DUMPLINGS
Baidu Encyclopedia 百度百科. "Quhan jiaoer tang" 祛寒娇耳汤 [Cold dispelling ear soup]. 2022 https://baike.baidu.com/item/祛寒娇耳汤/8771784.

Eberhard, Wolfram. *The Local Cultures of South and East China.* Leiden: E. J. Brill, 1968.

Jenny. "Hundun he jiaozi de qubie" 馄饨和饺子的区别 [The differences between wontons and jiaozi]. *Chinese Recipes* (blog), Eazzychinese, June 30, 2021. https://www.eazzychinese.com/馄饨和饺子的区别.

EGG ROLLS AND SPRING ROLLS
Auffrey, Richard. "The Origin of the Chinese Egg Roll." *The Passionate Foodie* (blog). October 27, 2021. https://passionate-foodie.blogspot.com/2021/10/the-origin-of-chinese-egg-roll.html.

Chef One Foods. "What Is the Difference Between Spring Rolls and Egg Rolls". *Chef One* (blog). December 9, 2019. https://chefonefoods.com/what-is-the-difference-between-spring-rolls-and-egg-rolls/.

Composition Encyclopedia 优秀作文. "Chunjuan chuanshuo chunjuan zuofa" 春卷传说 春卷的做法" [Spring roll legends and recipe]. May 10, 2021. http://dapigu.net/read-627887.html.

Kalmusky, Katie. "What's the Difference between Spring Rolls and Summer Rolls?" Culture Trip. June 28, 2018. https://theculturetrip.com/asia/vietnam/articles/spring-rolls-and-summer-rolls-whats-the-difference/.

Leung, Janice. "Legends: Spring Rolls." *South China Morning Post*, January 10, 2013. https://www.scmp.com/lifestyle/food-drink/article/1123854/legends-spring-rolls.

Lifestyle Guide. "Chunjuan yu danjuan: chayi zongjie" 春卷与蛋卷：差异总结 [Spring rolls and egg rolls: what's the difference]. Accessed February 2022. https://zh.jf-prior-velho.pt/spring-roll-vs-egg-roll.

Liu Ying 流萤. "Chi chunjuan de xisu" 吃春卷的习俗 [The customs of eating spring rolls]. Gugong lishi wang 故宫历史网. November 13, 2021. https://www.gugong.net/wenhua/28250.html.

Lu Wanwan 鲁万万. "Taiwan Qingmingjie chi de 'runbing' shi shenme?" 台湾清明节吃的 '润饼' 是什么? [What is the 'run-bing' eaten during the Qingming Festival in Taiwan?]. Zhonguo Taiwan wang 中国台湾网. April 12, 2019. http://www.taiwan.cn/plzhx/wyrt/201904/t20190412_12155854.htm.

TVBS News. "Runbing de youlai shi guanyu ai yu caihua de gushi" 潤餅的由來 是關於愛與才華的故事 [The origin of the runbing is a story about love and talent]. Streamed live on March 31, 2017. YouTube Video, 1:03. https://www.youtube.com/watch?v=tWMW8Lnus7w.

SCALLION PANCAKES

China Tea Network. "Longgai si qianshuo chasheng—Jingling congxiang bing"龙盖寺前说茶圣——竟陵葱香饼 [The god of tea at the gate of Longgai Temple—jingling scallion pancake]. November 6, 2011. http://www.zgchawang.com/culture/show-89.html.

Hungry Howie's. "Did Pizza Actually Originate in China?" August 28, 2017. https://www.hungryhowies.com/blog/did-pizza-actually-originate-China

Liu, Jerry. "Taiwanese Scallion Pancake." *Jerry Liu's English 015 Blog*, Sites at Penn State. April 7, 2014. https://sites.psu.edu/jerryliuenglish15/2014/04/07/taiwanese-scallion-pancakes/.

Lotte Plaza Market. "The History of the Chinese Scallion Pancake." October 27, 2017. https://www.lotteplaza.com/fun-food-facts/chinese-food/history-chinese-scallion-pancake/.

Renyu Haitang人鱼海棠. "Make Bolou, congyoubing yu pisa 马可·波罗、葱油饼与披萨" [Marco Polo, pizza, and scallion pancakes]. Jian Shu 简书. February 9, 2019. https://www.jianshu.com/p/03e2cb5b4d61.

Team Pizzeria Ortica. "Did Pizza Originate in China? Uncovering the Old Tale." Pizzeria Ortica. October 20, 2021. https://pizzeriaortica.com/did-pizza-originate-in-china/.

Tengxun 腾讯."Congyoubing, bianbu dongxinanbei zhong de yongdun dou xiang mashang chi dao ta" 葱油饼，遍布东西南北中的拥趸都想马上吃到它 [Scallion pancakes, what fans all over the world want to eat]. December 3, 2020. https://new.qq.com/omn/20200311/20200311A0Q89H00.html.

Sakamoto, Rumi and Stephen Epstein. "The True Origins of Pizza: Irony, the Internet and East Asian Nationalisms ピッツァの真の起源――イロニー、インターネット、東アジアの国家主義." *The Asia-Pacific Journal* 9, no. 5 (October 31, 2011): first-last page. https://apjjf.org/2011/9/44/Rumi-SAKAMOTO/3629/article.html.

Week in China. "Congyou Bing (Scallion Pancakes 葱油饼)." China in 50 Dishes. 2019. https://www.weekinchina.com/chapter/china-in-50-dishes/huaiyang-dishes/congyou-bing-scallion-pancakes葱油饼/.

Xiu Ouyang 歐陽脩. "Xin Tang shu juan yibai jiushiliu liezhuan di yibai ershiyi yinyi" 新唐书 卷一百九十六 列傳第一百二十一 隱逸 [New book of tang, volume 196, biographies 121: recluses]. Chinese Notes.

FRIED SHRIMP

Costas Inn. "A Look at the History of Shrimp." August 23, 2019. https://www.costasinn.com/seafood-facts/a-look-at-the-history-of-shrimp/.

Dachi dawan 大吃大玩. "Xiabingxiejing de chuanshuo— zheme meiwei" 虾兵蟹将的传说~ 这么美味" [Legend of shrimp soldiers and crab generals—so delicious] *Sina* (blog). August 29, 2018. https://k.sina.cn/article_6418704055_17e95a6b700100b3kp.html.

Dongpo xiansheng 东坡先生."Minjian chuanshuo zhong, weishenme zongshi xiabingxiejiang, gui wei chengxiang? Yuanlai hen you zhihui" 民间传说中，为什么总是虾兵蟹将，龟为丞相？原来很有智慧 [In folklore, why are shrimps soldiers, crabs generals, and turtles advisors? The reason is quite smart]. Jintian Toutiao 今天头条. July 21, 2018. https://www.toutiao.com/article/6582807866145505799/?&source=m_redirect.

Food of History. "Cooking Shrimp: An Everyday Primer." March 19, 2017. http://foodofhistory.com/2017/03/cooking-shrimp-primer/.

Jiazi meishi 茄字美食. "Guanyu wo da Zhonghua chi xia de lishi xiao houbanmen liaojie duoshao ne? 关于我大中华吃虾的历史小伙伴们了解多少呢？" [How much do you know about the history of eating shrimp culture?]. *Sina* (blog). March 11, 2019. https://k.sina.cn/article_6430096046_17f437aae00100pdfl.html.

Reynolds, Doris. "Let's Talk Food: Shrimp is Favorite Seafood Worldwide." *Naples Daily News*, September 19, 2012. https://archive.naplesnews.com/columnists/lifestyle/doris-reynolds/lets-talk-food-shrimp-is-favorite-seafood-worldwide-ep-387378323-331595892.html/.

Yum of China. "Chinese Shrimp Stir Fry: Authentic Cantonese Style." February 24, 2022. https://www.yumofchina.com/chineese-shrimp/.

WONTON SOUP

Anderson, E. N. "Some Basic Cooking Strategies." In *The Food of China*, edited by Ellen G. Landau, 182–93. New Haven: Yale University Press, 1988. http://www.jstor.org/stable/j.ctt32bq1r.14.

Chuang Tzu. *Wandering on the way: early Taoist tales and parables of Chuang Tzu*. Translated by Victor H. Mair. New York: Bantam Books, 1994.

Ding Mengyu 丁梦钰. "Dongzhi daodi shi chi jiaozi haishi chi hundun? Jing zheme jiangjiu" 冬至到底是吃饺子还是吃馄饨？竟这么讲究 [Do you eat dumplings or wontons during the Winter Solstice? It's important to know]. Guoxue Pindao 国学频道. December 21, 2017. https://iguoxue.ifeng.com/54384293/news.shtml?&back&back.

Girardot, Norman J. *Myth and Meaning in Early Taoism*. Univ of California Press, 1983.

Shijing mishi ji市井觅食记. "Beifang de hundun vs nanfang de yuntun he chaoshou, chabie yuanlai zai zheli, wangyou: meifan bi" 北方的馄饨VS南方的云吞和抄手，差别原来在这里，网友：没法比 [Northern wontons vs. southern wontons: the differences are here. Netizens say there is no comparison]. Sohu 搜狐. May 30, 2021. https://www.sohu.com/a/469481440_100140727.

Watts, Alan. *The Way of Zen*. New York: Pantheon, 1957.

CROSSING THE BRIDGE NOODLE SOUP

Baidu Encyclopedia 百度百科. "Guo qian mixian" 过桥米线 [Crossing bridge rice noodles]. 2022. https://baike.baidu.com/item/过桥米线/120893.

Jucan Wang 聚餐网. "Guo qian mixian de chuanshuo过桥米线的传说" [The legend of crossing the bridge rice noodles]. October 2014, 24. https://www.jucanw.com/mszx/mszx/2445.html.

Shirley. "Guo Qiao Mi Xian (Crossing Bridge Noodles)." *HomeNaturallyMade* (blog). June 26, 2022. https://homenaturally-made.com/guo-qiao-mi-xian/.

Smile to explain that 微笑诠释那一份. "Guo qian mixian de chuanshuo" 过桥米线的传说 [The legend of crossing the bridge noodles]. Meishijia 美食杰. February 1, 2007. https://www.meishij.net/wenhua/diangu/33489.html.

WildChina. "The Story of Yunnan's Crossing the Bridge Noodles." August 19, 2013. https://wildchina.com/2013/08/crossing-the-bridge-noodles/.

Wonders of Yunnan. "The Across-the-Bridge Rice Noodles." June 28, 2017. http://wondersofyunnan.com/blog/posts/the-cross-bridge-rice-noodles.

Yang Xin. "Crossing-Bridge Rice Noodles." ChinaCulture. http://en.chinaculture.org/chineseway/2011-08/26/content_422542.htm.

HOT AND SOUR SOUP
Liang Jinghong Secai yu Sheji 梁景红色彩与设计."Hula tang de lishi qiyuan" 胡辣汤的历史起源 [The historical origins of hot pepper soup]. Baidu Zhidao 百度知道. June 9, 2016. https://zhidao.baidu.com/question/985465564251248379.html.

Wutongzi 梧桐子. "La tang chuanshuo" 辣汤传说 [Hot soup legends]. May 9, 2014. http://www.wutongzi.com/a/29460.html.

Zhangj. "Hula tang de gushi" 胡辣汤的故事 [The story of hot pepper soup] 52. Wo Ai Lishi 我爱历史. December 4, 2020. https://www.52lishi.com/article/63950.html.

BIRD'S NEST SOUP
Galarneau, Andrew Z. "Bird's Nest Soup Is a Spoonful of Legend." *Buffalo News*, July 23, 2020. https://buffalonews.com/entertainment/dining/bird-s-nest-soup-is-a-spoonful-of-legend/article_a9022df6-913d-54b6-b8d6-6f3185def6d7.html.

Nat Geo Wild. "Salivating for a New Nest: Wild Borneo." Streamed live on January 3, 2017. YouTube video, 1:58. https://www.youtube.com/watch?v=ngPs3kINUXE.

The Nest House. "History of Birds Nest Soup: History of Birdnest." Accessed February 2022. http://nesthouse.com.my/history-of-birds-nest-soup/.

Tese pan wang 特色盘网. "Yanwo chuanshuo gushi" 燕窝传说故事 [The legend of bird's nest soup]. March 1, 2021. https://www.tspweb.com/key/燕窝的故事.html.

SIZZLING RICE SOUP
Chinese Text Project. "Sanguozhi Zhuge: liang chuan" 三国志, 诸葛亮传 [Records of the three kingdoms: Zhuge Liang's biography]. Chinese Text Project.

Han, Richard. "Three Visits to the Cottage: San Gu Mao Lu." *Chinese Story Collection* (blog). September 24, 2016. http://chinese-story-collection.blogspot.com/2016/09/three-visits-to-cottage-san-gu-mao-lu.html.

Sweetheart Loves Xiaolongbao 甜心爱吃小笼包. "Gangben suci de guoba, bujinjin shi lingshi, ye keyi shi meiwei jiaoyao" 嘎嘣酥脆的锅巴,不仅仅是零食,也可以是美味佳肴 [Crunchy scorched rice, not just a snack, but also a delicious food]. Zhihu 知乎. April 16, 2017. https://zhuanlan.zhihu.com/p/26389778.

RICE
Chen, Stephen. "Ancient Dog Festival Celebrates Legend of Heaven-Sent Canine in China." *South China Morning Post*, September 3, 2017. https://www.scmp.com/news/china/policies-politics/article/2109554/chinese-tribes-ancient-dog-lifting-festival-honours.

Duarte, Ruben. "How Rice Became a Staple in Asian Cuisine." *BFF Asian Grill & Sports Bar* (blog). December 1, 2020. https://bffasiangrill.com/how-rice-became-a-staple-in-asian-cuisine.

Earthstoriez. "China: On the Origin of Rice 稻—Myths, History and Folklore." 2014. https://www.earthstoriez.com/myths-history-folklore-rice-china/.

Kawagoe, Aileen. "Earliest Origins of Rice: South Korea vs. China? China vs. India?" *Heritage of Japan* (blog). July 10, 2012. https://heritageofjapan.wordpress.com/yayoi-era-yields-up-rice/the-advent-of-agriculture-and-the-rice-revolution/life-on-a-wet-rice-farming-village/south-korean-discovery-of-rice-older-than-chinas.

MandaLingua. "Rice—More Than Just a Grain.". Inforce Group. July 13, 2018. https://mandalingua.com/en/china-guide/chinese-culture/highlights/rice/.

Novarroz. "Myths and Legends." https://www.novarroz.pt/en/the-world-of-rice/rice-around-the-globe/4-myths-and-legends.

Rost, Thomas L. "Where Rice Came From." Rice Anatomy. 1997. https://labs.plb.ucdavis.edu/rost/rice/introduction/intro.html.

Sartor, Valerie. "The World of Rice." *Beijing Review*, November 16, 2020. http://www.bjreview.com.cn/eye/txt/2010-12/13/content_319027.htm.

Seres Collection. "The Beginning of Chinese Civilisation: A Bowl Full of Rice." March 3, 2017. https://shop.serescollection.com/blogs/news/the-beginning-of-chinese-civilisation-a-bowl-full-of-rice.

Taryo, Obayashi, "Rice in Myth and Legend," *UNESCO Courier: A Window Open on the World*, XXXVII, 12, p. 9–13, illus. 1984. https://unesdoc.unesco.org/ark:/48223/pf0000061956.

Zhao Yanqinq. "The Mesmerizing Culture of the Miao People." *China Today*, November 19, 2021. http://www.chinatoday.com.cn/ctenglish/2018/cs/202111/t20211119_800263878.html.

NOODLES

San-J International. "Chow Mein vs. Lo Mein: What's the Difference and Common Recipes." *Tamari Soy Sauce Cooking Tips and Recipes: San-J (blog). July 20, 2022. https://san-j.com/blog/chow-vs-lo-mein/.*

Wilkinson, Endymion Porter. *Chinese History: A Manual.* Cambridge: Harvard University Asia Center, 2000.

Xue Haopeng. "Art of Chinese Noodles and Preservation for Traditions." CHN/ITAL370W Noodle Narratives: Summer 2019 (blog). August 10, 2019. CHNITAL370W Noodle Narratives Summer 2019.

Zhang, Na and Guansheng Ma. "Noodles, Traditionally and Today." *Journal of Ethnic Foods 3*, no 3 (September 2016): 209-212. ScienceDirect. https://doi.org/10.1016/j.jef.2016.08.003

TOFU

Chinese Text Project. "Bencao Ganmu" 本草纲目 [Compendium of materia medica].

———. "Taiping Huanyu Ji" 太平寰宇记. [Universal geography of the Taiping Era].

Ge Hong 葛洪. "Shenxian chuan" 神仙传 [Biographies of deities and immortals]. Chinese Text Project.

Pym, Jason. "Liu An: God of Tofu." *Jason Pym Illustration / Blog.* January 14, 2016. http://www.jasonpym.com/blog/2016/01/14/tofu1/.

Ziyan ziyu 字言字语. "Xianjia doufu chuanshuo gushi" 仙家豆腐传说故事 [The legend of immortal's (fairy tale) tofu]. Wangyi 网易. January 4, 2022. https://www.163.com/dy/article/GSQ74TDF0552T6Q2.html.

KUNG PAO CHICKEN

Baidu Wenku 百度文库. "Gongbaoji ding yu Ding Baozhen" 宫保鸡丁与丁宝桢 [Kung pao chicken and Ding Baozhen]. August 3, 2018. https://wenku.baidu.com/view/f53d0829453610661ed9f422.

Callos, Nick. "The Delicious History of Kung Pao Chicken: Chengdu's Signature Dish." Frayed Passport. August 4, 2022. https://frayedpassport.com/the-delicious-history-of-kung-pao-chicken/.

Chili House. "Everything You Wanted to Know about Kung Pao Chicken." *Chili House: San Francisco's Best Peking Duck & Chinese Food* (blog). April 5, 2021. www.chilihousesf.com/blog/everything-you-wanted-to-know-about-kung-pao-chicken/.

———. "A History of Tofu and Its Role in Chinese Food." *Chili House: San Francisco's Best Peking Duck & Chinese Food* (blog). April 5, 2021. https://www.chilihousesf.com/blog/a-history-of-tofu-its-role-in-chinese-food/.

Dunlop, Fuchsia. "Kung Pao Chicken's Legacy, from the Qing Dynasty to Panda Express." *Los Angeles Times*, November 7, 2019. https://www.latimes.com/food/story/2019-11-07/kung-pao-chicken-history-recipe-gong-bao.

Shi Jizhong 史继忠. "Ding Baozhen: wuwei de fengjian dachen 丁宝桢, 无畏的封疆大臣" [Ding Baozhen: an outstanding minister of the Qing Dynasty]. Cenes of Guizhou. https://web.archive.org/web/20080820015340/http://www.chinaguizhou.gov.cn/scenes05/dbz.htm.

Tiao Se Pan Wang 调色盘网. "Yiqi liaojie meishi beihou de gushi" 一起了解美食背后的故事 [Let's learn the story behind foods together]. December 5, 2020. https://www.tspweb.com/key/宫保鸡丁的故事.html.

Zhang, Na and Guansheng Ma. "Noodles, Traditionally and Today." *Journal of Ethnic Foods 3*, no 3 (September 2016): 209-212. ScienceDirect. https://doi.org/10.1016/j.jef.2016.08.003

Zhao Erxun 赵尔巽. *Qingshigao* 清史稿 [Draft history of the Qing Dynasty]. Ancient Chinese Poetry and Books. https://www.arteducation.com.tw/guwen/book_301.html.

SWEET AND SOUR PORK

Guangdong Tourism Bureau 广东省旅游局. "Gulu ruo" 咕噜肉 [Gulu pork]. Zhongguo Zhengfu Wang 中国政府网. 2018. http://www.gd.gov.cn/zjgd/lnms/gzms/content/post_111587.html.

Leung, Janice. "Legends: Sweet and Sour Pork: A Global Favorite, No Bones About It." *South China Morning Post*, January 3, 2013. https://www.scmp.com/lifestyle/food-drink/article/1118279/legends-sweet-and-sour-pork.

Qianyu Qianxun 千与千寻. "Tang cu paigu de lishi diangu" 糖醋排骨的历史典故 [The historical legend of sweet and sour pork]. Baidu Zhidao 百度知道. January 13, 2020. https://zhidao.baidu.com/question/29546666.html.

MU SHU PORK

Tiao Se Pan Wang 调色盘网. "Mu xu ruo de youlai" 木须肉的由来 [The origins of mu shu pork]. December 8, 2020. https://www.tspweb.com/key/木须肉的历史和典故.html.

PEKING DUCK

Dunlop, Fuchsia. "Peking Duck: The Complex History of a Chinese Classic." *National Geographic*, July 9, 2021. https://www.nationalgeographic.co.uk/travel/2021/07/peking-duck-the-complex-history-of-a-chinese-classic.

My Beijing China. "History of Beijing Roast Duck." https://www.mybeijingchina.com/travel-guide/beijing-duck/history-of-beijing-duck.htm.

Reinhard, Ashley. "What is the difference between a Pekin duck and a Peking duck?" Joe Jurgielewicz & Son. February 3, 2021. https://tastyduck.com/faq-items/what-is-the-difference-between-a-pekin-duck-and-a-peking-duck/.

Tengxun Wang 腾讯网. "Beijing kaoya de gushi yu chuanshuo" 北京烤鸭的故事与传说 [The story and legend of Peking duck]. 2020. https://new.qq.com/omn/20200109/20200109A0DTS400.html?pc.

——— 腾讯网. "Guanyu Beijing kaoya de 6 zhong qiyuan chuanshuo" 关于北京烤鸭的6种起源传说 [All about Peking duck's six different origin legends]. 2018. https://new.qq.com/omn/20200425/20200425A0A3GS00.html.

Xu, Shitao, comp. *Origin of Chinese Cuisine.* Illustrated by Chunjiang Fu. Translated by Jingyu Wu. Singapore, Singapore: Asiapac Books, 2003.

Yi Du 壹读. "Jingdian gushi lianhuanhua (kan qian nu mai yuanjia maizhu) 經典故事連環畫(看錢奴買冤家債主) [Historical stories in comic form, a miser buys a hostile creditor]. July 24, 2015. https://read01.com/248jaM.html.

BEEF AND BROCCOLI

Daddy Lau. "Dad's Perfect Chinese broccoli (蠔油芥蘭): Gai Lan with Oyster Sauce!" Made With Lau. Streamed live on December 15, 2020. YouTube video, 18:53. https://www.youtube.com/watch?v=zi3FB2NtLCc&t=88s.

Gao Zhiwei 高志伟. "Guanyu gailan de renwen nei han: yi ke yao shi tongyuan xiao qingcai de chuanqi xiao gushi" 关于芥蓝的人文内涵：一棵药食同源小青菜的传奇小故事 [Humans and Chinese broccoli: a medicinal and mystical story]. Baidu 百度百科. July 29, 2019. https://wapbaike.baidu.com/tashuo/browse/content?id=69510a16e885351b68c4eca9.

Sabrina and Bianca. "Beef and Broccoli." 196 flavors. January 13, 2022. https://www.196flavors.com/beef-and-broccoli/.

Sohu 搜狐. "'Taoshan gailan,' youming taoshan gelan, shengchan yu jieyang tao shanxiang" '桃山芥蓝'，又名桃山格蓝，盛产于揭阳桃山乡" ['Taoshan Chinese broccoli,' also known as Taoshan 'gelan' is abundant in Jieyan, Taoshan]. December 8, 2021. https://www.sohu.com/a/506417892_120089512.

World Crops. "Chinese Broccoli." UMass Center for Agriculture, Food and the Environment. https://worldcrops.org/crops/chinese-broccoli.

EMPRESS CHICKEN

Bai Ju-Yi 白居易. "The Song of Everlasting Regret." Translated by Ying Sun. Poems of Tang Dynasty with English Translations. November 11, 2008. http://www.musicated.com/syh/TangPoems/EverlastingRegret.htm.

Baike Kuai Dong 百科快懂. "Guifei ji 贵妃鸡" [Empress chicken]. October 1, 2017. https://www.baike.com/wiki-id/3464267369074811110?prd=attribute&view_id=27wk79onch7a4g.

Hinsch, Bret. *Women in Tang China.* Lanham, MA: Rowman & Littlefield, 2020.

Lao Fan Gu 老饭骨. "State Banquet Master Chef—Guifei Chicken: Crispy Skin and Tender and Juicy Meat." Livestreamed on July 15, 2020. YouTube video, 6:40. https://www.youtube.com/watch?v=_ybXYdvgTME.

Meishijie 美食杰. "Guifei ji de zuofa" 贵妃鸡的做法 [Empress chicken recipe]. January 20, 2007. https://www.meishij.net/china-food/caixi/jingcai/3841.html.

Qinggan Qian Yu 情感千语. "Dou zhidao guifei ji shi yi dao hangzhuo meiwei, Yang guigei yu guifei ji you you zheme yang de gushi ne 都知道贵妃鸡是一道杭州美味，杨贵妃与贵妃鸡又有着怎样的故事呢" [Everyone knows of Hangzhou's tasty empress chicken; what is the story of Yang Guifei and empress chicken?]. *Sina* (blog). January 1, 2020. https://k.sina.cn/article_6839339616_197a80a6000100nvmf.html?from=food.

GENERAL TSO'S CHICKEN

Baidu Encyclopedia 百度百科. "Zuo Zongtang" 左宗棠 [General Zuo]. 2011. https://baike.baidu.com/item/左宗棠/66874.

Claiborne, Craig. "T. T. Wang, Influential Master of Chinese Kitchen, Dies at 55." *New York Times*, February 19, 1983. https://www.nytimes.com/1983/02/19/obituaries/tt-wang-influential-master-of-chinese-kitchen-dies-at-55.html.

Dunlop, Fuchsia. "Hunan Resources" *The New York Times Magazine*. February 5, 2007 https://www.nytimes.com/2007/02/04/magazine/04food.t.html?_r=1&scp=1&sq=fuchsia%20dunlop&st=cse

Grimes, William. "Peng Chang-Kuei, Chef behind General Tso's Chicken, Dies at 98." *New York Times*, December 2, 2016. https://www.nytimes.com/2016/12/02/world/asia/general-tso-chicken-peng-chang-kuei.html.

Lam, Francis. "The Curious History of General Tso's chicken." *Salon*. January 6, 2010. /http://www.salon.com/food/francis_lam/2010/01/05/history_of_general_tsos_chicken.

Lopez, German. "Why General Tso's Chicken Is So Popular in America—But Not Mainland China." Vox. December 28, 2016. https://www.vox.com/culture/2016/12/28/14058702/general-tsos-chicken-origin.

Pletcher, Kenneth. "Zuo Zongtang." *Encyclopedia Britannica*, November 6, 2021. https://www.britannica.com/biography/Zuo-Zongtang.

Ricardo. "The History of General Tao." Ricardo Media. https://www.ricardocuisine.com/en/articles/special-feature/1194-the-history-of-general-tao.

Taylor, Rupert. "The Story of General Tso's Chicken." Delishably. December 26, 2017. https://delishably.com/meat-dishes/The-Story-of-General-Tsos-Chicken.

Xiong Zijie 熊子杰. "Damingdingding de Zuo Zongtangji, weihe ruci shou Meiguo ren huanying?" 大名鼎鼎的"左宗棠鸡",为何如此受美国人欢迎? [Why is the famous 'General Tso's chicken popular with Americans?]. Excerpted from *Ni Bu Zhidao de Taiwan* 你不知道的台湾 [The Taiwan you don't know] in Sohu 搜狐. October 29, 2019. https://www.sohu.com/a/350420669_260616.

MAPO TOFU
Baidu Encyclopedia 百度百科. "Mapo doufu 麻婆豆腐" [Mapo tofu]. September 15, 2018. https://baike.baidu.com/item/麻婆豆腐/30888.

Callos, Nick. "The Delicious History of Mapo Tofu: Chengdu's Signature Dish." Frayed Passport. August 7, 2022. https://frayedpassport.com/the-delicious-history-of-mapo-tofu-chengdus-signature-dish/.

Jucan Wang 聚餐网. "Mapo duofu de youlai he lishi diangu" 麻婆豆腐的由来和历史典故 [Mapo tofu's origins and history]. April 8, 2014. https://www.jucanw.com/mszx/mszx/1354.html.

Sun Jiahui. "The Making of Mapo Tofu." *China Daily*, September 6, 2015. https://www.chinadaily.com.cn/kindle/2015-09/06/content_21798522.htm.

Pu Ji 普濟. "Mapo duofu: Yingyu ye nian Mapo Tofu, qishi Chengdu Wanfu Qiao Chen Mapo bingbu shi mapo" 麻婆豆腐：英語也念 Mapo Tofu，其實成都萬福橋陳麻婆並不是麻婆 [Mapo tofu in English is also pronounced mapo tofu; in fact, the Chengdu Wanfu Lady Chen Mapo isn't mapo]. Ai Jianggu 愛講古. July 9, 2021. https://aijianggu.com/proverb/251999.html.

CHOP SUEY
Anderson, E. N. *The Food of China*. New Haven: Yale University Press, 1988.

Avey, Tori. "Food of the California Gold Rush." *The History Kitchen* (blog). Public Broadcasting Station. January 20, 2015. https://www.pbs.org/food/the-history-kitchen/food-california-gold-rush/.

Brown, Miranda. "The Hidden, Magnificent History of Chop Suey." Gastro Obscura. Atlas Obscura. July 1, 2022. https://www.atlasobscura.com/articles/chop-suey-history.

Chang, Iris. *The Chinese in America: A Narrative History*. New York: Penguin Books, 2003.

Coe, Andrew. "Mixed Bits: The True History of Chop Suey." *American Heritage* 62, no. 5 (2017). www.americanheritage.com/mixed-bits-true-history-chop-suey#3.

Conlin, Joseph Robert. *Bacon, Beans, and Galantines: Food and Foodways on the Western Mining Frontier*. Reno: University of Nevada Press, 1986.

Lee, Alexander. "A History of Chop Suey." Historian's Cookbook. *History Today* 69, no. 10 (October 2019). https://www.historytoday.com/archive/historians-cookbook/history-chop-suey.

Li, Shu-fan. *Hong Kong Surgeon*. New York: Dutton, 1964.

Liu, Haiming. *From Canton Restaurant to Panda Express: A History of Chinese Food in the United States*. New Brunswick, NJ: Rutgers University Press, 2015.

Mendelson, Anne. *Chow Chop Suey: Food and the Chinese American Journey*. New York: Columbia University Press, 2016.

BEGGAR'S CHICKEN

Baike Gushi 百科故事. "Jiaohua ji de chuanshuo" 叫化鸡的传说 [Beggar's chicken legend]. November 8, 2016. https://www.niaoleiba.com/story/wuv.html.

Basler, Barbara. "Fare of the Country: Hong Kong's Mystery Chicken." *New York Times*, April 8, 1990. https://www.nytimes.com/1990/04/08/travel/fare-of-the-country-hong-kong-s-mystery-chicken.html.

Hangzhou at West Lake. "Jin Sha Beggar's Chicken: The Legend behind the Dish." Four Seasons Hotel. Accessed February 2022. https://www.fourseasons.com/hangzhou/dining/restaurants/jin_sha/beggars-chicken-the-legend-behind-the-dish/

Leo 女王. "Jiaohua ji de youlai" 叫化鸡的由来 [Beggar's chicken origins]. Meishijia 美食杰. June 1, 2016. https://www.meishij.net/diangu/jiaohuajideyoulai.html.

Weilei 味蕾. "Jiaohua ji de youlai" 叫化鸡的由来" [Beggar's chicken origins]. *Epoch Times*, June 9, 2015. https://www.epochtimes.com/gb/15/6/9/n4453406.htm.

DRAGON AND PHOENIX

Baidu Encyclopedia 百度百科. "Longfengchengxiang" 龙凤呈样 [Dragon and phoenix are good fortune]. Baidu. 2016. https://baike.baidu.com/item/龙凤呈样/7661723.

Liu, Xiang 刘向. *Liexian Zhuan* 列仙转 [Biographies of immortals]. Translated by Jin Ling Zhang. The Project Gutenberg. https://www.gutenberg.org/cache/epub/25414/pg25414.html.

BUDDHA'S DELIGHT

360 Company 快资讯. "Suyan Luohan cai mingcheng de laili: yu Fojiao you sha guanxi?" 素筵罗汉菜名称的来历:与佛教有啥关系? [The origin of the name for the Luohan vegetarian feast: what does it have to do with Buddhism?]. March 12, 2021. https://www.360kuai.com/pc/9566731615590330d?cota=4&kuai_so=1&tj_url=so_rec&sign=360_e39369d1.

Tip of the Tongue Stories 舌尖上的故事. "Luohan zhai: Fomen zui shechi de yidao su zhai" 舌尖上的故事 羅漢齋——佛門最奢侈的一道素齋 [Luohan vegetarian cuisine, the most extravagant dish in Buddhism]. Yi Du 壹读. October 26, 2017. https://read01.com/GPJnAx5.html.

Vegetarian Buddhist Culture Communication Network 素食佛学文化传播网. "Luohan zhai de mingzi youlai" 罗汉斋的名字由来 [The origins of Buddha's delight]. December 24, 2012. https://www.97su.cn/8/85838.

ORANGES

Danni 丹妮. "Zhongguo guonian chide jili shiwu: ni zhidao dou you shenme yuyi ma?" 中国过年吃的吉利食物 你知道都有什么寓意吗?[Chinese New Year auspicious foods: do you know their meanings?]. *China Daily*, January 19, 2018. http://language.chinadaily.com.cn/2018-01/29/content_35602661.htm.

Flower Encyclopedia 花百科"Ganju de huayu he chuanshuo" 柑橘的花语和传说 [The legendary origin of citrus]. February 13, 2022. https://www.huabaik.com/view/24845.html.

Flower Network 花语网. "Ganju de huayu he chuanshuo" 柑橘的花语和传说 [The legendary origin of citrus]. September 5, 2019. https://www.52zzl.com/zhiwu/24810.html.

Keefe, Jackson. "Oranges: Chinese Symbol of Abundance and Happiness." The S Media. January 13, 2022. https://thesmedia.id/posts/oranges-chinese-symbol-of-abundance-and-happiness.

Liu Qiaoxiong 刘巧雄 "Juzi zhou de lishi chuanshou" 橘子洲的历史传说 [The legend of Tangerine Island]. Taigong Hu 太公胡. March 6, 2016. https://www.takunghn.com/s/6627.html.

Wang Rulai 王瑞来. "Juzi weishenme you xie zuo juzi" '橘子' 为什么又写作' 桔子'? [Why is tangerine written in two ways?]. Sohu 搜狐. Accessed April 2022. https://www.sohu.com/a/195959378_617374.

Xinxian 新鲜. "Ganju de minjian chuanshuo: ganju de youlai" 柑橘的民间传说：" 柑橘" 的由来 [Citrus folk tales: the origin of citrus]. Zhi Hu 知乎. January 30, 2021. https://zhuanlan.zhihu.com/p/348284237.

RED BEAN SOUP

"Hongdou tang yong chi xiao dou zou ma hongdou tang yong de shi na zhong dou 红豆汤用赤Liang Faner 靓范儿. "Xiaodou zuo hongdou tang yong de shi na zhong dou" 小豆做吗 红豆汤用的是哪种豆 [Is red bean soup made with adzuki beans? What type of bean is used for red bean soup]. May 1, 2017. https://www.liangfaner.com/jiankangshenghuo/jiankangyangsheng/56893.html.

Hu Xianguo 胡献国. "Song Renzong yu chixiaodou" 宋仁宗与赤小豆 [Song Renzong and adzuki beans]. *Sina* (blog). July 31, 2019. https://m.fx361.com/news/2019/0731/5367862.html.

Sohu 搜狐. "Zhongyao gushi: 'Hongdou' sheng nanguo, 'xiangsi' zui duanchang" 中药故事：' 红豆' 生南国，' 相思' 最断肠 [A traditional Chinese medicine story: red beans are born in the South, the acacia (lovesickness) is most heartbreaking]. August 12, 2018. https://www.sohu.com/a/246740272_100239378.

ICE CREAM

Atong and the Dungeon 阿通与地下城. "Yuanchao qi shi, yidai chihuo Hubilie faming bingjiling he shuai yangruo" 元朝奇事，一代"吃货"忽必烈发明冰激凌和涮羊肉 [A Yuan Dynasty wonder, the first foodie Kublai Khan invents ice cream]. *Sina* (blog). November 13, 2020. https://k.sina.cn/article_6420797780_17eb5995400100okso.html.

Daily News 天天要闻. "Guren xiatian ye neng chi dao lengyin? Yuanchao hai you bingqilin! 古人夏天也能吃到冷饮？元朝还有' 冰淇淋'!" [Can the Ancients also have cold drinks during the summer? The Yuan Dynasty also had ice cream!]. June 29, 2020. https://daydaynews.cc/zh-hans/history/641952.html.

History and Culture Pavilion 历史文化阁. "Meiyou dian de gudai, guren xiatian yong de bing laizi nali? Kan wan budebu peifu guren zhihui" 没有电的古代，古人夏天用的冰来自哪里？看完不得不佩服古人智慧 [In ancient times without electricity, how did ancient people have ice? Once you read this, you'll have to admire them]. Sohu 搜狐. February 26, 2021. https://www.sohu.com/a/452844298_120340030.

Madieer 马迭尔食品. "Gudai ren de xia ri chi bing shi" 古代人的夏日吃冰史 [The history of ancient people eating ice during the summer]. Sohu 搜狐. April 21, 2020. https://www.sohu.com/a/389722393_100183506.

Shaunak, Aran. "The History of Ice Cream: From Milk Ice to Magnums." Foodunfolded. September 24, 2020. https://www.foodunfolded.com/article/the-history-of-ice-cream-from-milk-ice-to-magnums.

Toussaint-Samat, Maguelonne. *A History of Food*. Translated by Anthea Bell. Malden, MA: Wiley-Blackwell, 2009.

FORTUNE COOKIES

Frost, Natasha. "Did Mooncakes Help the Chinese Overthrow the Mongols?" Gastro Obscura. Atlas Obscura. November 14, 2017. https://www.atlasobscura.com/articles/mooncakes-china-mongols-manchu-metaphor-uprising.

Jenne, Jeremiah. "Mongols, the Ming, and the Myth of the Mooncake Rebellion." Radii. September 13, 2019. https://radii-china.com/mongols-the-ming-and-the-myth-of-the-mooncake-rebellion/.

Mulcrone, Kate. "The Complicated History of Fortune Cookies." Eat This Not That!. July 20, 2020. https://www.eatthis.com/fortune-cookie-origin/.

Ono, Gary T. "Japanese American Fortune Cookie: A Taste of Fame or Fortune - Part 1." *Discover Nikkei*, October 31, 2007. http://www.discovernikkei.org/en/journal/2007/10/31/fortune-cookie/.

Scaglione, Joe. "The Fortune Cookie Trials." *The Technical* (blog). Medium. November 22, 2021. https://medium.com/the-technical/the-fortune-cookie-trials-c374c63dbea9.

ACKNOWLEDGMENTS

Many thanks to:

- my family, especially my mom, who shared our heritage with me in the way I express it now—through food and stories
- my husband, Alex, who put up with my cranky moods while I worked feverishly on this
- my daughter, Hazel, who not only posed but gave a highly critical eye to all the art, helping me much improve it (yes, you were right—adding the flower pattern on the dresses did make it better)
- my agent, Rebecca Sherman, who encouraged me to re-pursue this idea
- my research assistant, Izabelle Brande; without her assistance and Chinese language mastery I could not have done this book half as well nor made my deadlines!
- Minghan Levine and her mother, Leah, for allowing me to use her as a model
- Lewis Poma for helping to put together the bibliography and saving me hours of work!
- Everyone at Little, Brown Books for Young Readers, especially Megan Tingley, Dave Caplan, Jackie Engel, Victoria Stapleton, Emilie Polster, Shawn Foster, Danielle Canterella, Marisa Russell, Christie Michel, Bill Grace, Andie Divelbiss, and Cheryl Lew, for believing in this book and the original pitch. I am truly, truly grateful
- Saho Fujii for her beautiful art direction and design
- Lillian Sun for helping to make this book a beautiful physical object
- Andy Ball for his patience, as I'm sure the schedule was a nail-biter as I pushed the deadlines to their limit!
- Lily Choi for her encouraging and very helpful first read of the manuscript
- Jennifer So and Annie McDonnell for their great attention to detail and fact-checking skills! I know with both of you I can rest much easier!
- Ruqayyah Daud for her help managing all the little details and being the "cc that made sure things didn't fall through the cracks"
- my editor and book friend forever Alvina Ling...for everything!

INDEX